WIZARD BEACH™

BOOM! STUDIOS

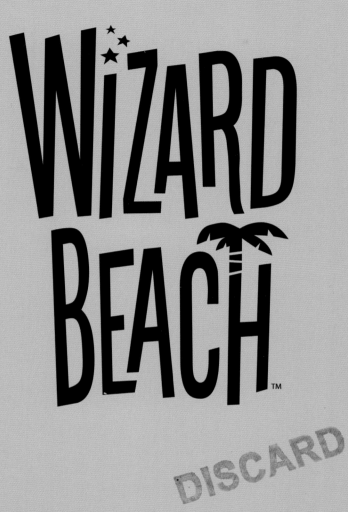

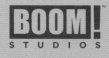

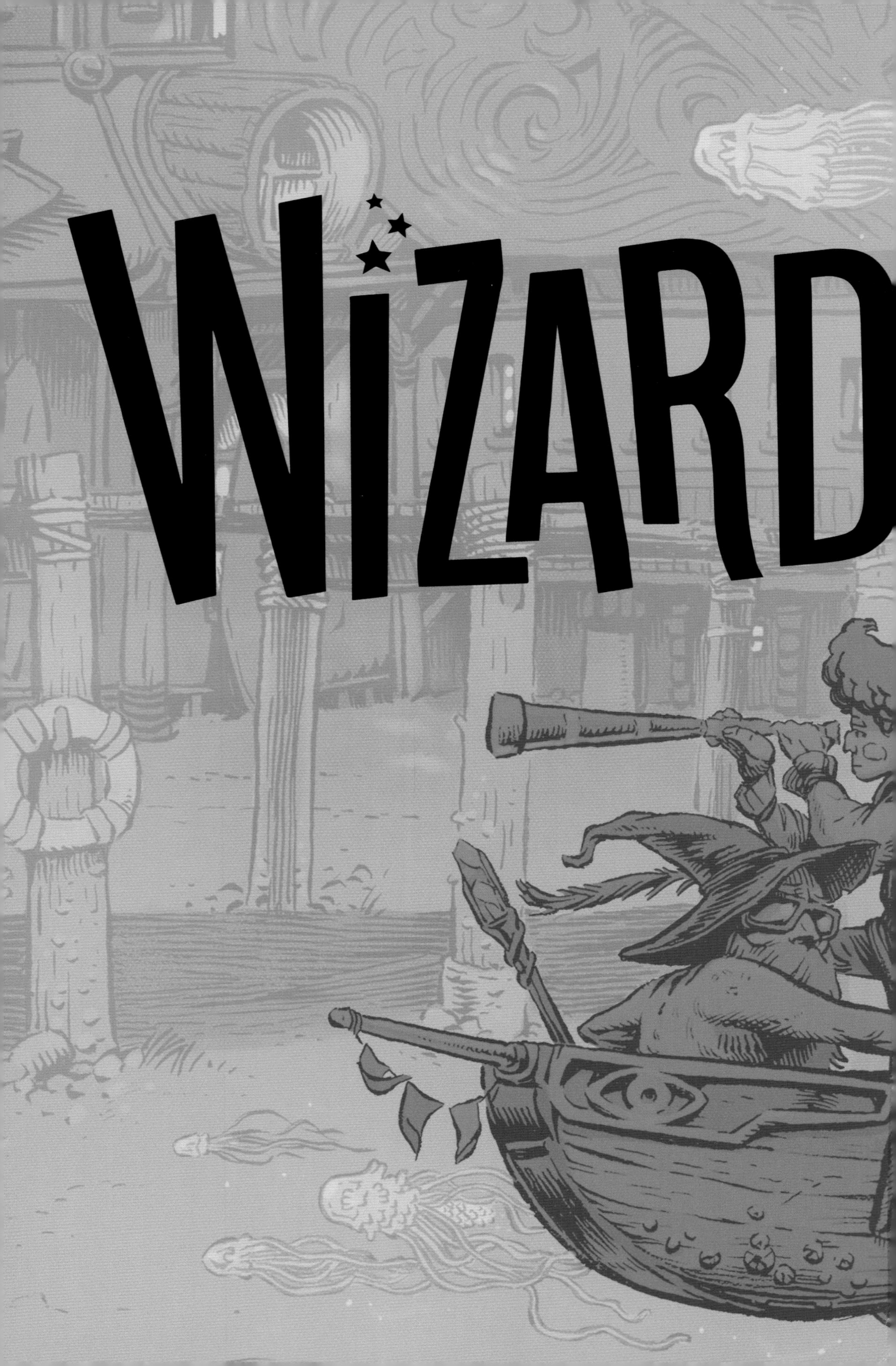
WIZARD

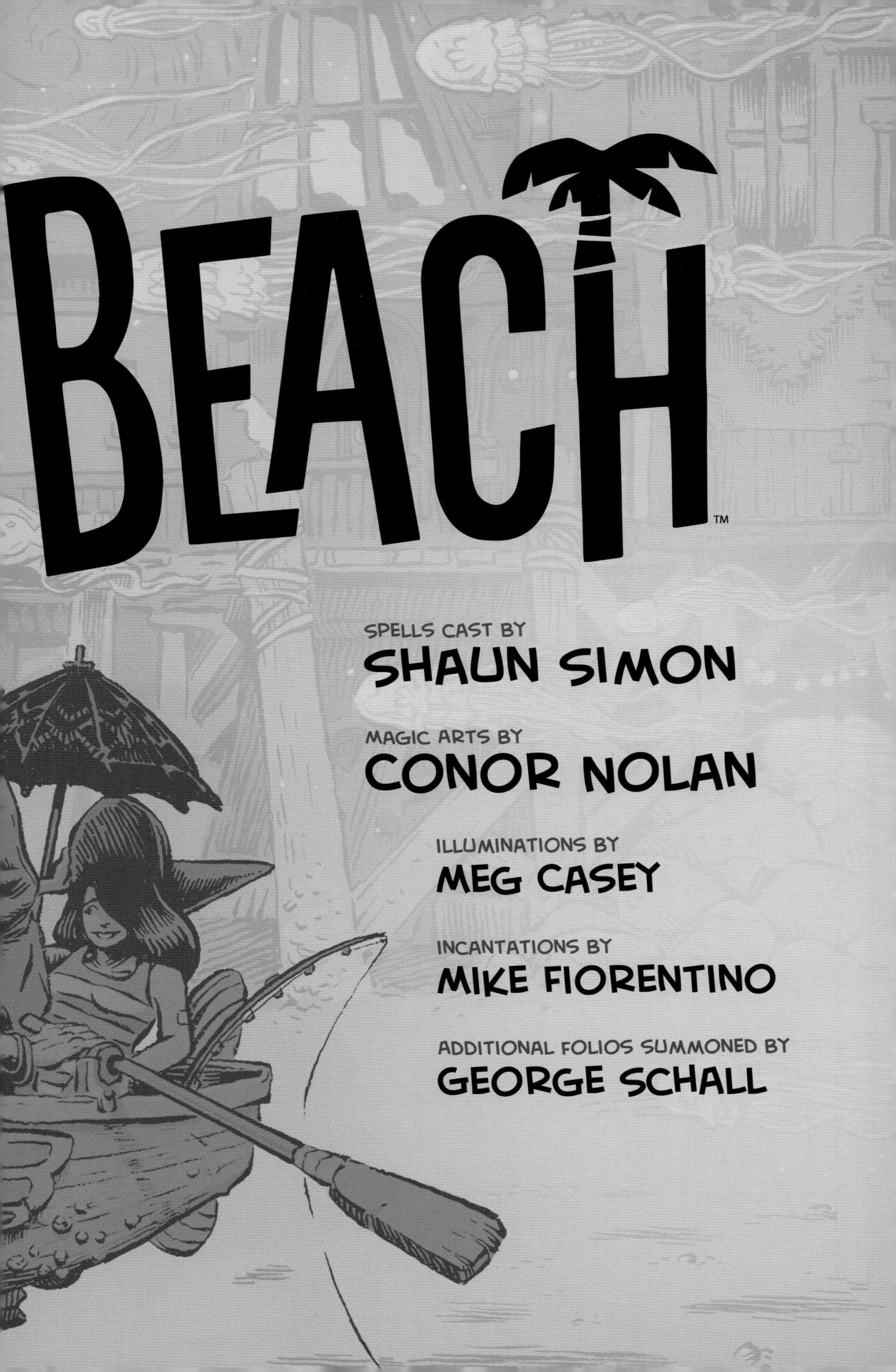

BEACH™

SPELLS CAST BY
SHAUN SIMON

MAGIC ARTS BY
CONOR NOLAN

ILLUMINATIONS BY
MEG CASEY

INCANTATIONS BY
MIKE FIORENTINO

ADDITIONAL FOLIOS SUMMONED BY
GEORGE SCHALL

COVER BY
CONOR NOLAN

BACK COVER ART, LOGO DESIGN AND
PAGES 41, 46, 63, 68, 84, 92, 120, AND 122 BY
GEORGE SCHALL

SERIES DESIGNER
MICHELLE ANKLEY

COLLECTION DESIGNER
SCOTT NEWMAN

EDITOR
SIERRA HAHN

SPECIAL THANKS TO CHRIS ROSA.

Ross Richie CEO & Founder
Joy Huffman CFO
Matt Gagnon Editor-in-Chief
Filip Sablik President, Publishing & Marketing
Stephen Christy President, Development
Lance Kreiter Vice President, Licensing & Merchandising
Arune Singh Vice President, Marketing
Bryce Carlson Vice President, Editorial & Creative Strategy
Scott Newman Manager, Production Design
Kate Henning Manager, Operations
Spencer Simpson Manager, Sales
Sierra Hahn Executive Editor
Jeanine Schaefer Executive Editor
Dafna Pleban Senior Editor
Shannon Watters Senior Editor
Eric Harburn Senior Editor
Chris Rosa Editor
Matthew Levine Editor
Sophie Philips-Roberts Associate Editor
Gavin Gronenthal Assistant Editor
Michael Moccio Assistant Editor
Gwen Waller Assistant Editor

Amanda LaFranco Executive Assistant
Jillian Crab Design Coordinator
Michelle Ankley Design Coordinator
Kara Leopard Production Designer
Marie Krupina Production Designer
Grace Park Production Designer
Chelsea Roberts Production Design Assistant
Samantha Knapp Production Design Assistant
Paola Capalla Senior Accountant
José Meza Live Events Lead
Stephanie Hocutt Digital Marketing Lead
Esther Kim Marketing Coordinator
Cat O'Grady Digital Marketing Coordinator
Amanda Lawson Marketing Assistant
Holly Aitchison Digital Sales Coordinator
Morgan Perry Retail Sales Coordinator
Megan Christopher Operations Coordinator
Rodrigo Hernandez Mailroom Assistant
Zipporah Smith Operations Assistant
Breanna Sarpy Executive Assistant

WIZARD BEACH, October 2019. Published by
BOOM! Studios, a division of Boom Entertainment,
Inc. Wizard Beach is ™ & © 2019 Conor Nolan & Shaun
Simon. Originally published in single magazine
form as WIZARD BEACH #1-5 ™ & © 2018, 2019. All
rights reserved. BOOM! Studios™ and the BOOM!
Studios logo are trademarks of Boom Entertainment, Inc., registered in various
countries and categories. All characters, events, and institutions depicted herein
are fictional. Any similarity between any of the names, characters, persons, events,
and/or institutions in this publication to actual names, characters, and persons,
whether living or dead, events, and/or institutions is unintended and purely
coincidental. BOOM! Studios does not read or accept unsolicited submissions of
ideas, stories, or artwork.

BOOM! Studios, 5670 Wilshire Boulevard, Suite 400, Los Angeles, CA 90036-5679.
Printed in China. First Printing.

ISBN: 978-1-68415-473-9, eISBN: 978-1-64144-590-0

DEDICATED TO MY PARENTS.
CONOR

TO JACK, EMILY, JULIET, AND ZOEY.
SHAUN

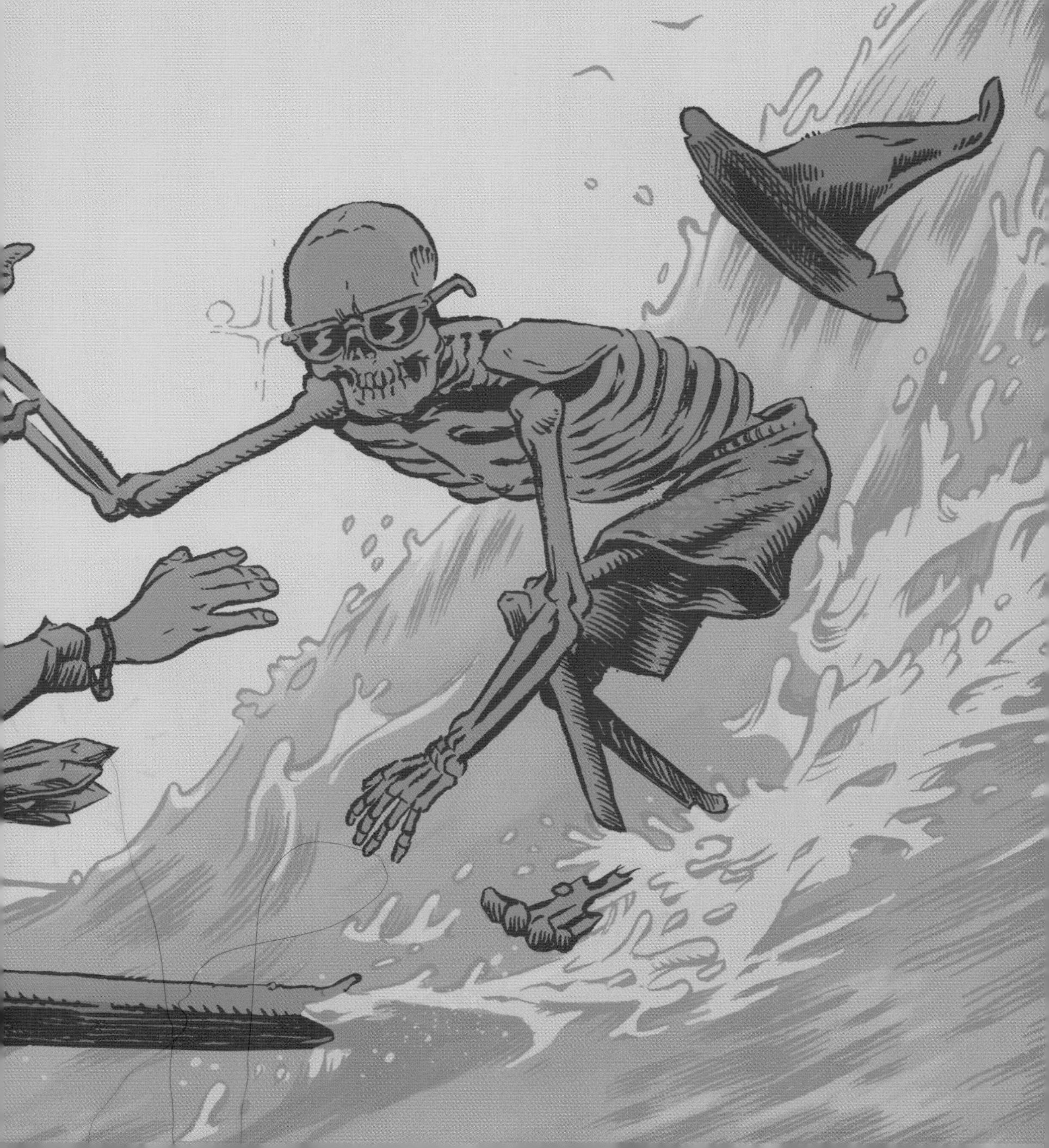

COVER BY
CONOR NOLAN

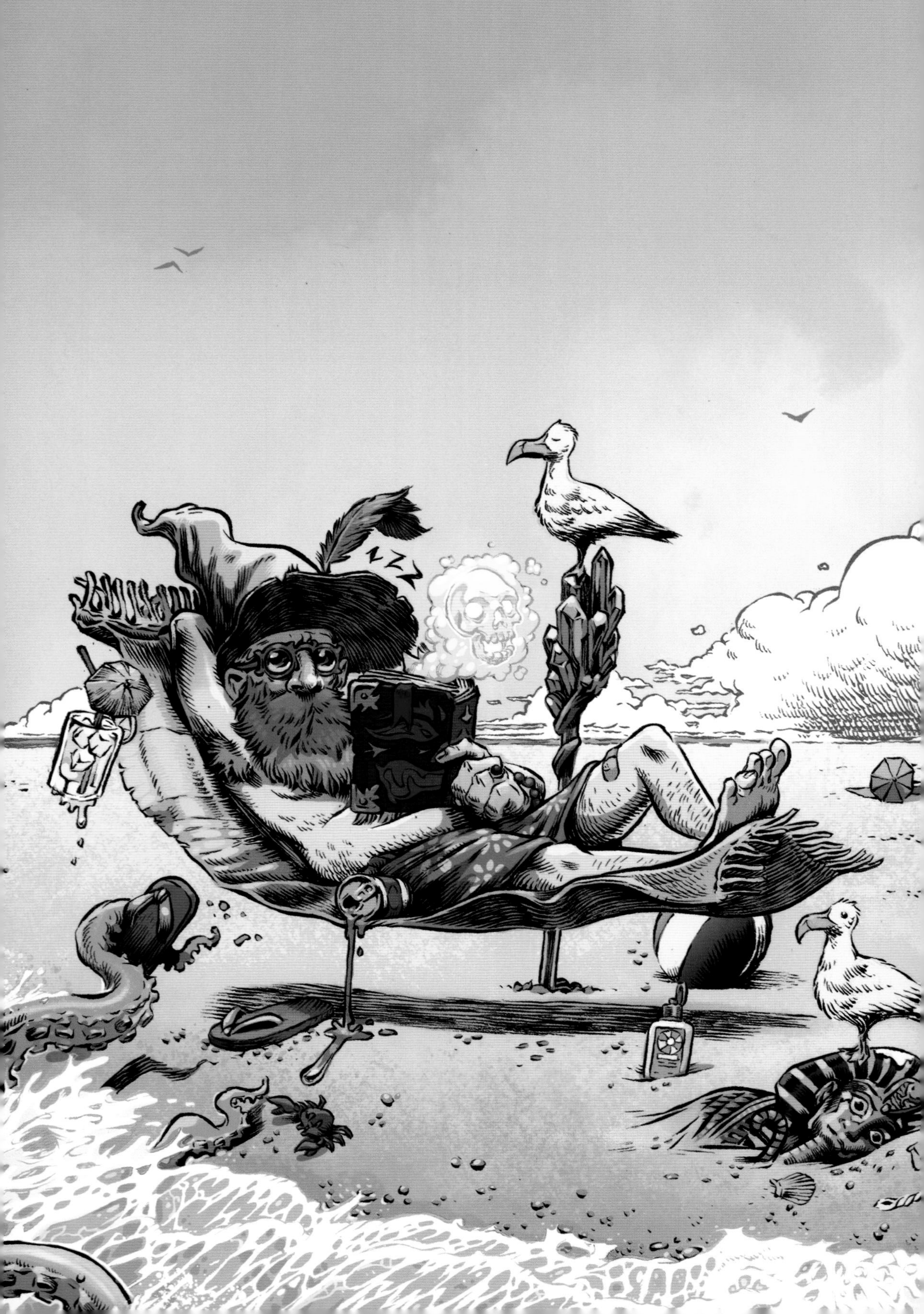
ZZZ

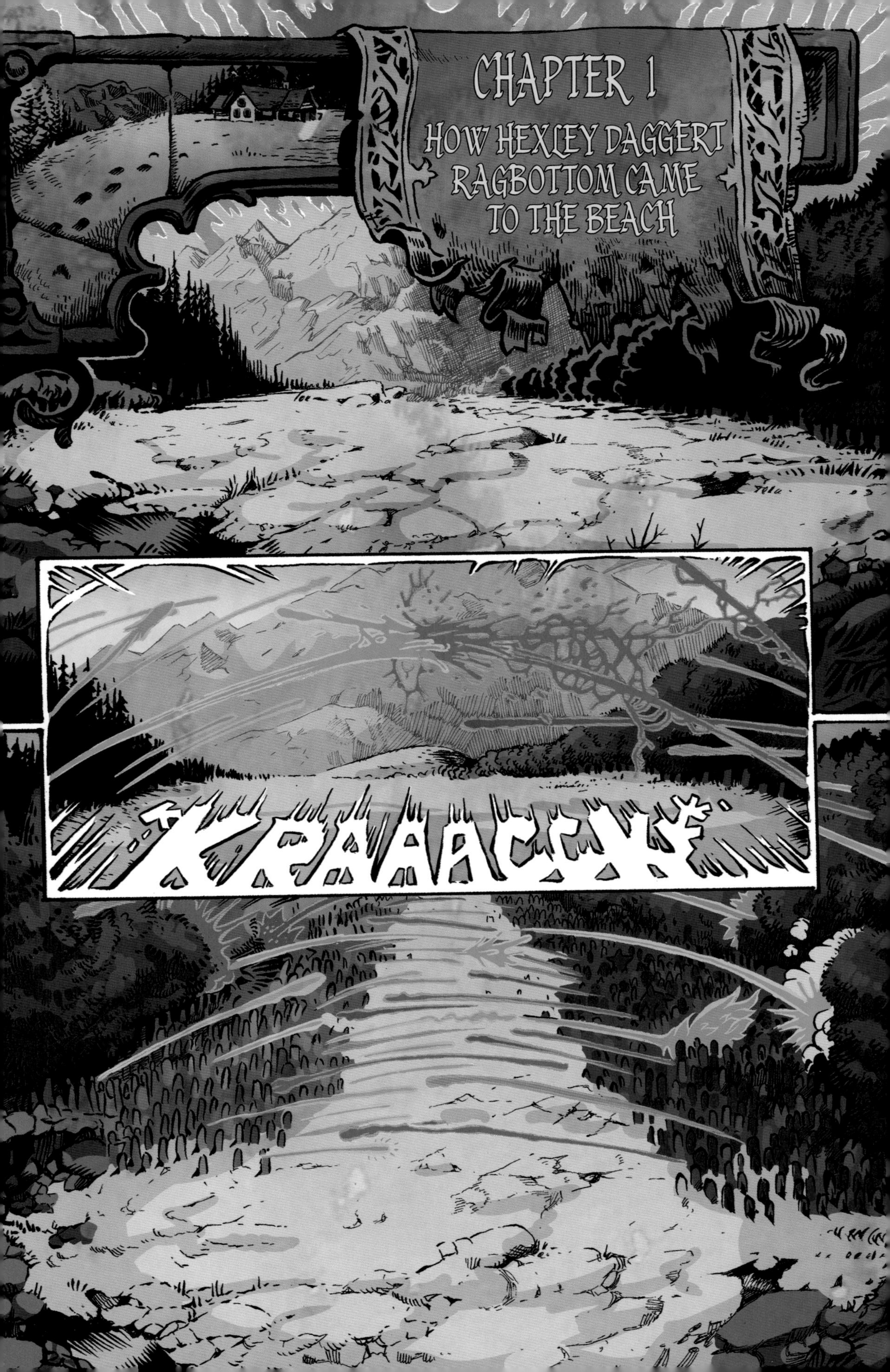
CHAPTER 1
HOW HEXLEY DAGGERT RAGBOTTOM CAME TO THE BEACH
KRAACCK!

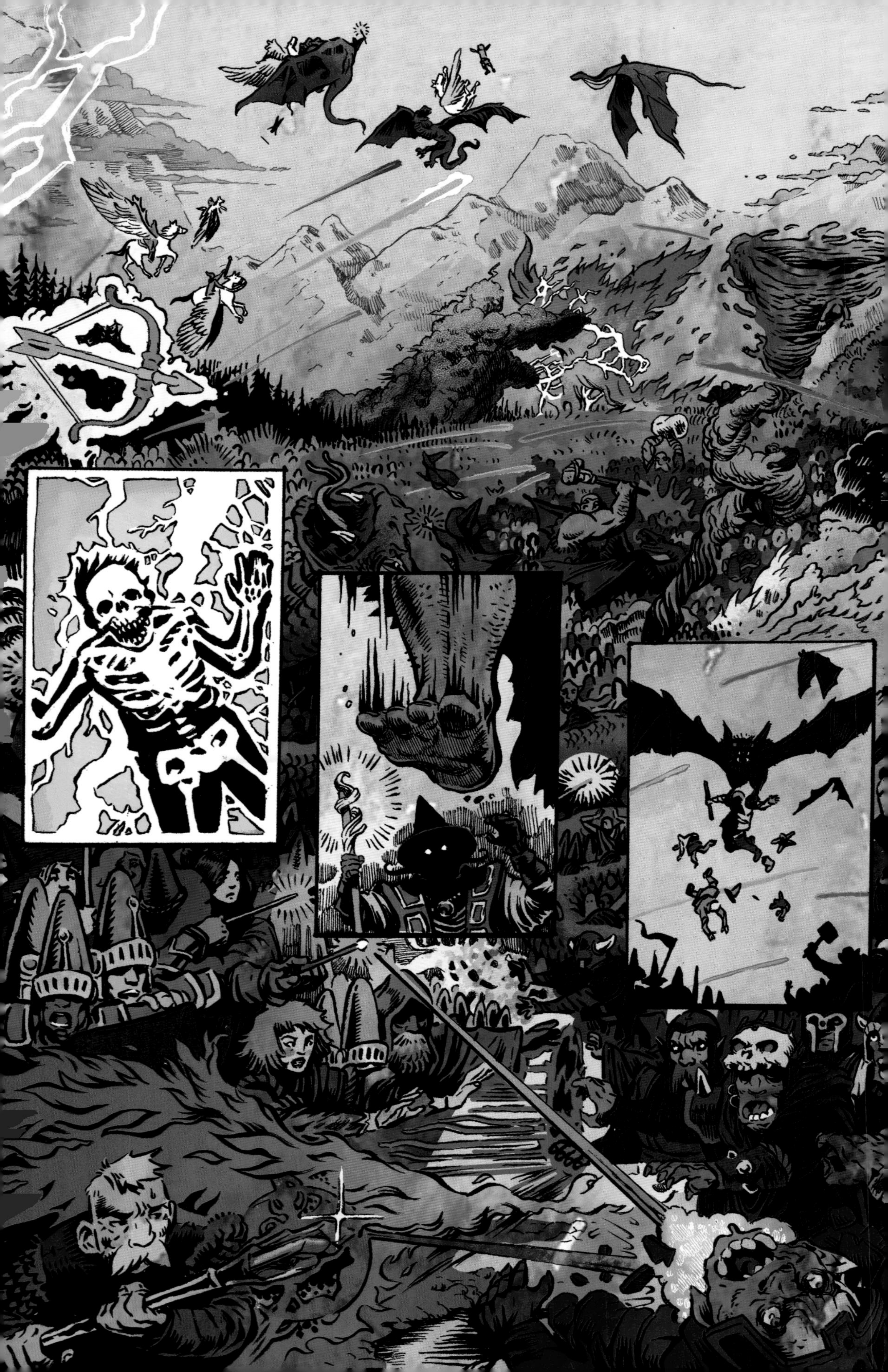

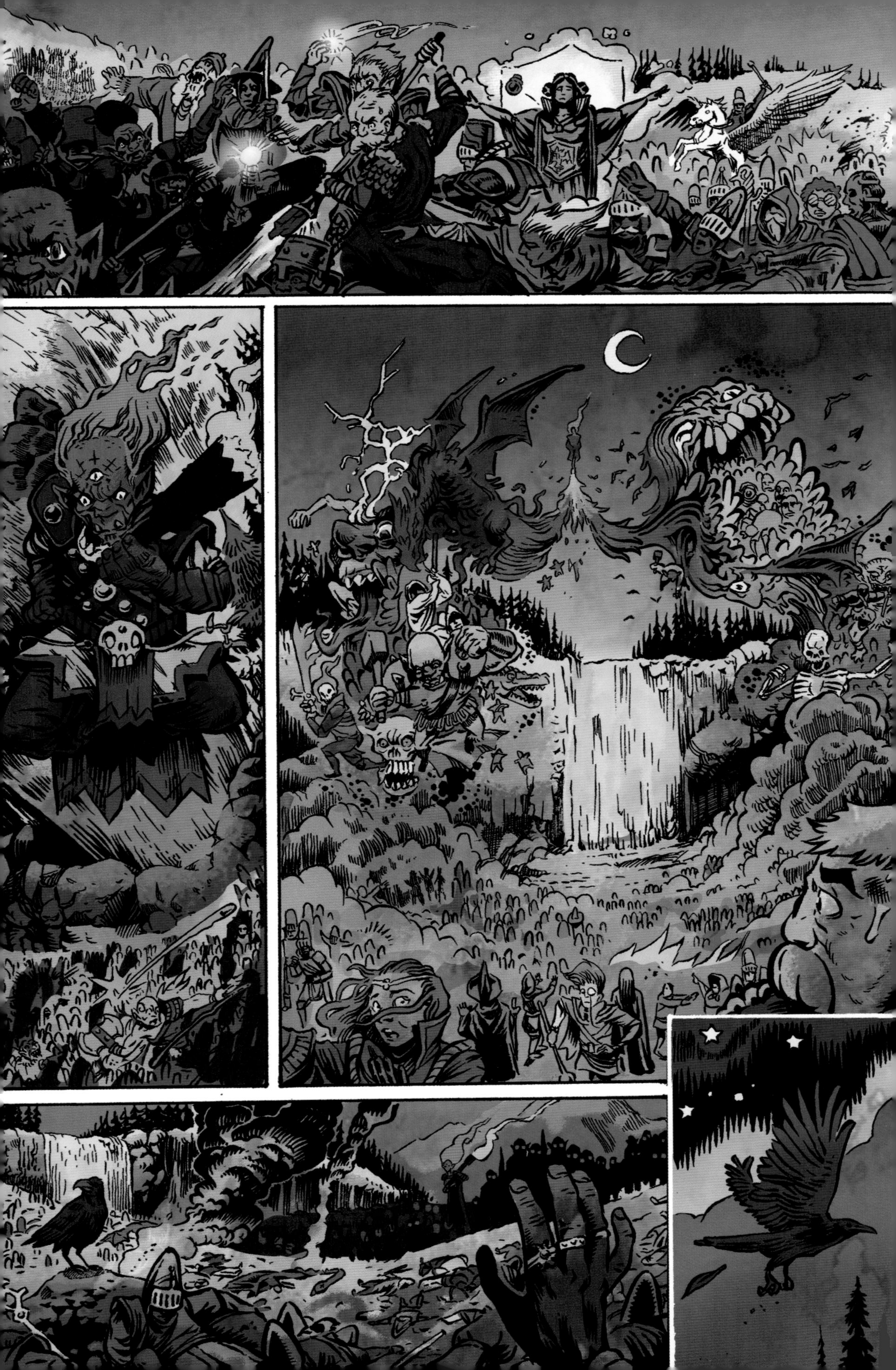

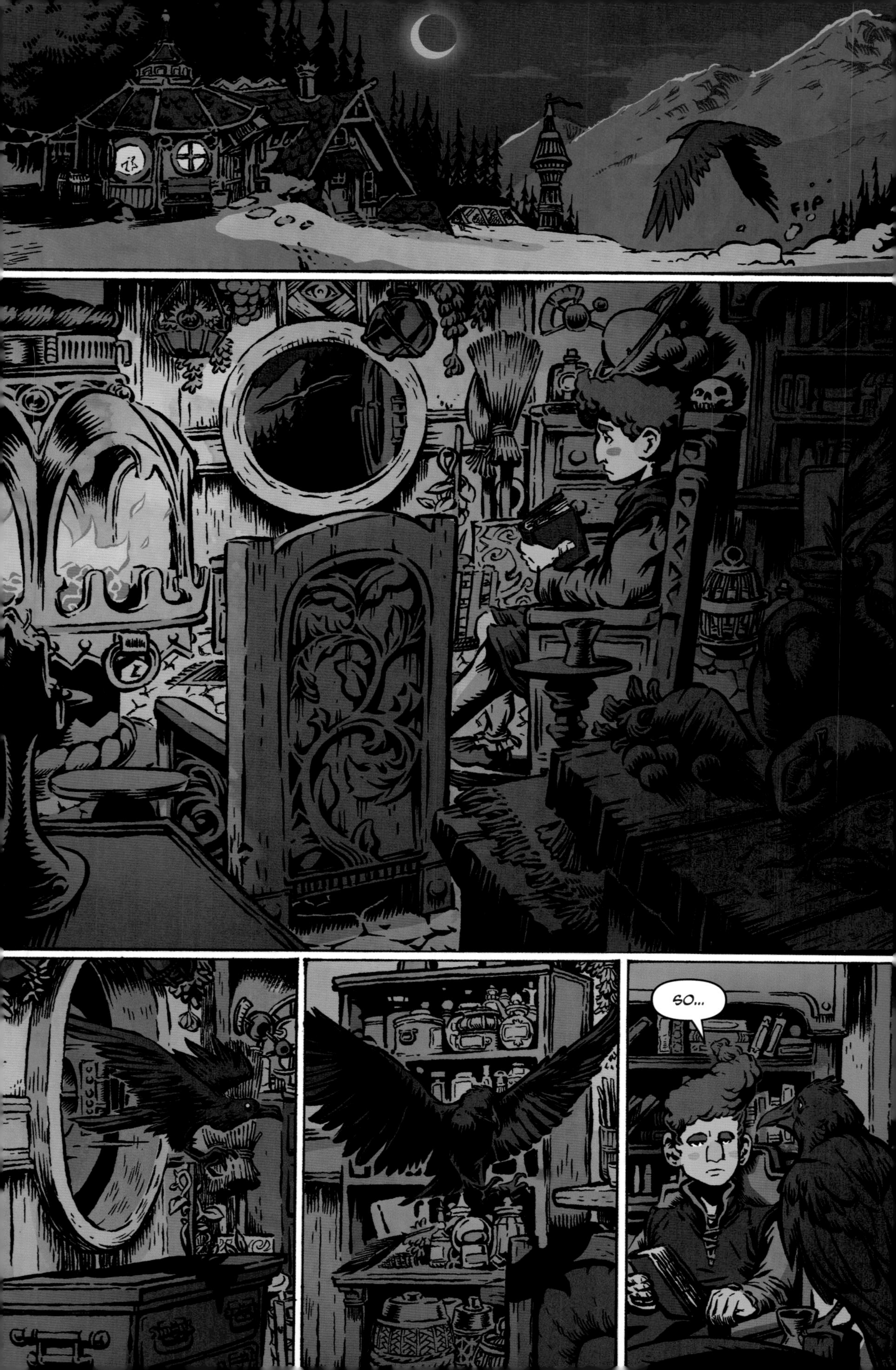
FIP
SO...

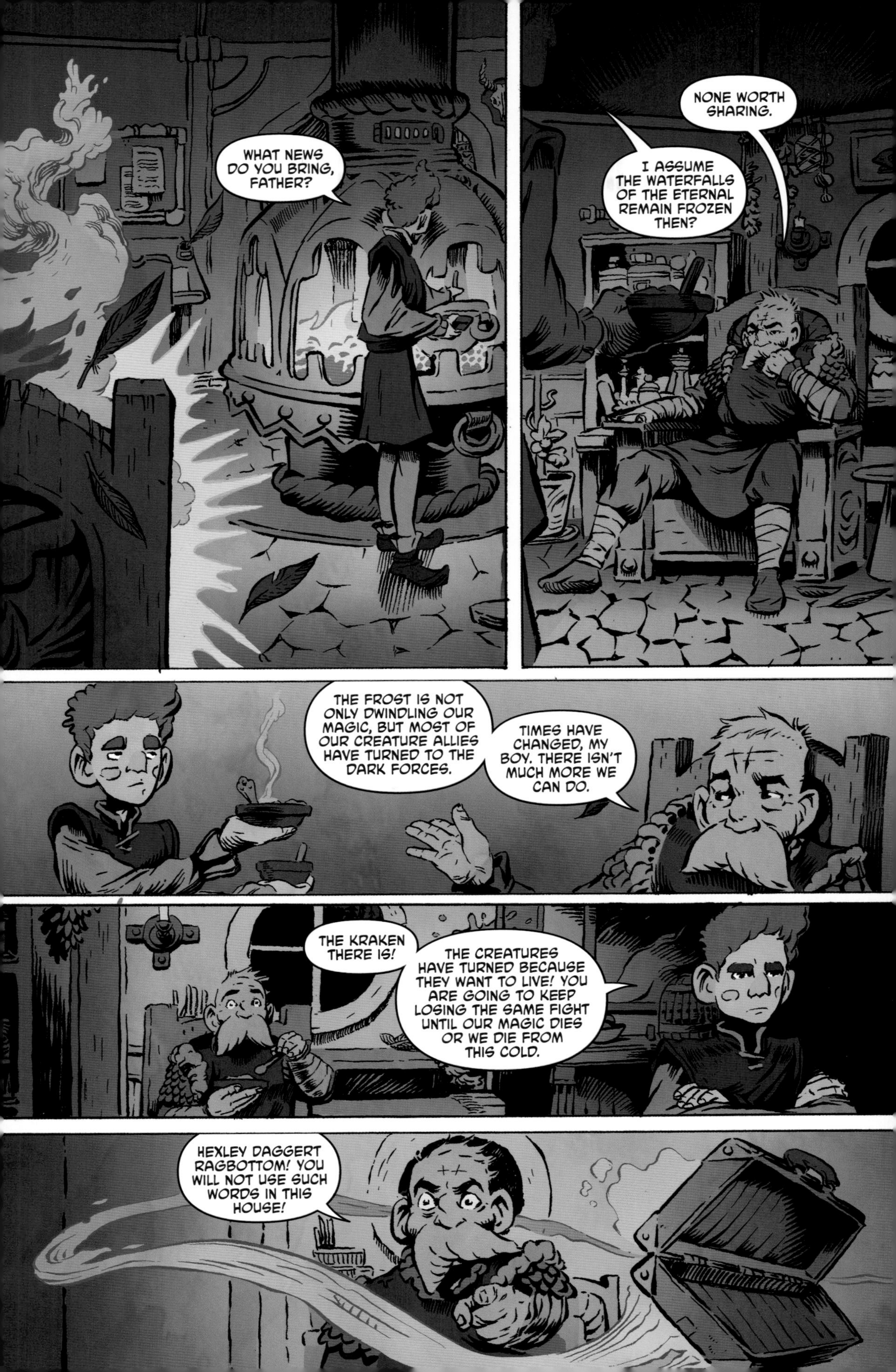
WHAT NEWS DO YOU BRING, FATHER?
NONE WORTH SHARING.
I ASSUME THE WATERFALLS OF THE ETERNAL REMAIN FROZEN THEN?
THE FROST IS NOT ONLY DWINDLING OUR MAGIC, BUT MOST OF OUR CREATURE ALLIES HAVE TURNED TO THE DARK FORCES.
TIMES HAVE CHANGED, MY BOY. THERE ISN'T MUCH MORE WE CAN DO.
THE CREATURES HAVE TURNED BECAUSE THEY WANT TO LIVE! YOU ARE GOING TO KEEP LOSING THE SAME FIGHT UNTIL OUR MAGIC DIES OR WE DIE FROM THIS COLD.
THE KRAKEN THERE IS!
HEXLEY DAGGERT RAGBOTTOM! YOU WILL NOT USE SUCH WORDS IN THIS HOUSE!

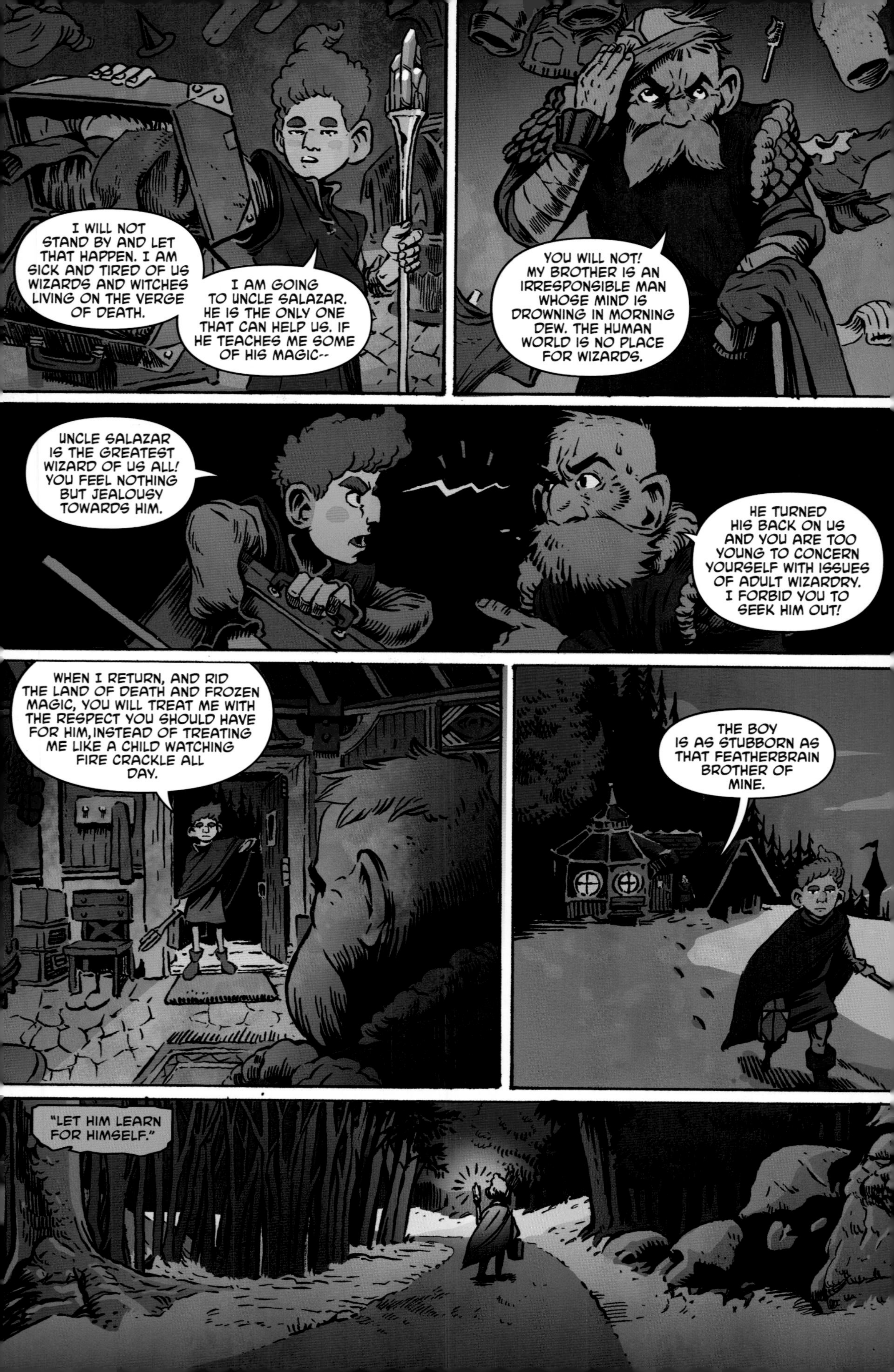
I WILL NOT STAND BY AND LET THAT HAPPEN. I AM SICK AND TIRED OF US WIZARDS AND WITCHES LIVING ON THE VERGE OF DEATH.
I AM GOING TO UNCLE SALAZAR. HE IS THE ONLY ONE THAT CAN HELP US. IF HE TEACHES ME SOME OF HIS MAGIC--
YOU WILL NOT! MY BROTHER IS AN IRRESPONSIBLE MAN WHOSE MIND IS DROWNING IN MORNING DEW. THE HUMAN WORLD IS NO PLACE FOR WIZARDS.
UNCLE SALAZAR IS THE GREATEST WIZARD OF US ALL! YOU FEEL NOTHING BUT JEALOUSY TOWARDS HIM.
HE TURNED HIS BACK ON US AND YOU ARE TOO YOUNG TO CONCERN YOURSELF WITH ISSUES OF ADULT WIZARDRY. I FORBID YOU TO SEEK HIM OUT!
WHEN I RETURN, AND RID THE LAND OF DEATH AND FROZEN MAGIC, YOU WILL TREAT ME WITH THE RESPECT YOU SHOULD HAVE FOR HIM, INSTEAD OF TREATING ME LIKE A CHILD WATCHING FIRE CRACKLE ALL DAY.
THE BOY IS AS STUBBORN AS THAT FEATHERBRAIN BROTHER OF MINE.
"LET HIM LEARN FOR HIMSELF."

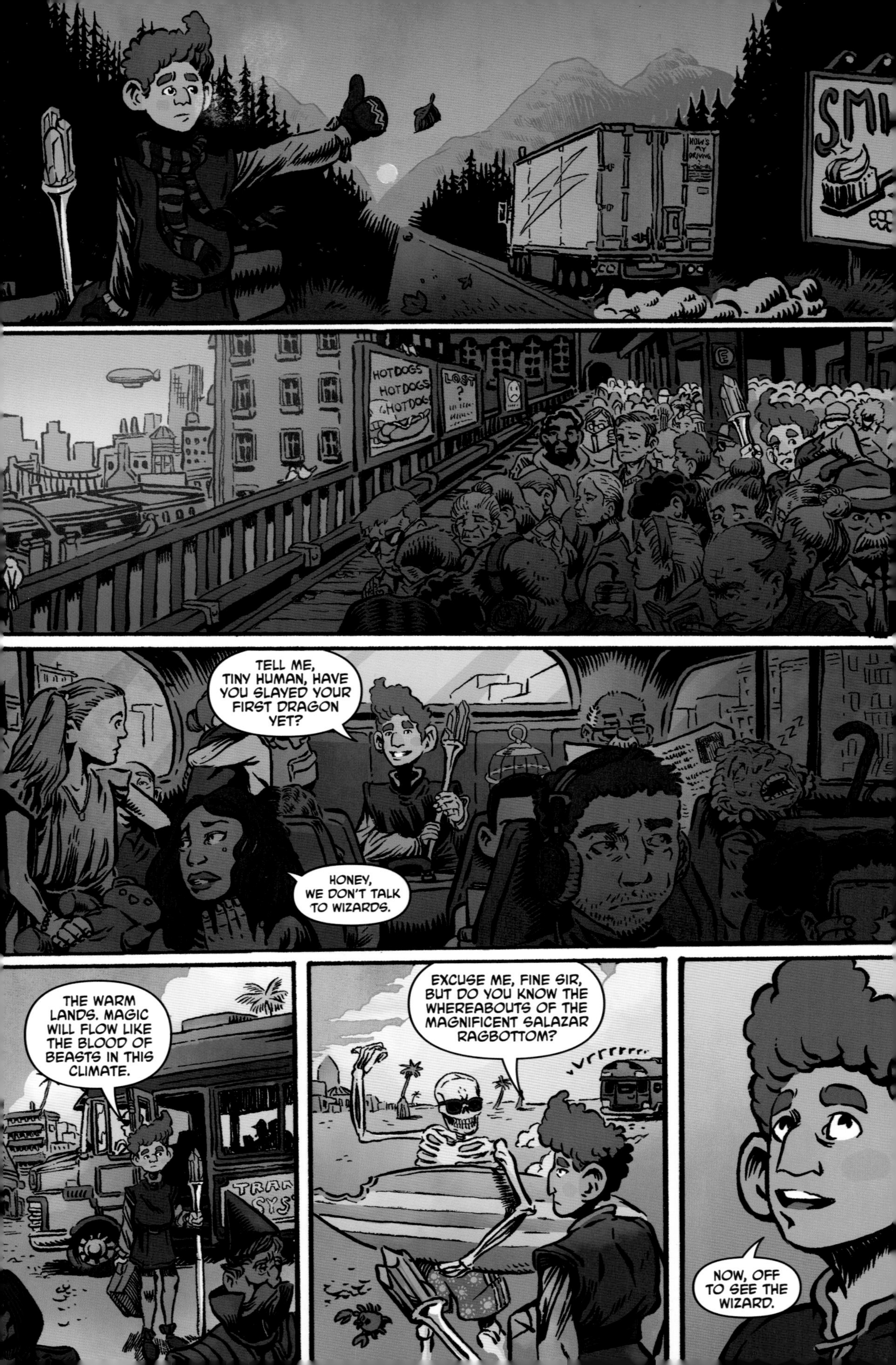
HOT DOGS
HOT DOGS
HOT DOGS
LOST ?
TELL ME, TINY HUMAN, HAVE YOU SLAYED YOUR FIRST DRAGON YET?
HONEY, WE DON'T TALK TO WIZARDS.
THE WARM LANDS. MAGIC WILL FLOW LIKE THE BLOOD OF BEASTS IN THIS CLIMATE.
EXCUSE ME, FINE SIR, BUT DO YOU KNOW THE WHEREABOUTS OF THE MAGNIFICENT SALAZAR RAGBOTTOM?
NOW, OFF TO SEE THE WIZARD.

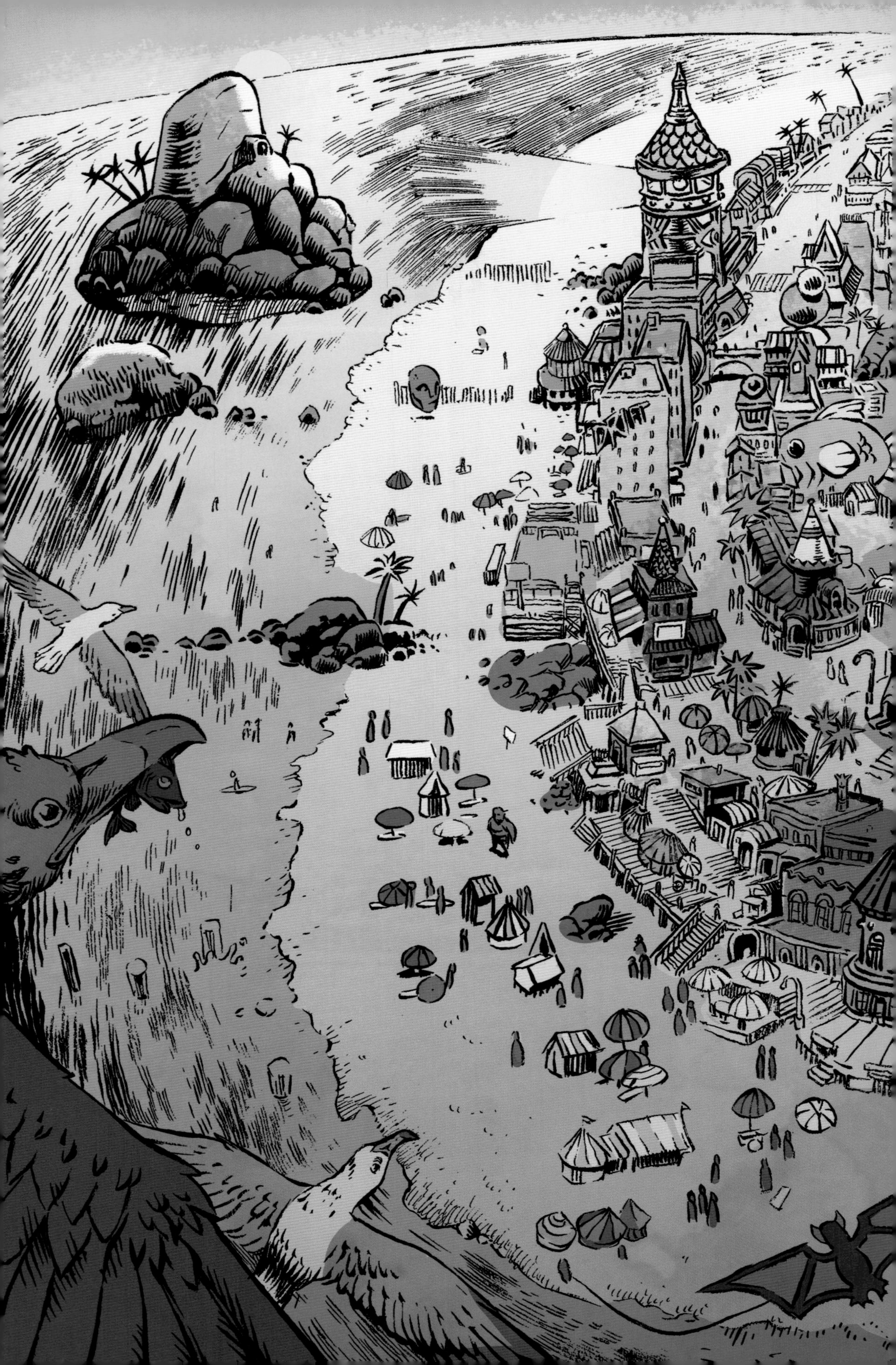

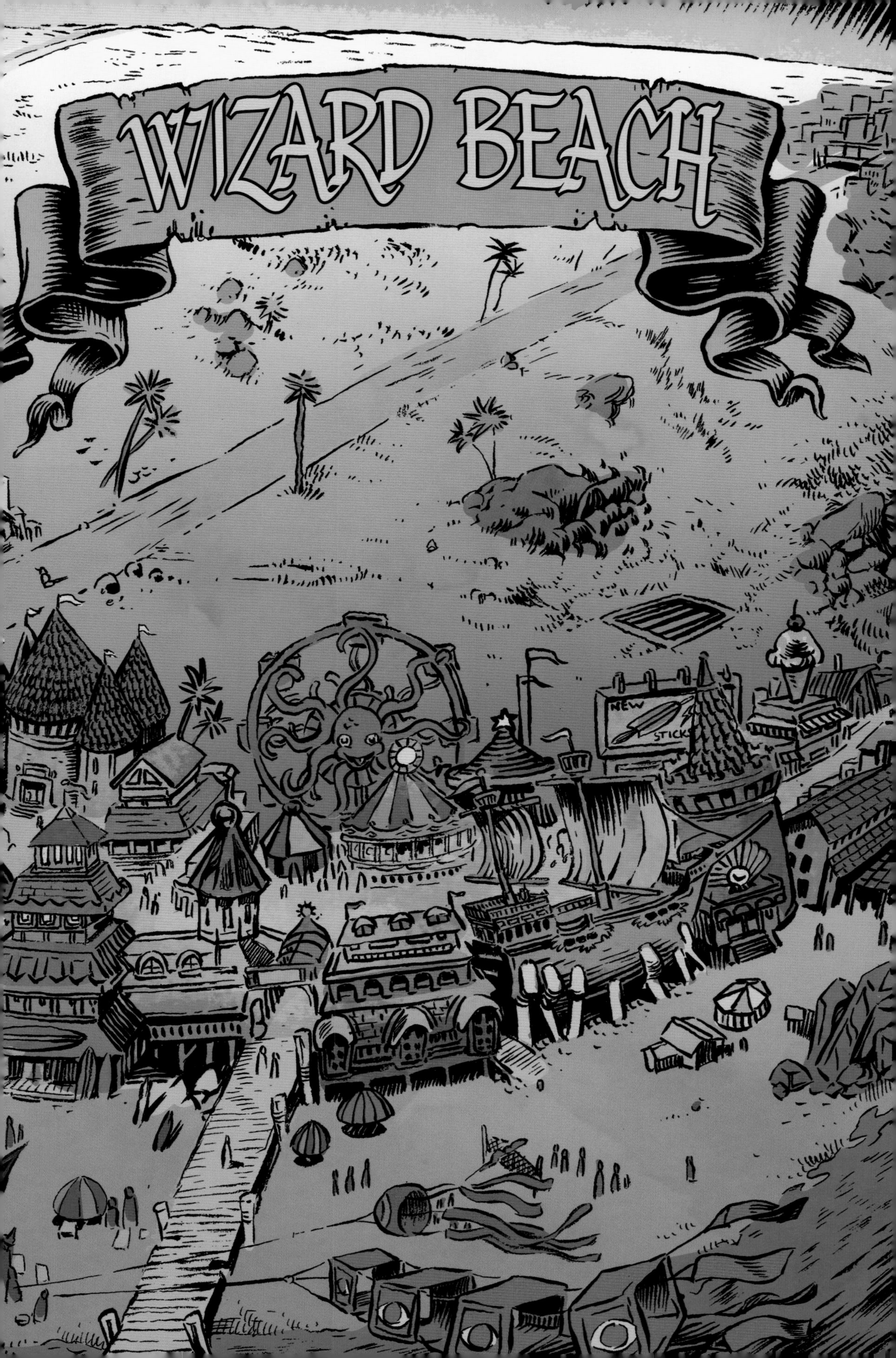
WIZARD BEACH
NEW
STICKS

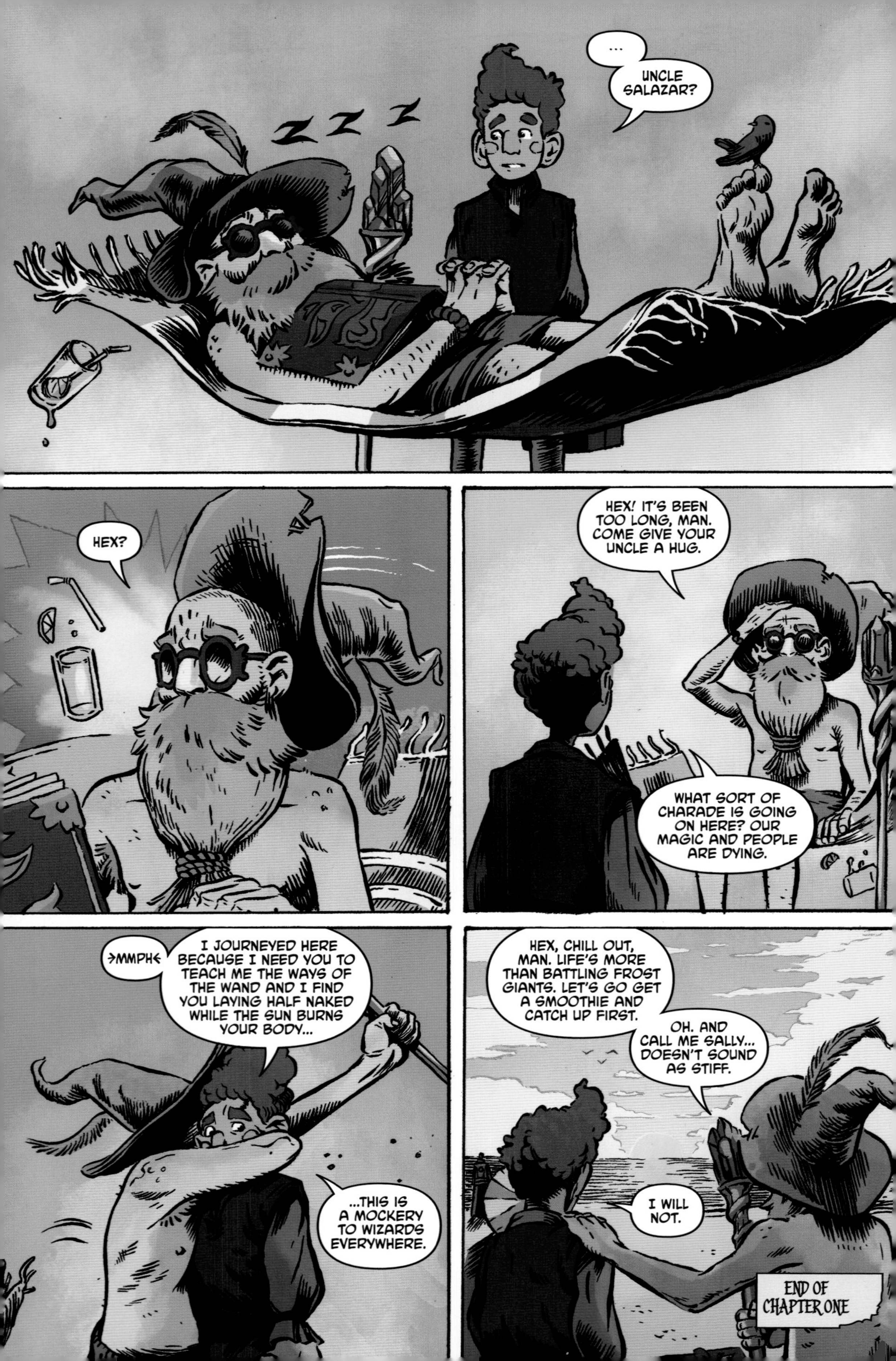

...
UNCLE SALAZAR?
Z Z Z
HEX?
HEX! IT'S BEEN TOO LONG, MAN. COME GIVE YOUR UNCLE A HUG.
WHAT SORT OF CHARADE IS GOING ON HERE? OUR MAGIC AND PEOPLE ARE DYING.
>MMPH<
I JOURNEYED HERE BECAUSE I NEED YOU TO TEACH ME THE WAYS OF THE WAND AND I FIND YOU LAYING HALF NAKED WHILE THE SUN BURNS YOUR BODY...
...THIS IS A MOCKERY TO WIZARDS EVERYWHERE.
HEX, CHILL OUT, MAN. LIFE'S MORE THAN BATTLING FROST GIANTS. LET'S GO GET A SMOOTHIE AND CATCH UP FIRST.
OH. AND CALL ME SALLY... DOESN'T SOUND AS STIFF.
I WILL NOT.
END OF CHAPTER ONE

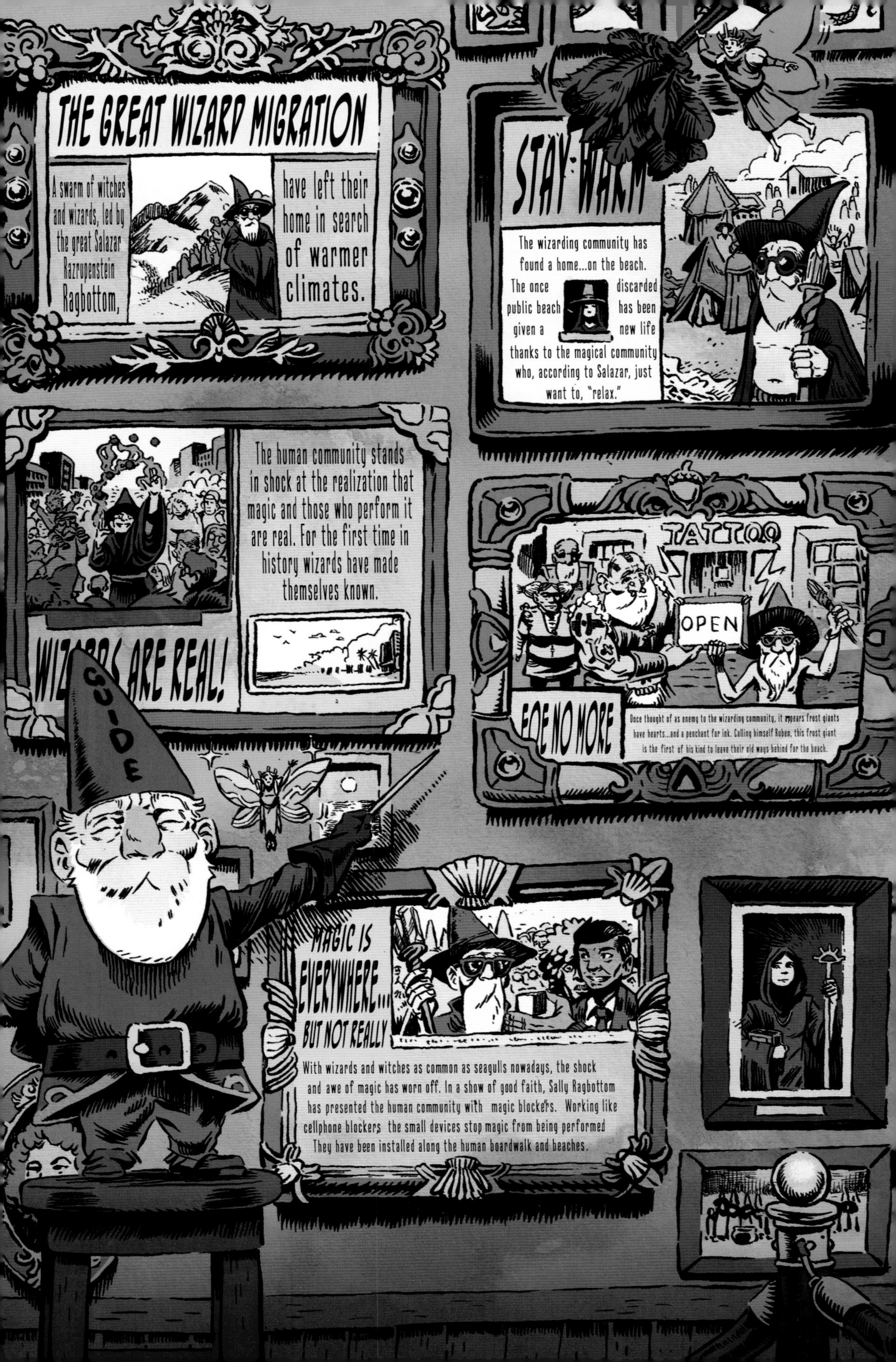
THE GREAT WIZARD MIGRATION
A swarm of witches and wizards, led by the great Salazar Razrupenstein Ragbottom,
have left their home in search of warmer climates.
STAY WARM
The wizarding community has found a home...on the beach. The once discarded public beach has been given a new life thanks to the magical community who, according to Salazar, just want to, "relax."
The human community stands in shock at the realization that magic and those who perform it are real. For the first time in history wizards have made themselves known.
WIZARDS ARE REAL!
TATTOO
OPEN
FOE NO MORE
Once thought of as enemy to the wizarding community, it appears frost giants have hearts...and a penchant for ink. Calling himself Ruben, this frost giant is the first of his kind to leave their old ways behind for the beach.
GUIDE
MAGIC IS EVERYWHERE... BUT NOT REALLY
With wizards and witches as common as seagulls nowadays, the shock and awe of magic has worn off. In a show of good faith, Sally Ragbottom has presented the human community with "magic blockers." Working like cellphone blockers, the small devices stop magic from being performed. They have been installed along the human boardwalk and beaches.

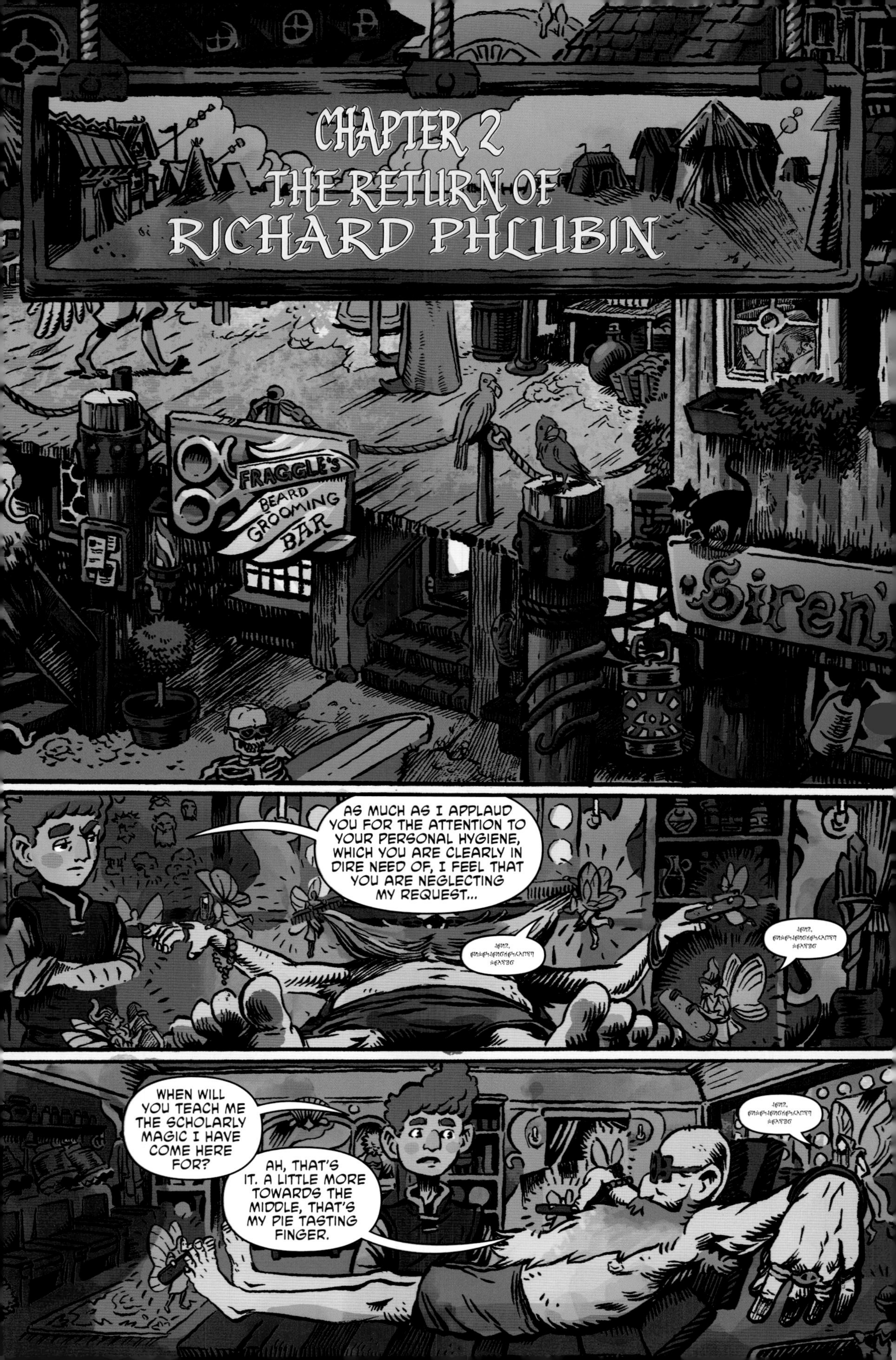
CHAPTER 2
THE RETURN OF
RICHARD PHLUBIN
FRAGGLE'S BEARD GROOMING BAR
AS MUCH AS I APPLAUD YOU FOR THE ATTENTION TO YOUR PERSONAL HYGIENE, WHICH YOU ARE CLEARLY IN DIRE NEED OF, I FEEL THAT YOU ARE NEGLECTING MY REQUEST...
WHEN WILL YOU TEACH ME THE SCHOLARLY MAGIC I HAVE COME HERE FOR?
AH, THAT'S IT. A LITTLE MORE TOWARDS THE MIDDLE, THAT'S MY PIE TASTING FINGER.

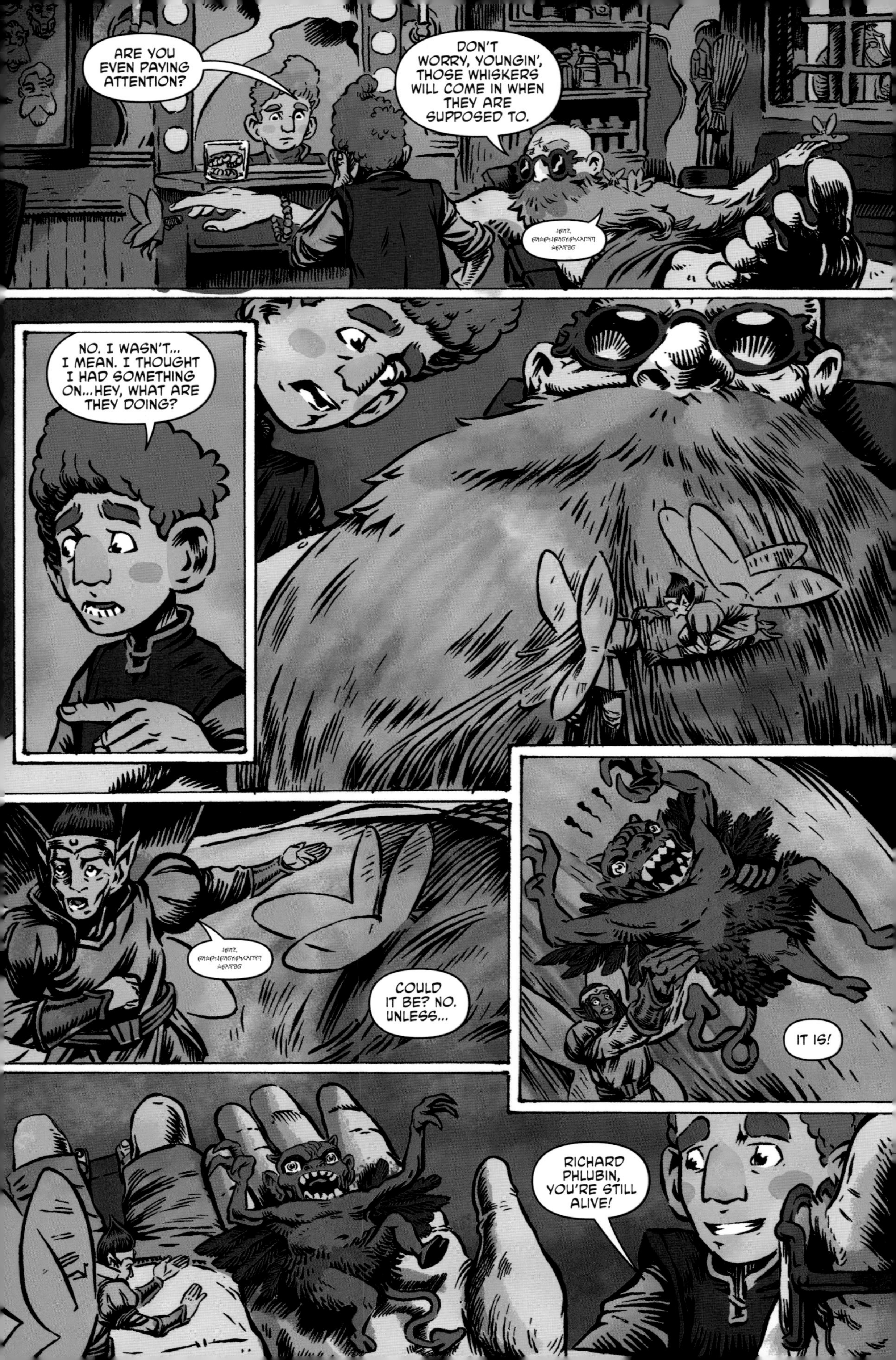
ARE YOU EVEN PAYING ATTENTION?
DON'T WORRY, YOUNGIN', THOSE WHISKERS WILL COME IN WHEN THEY ARE SUPPOSED TO.
NO. I WASN'T... I MEAN. I THOUGHT I HAD SOMETHING ON...HEY, WHAT ARE THEY DOING?
COULD IT BE? NO. UNLESS...
IT IS!
RICHARD PHLUBIN, YOU'RE STILL ALIVE!

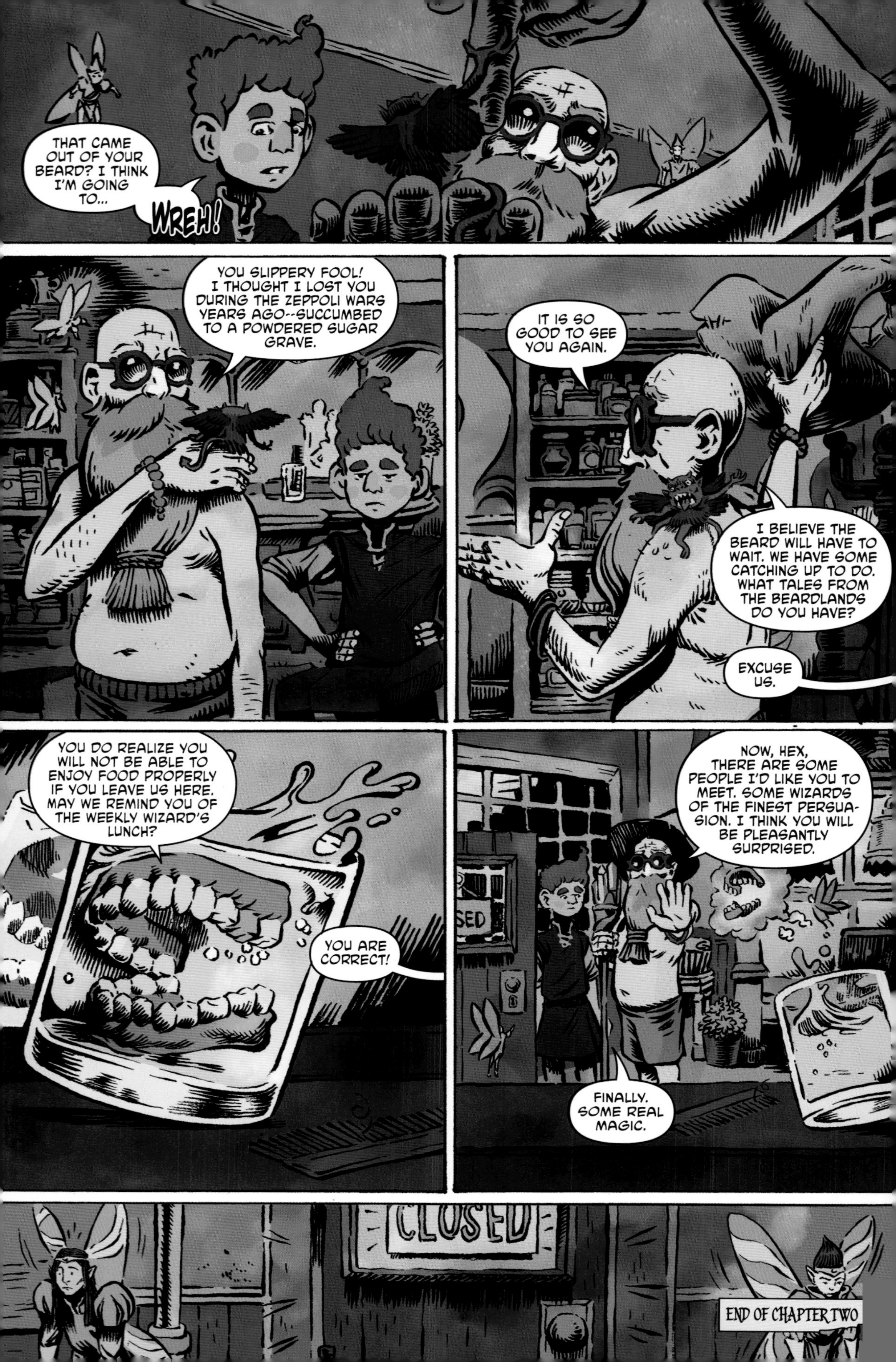
THAT CAME OUT OF YOUR BEARD? I THINK I'M GOING TO...
WREH!
YOU SLIPPERY FOOL! I THOUGHT I LOST YOU DURING THE ZEPPOLI WARS YEARS AGO--SUCCUMBED TO A POWDERED SUGAR GRAVE.
IT IS SO GOOD TO SEE YOU AGAIN.
I BELIEVE THE BEARD WILL HAVE TO WAIT. WE HAVE SOME CATCHING UP TO DO. WHAT TALES FROM THE BEARDLANDS DO YOU HAVE?
EXCUSE US.
YOU DO REALIZE YOU WILL NOT BE ABLE TO ENJOY FOOD PROPERLY IF YOU LEAVE US HERE. MAY WE REMIND YOU OF THE WEEKLY WIZARD'S LUNCH?
YOU ARE CORRECT!
NOW, HEX, THERE ARE SOME PEOPLE I'D LIKE YOU TO MEET. SOME WIZARDS OF THE FINEST PERSUASION. I THINK YOU WILL BE PLEASANTLY SURPRISED.
FINALLY. SOME REAL MAGIC.
CLOSED
END OF CHAPTER TWO

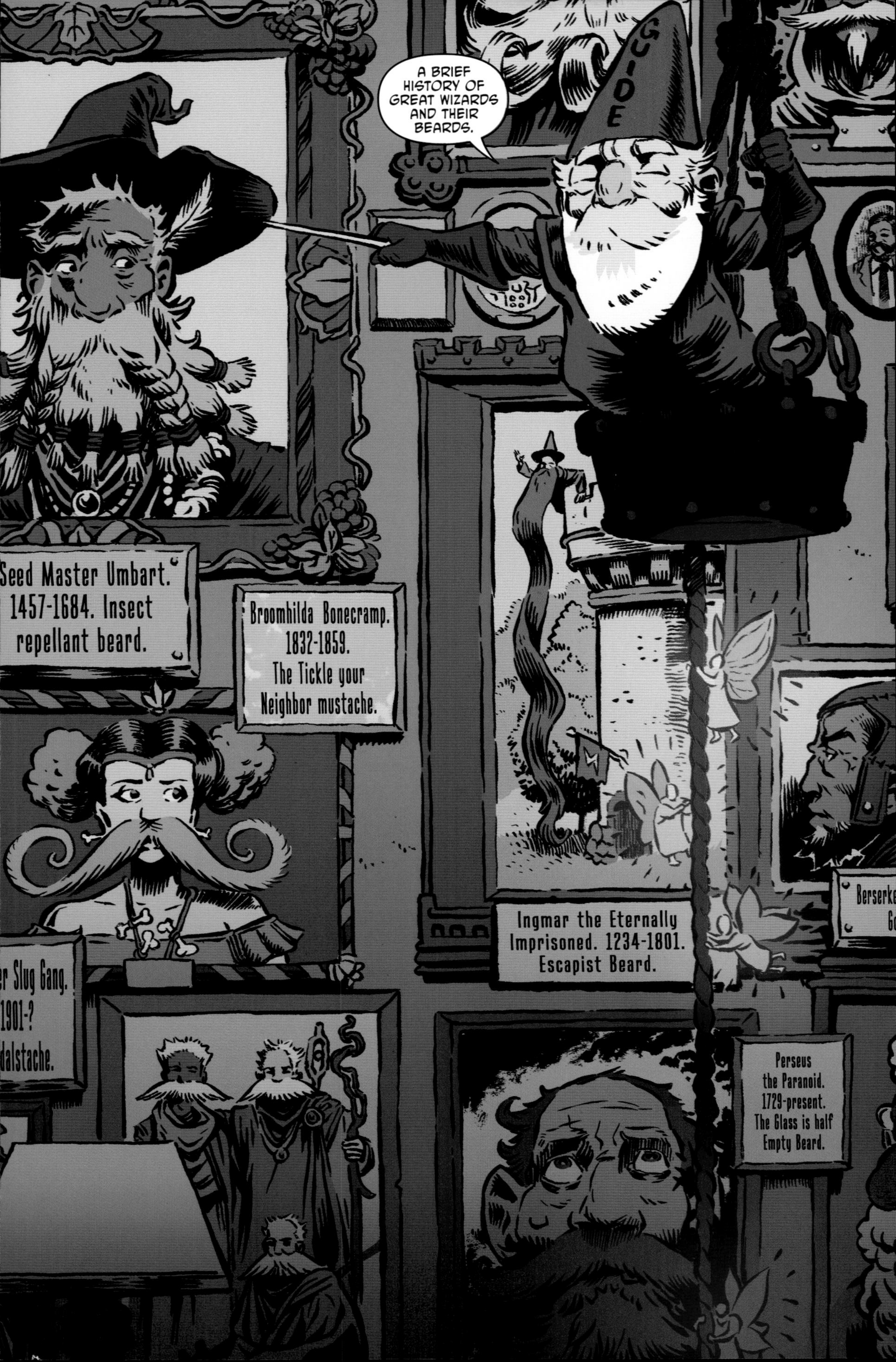

A BRIEF HISTORY OF GREAT WIZARDS AND THEIR BEARDS.
GUIDE
Seed Master Umbart. 1457-1684. Insect repellant beard.
Broomhilda Bonecramp. 1832-1859. The Tickle your Neighbor mustache.
Ingmar the Eternally Imprisoned. 1234-1801. Escapist Beard.
r Slug Gang. 1901-? dalstache.
Perseus the Paranoid. 1729-present. The Glass is half Empty Beard.
Berserke
Go

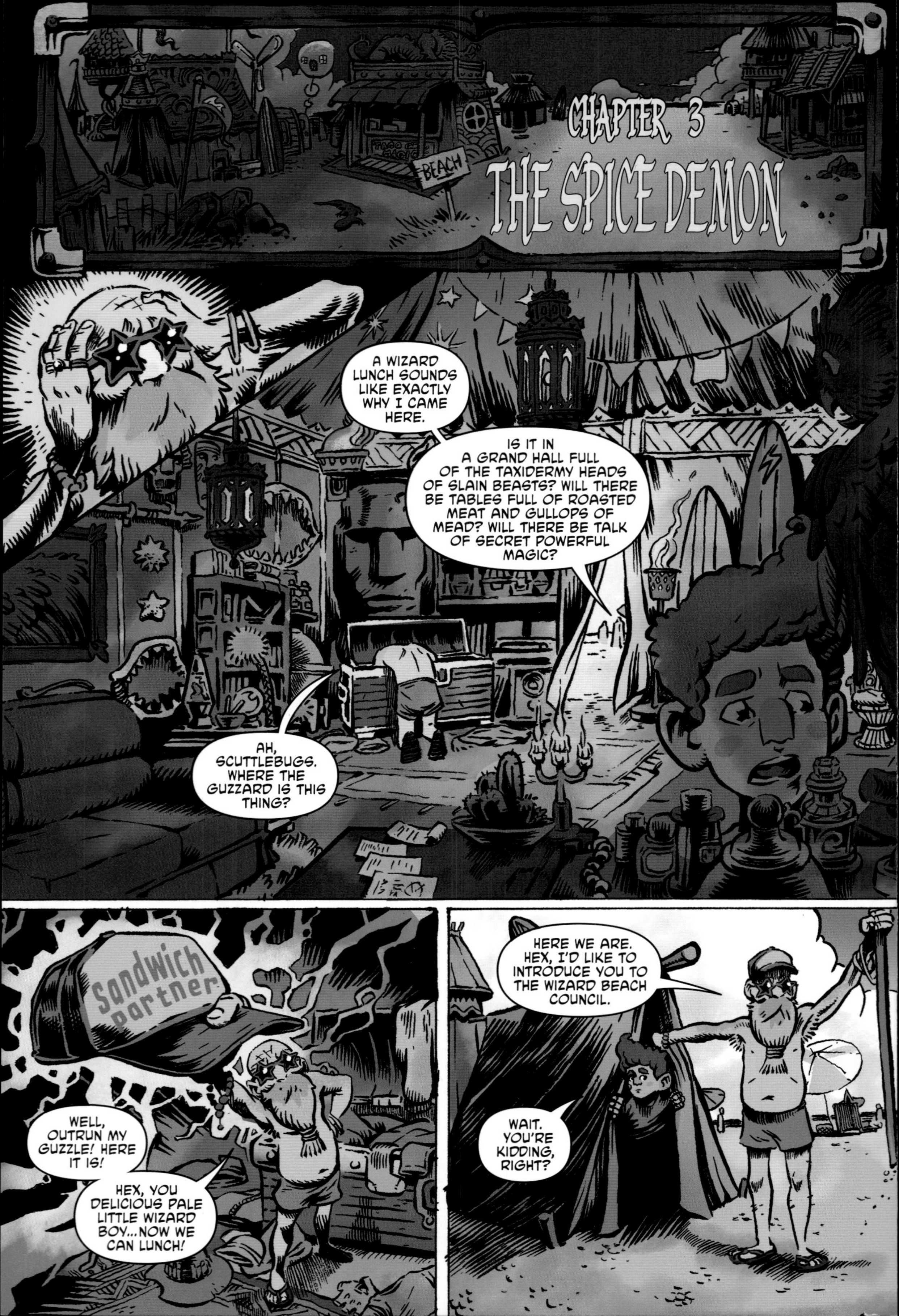
CHAPTER 3
THE SPICE DEMON
BEACH
A WIZARD LUNCH SOUNDS LIKE EXACTLY WHY I CAME HERE.
IS IT IN A GRAND HALL FULL OF THE TAXIDERMY HEADS OF SLAIN BEASTS? WILL THERE BE TABLES FULL OF ROASTED MEAT AND GULLOPS OF MEAD? WILL THERE BE TALK OF SECRET POWERFUL MAGIC?
AH, SCUTTLEBUGS. WHERE THE GUZZARD IS THIS THING?
Sandwich Partner
WELL, OUTRUN MY GUZZLE! HERE IT IS!
HEX, YOU DELICIOUS PALE LITTLE WIZARD BOY...NOW WE CAN LUNCH!
HERE WE ARE. HEX, I'D LIKE TO INTRODUCE YOU TO THE WIZARD BEACH COUNCIL.
WAIT. YOU'RE KIDDING, RIGHT?

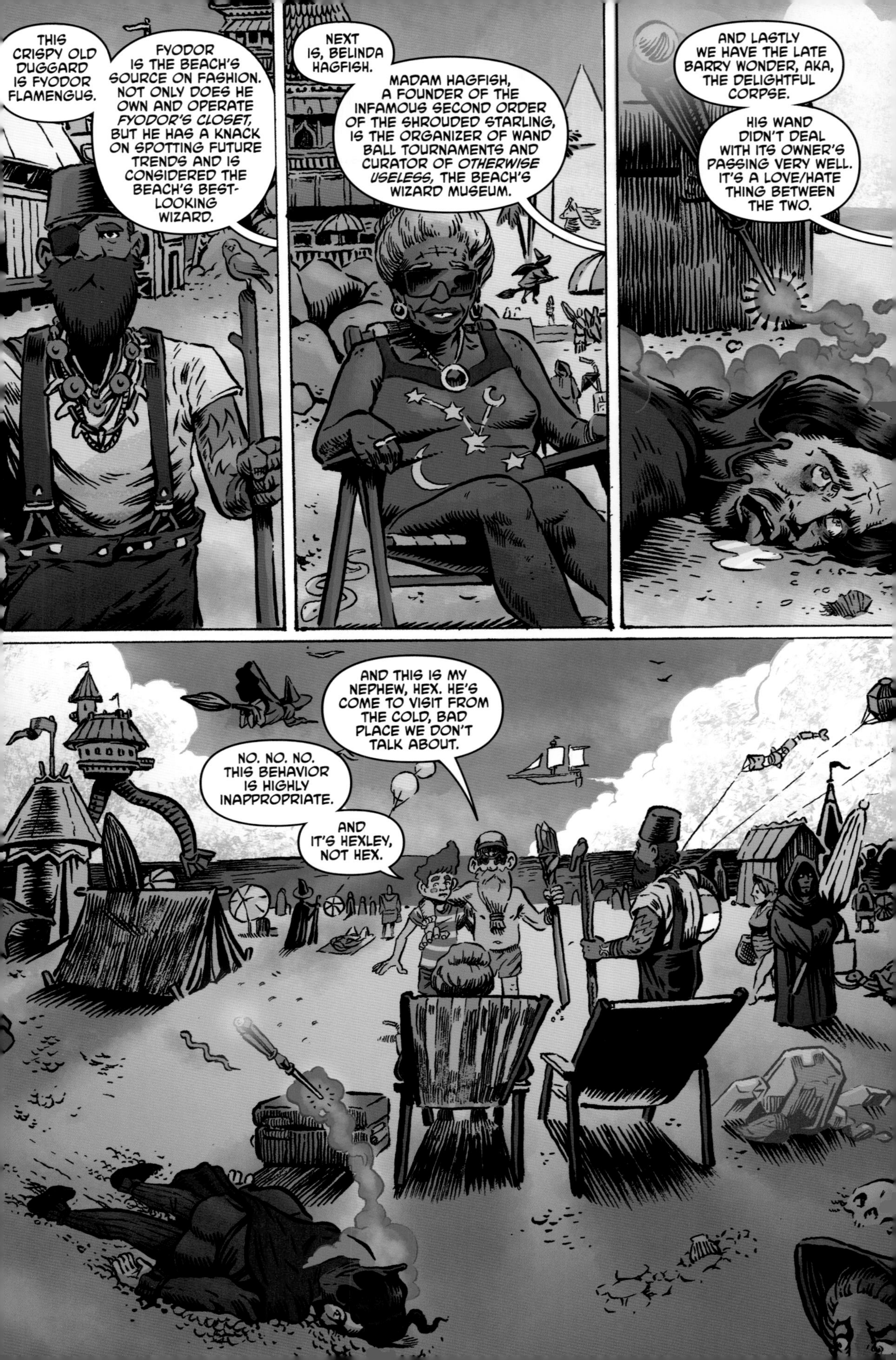
THIS CRISPY OLD DUGGARD IS FYODOR FLAMENGUS.
FYODOR IS THE BEACH'S SOURCE ON FASHION. NOT ONLY DOES HE OWN AND OPERATE *FYODOR'S CLOSET,* BUT HE HAS A KNACK ON SPOTTING FUTURE TRENDS AND IS CONSIDERED THE BEACH'S BEST-LOOKING WIZARD.
NEXT IS, BELINDA HAGFISH.
MADAM HAGFISH, A FOUNDER OF THE INFAMOUS SECOND ORDER OF THE SHROUDED STARLING, IS THE ORGANIZER OF WAND BALL TOURNAMENTS AND CURATOR OF *OTHERWISE USELESS,* THE BEACH'S WIZARD MUSEUM.
AND LASTLY WE HAVE THE LATE BARRY WONDER, AKA, THE DELIGHTFUL CORPSE.
HIS WAND DIDN'T DEAL WITH ITS OWNER'S PASSING VERY WELL. IT'S A LOVE/HATE THING BETWEEN THE TWO.
AND THIS IS MY NEPHEW, HEX. HE'S COME TO VISIT FROM THE COLD, BAD PLACE WE DON'T TALK ABOUT.
NO. NO. NO. THIS BEHAVIOR IS HIGHLY INAPPROPRIATE.
AND IT'S HEXLEY, NOT HEX.

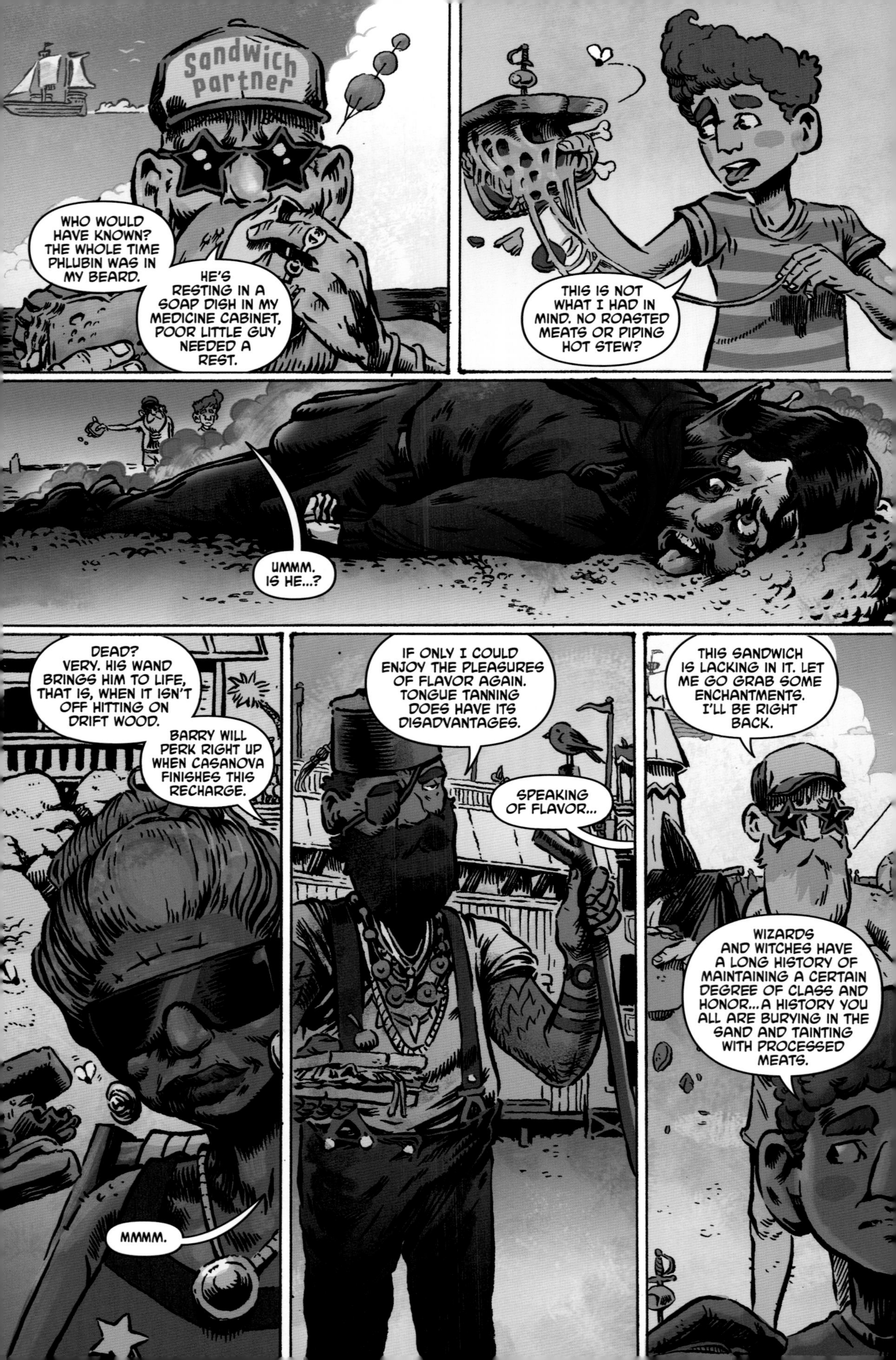

SANDWICH PARTNER
WHO WOULD HAVE KNOWN? THE WHOLE TIME PHLUBIN WAS IN MY BEARD.
HE'S RESTING IN A SOAP DISH IN MY MEDICINE CABINET, POOR LITTLE GUY NEEDED A REST.
THIS IS NOT WHAT I HAD IN MIND. NO ROASTED MEATS OR PIPING HOT STEW?
UMMM. IS HE...?
DEAD? VERY. HIS WAND BRINGS HIM TO LIFE, THAT IS, WHEN IT ISN'T OFF HITTING ON DRIFT WOOD.
BARRY WILL PERK RIGHT UP WHEN CASANOVA FINISHES THIS RECHARGE.
MMMM.
IF ONLY I COULD ENJOY THE PLEASURES OF FLAVOR AGAIN. TONGUE TANNING DOES HAVE ITS DISADVANTAGES.
SPEAKING OF FLAVOR...
THIS SANDWICH IS LACKING IN IT. LET ME GO GRAB SOME ENCHANTMENTS. I'LL BE RIGHT BACK.
WIZARDS AND WITCHES HAVE A LONG HISTORY OF MAINTAINING A CERTAIN DEGREE OF CLASS AND HONOR...A HISTORY YOU ALL ARE BURYING IN THE SAND AND TAINTING WITH PROCESSED MEATS.

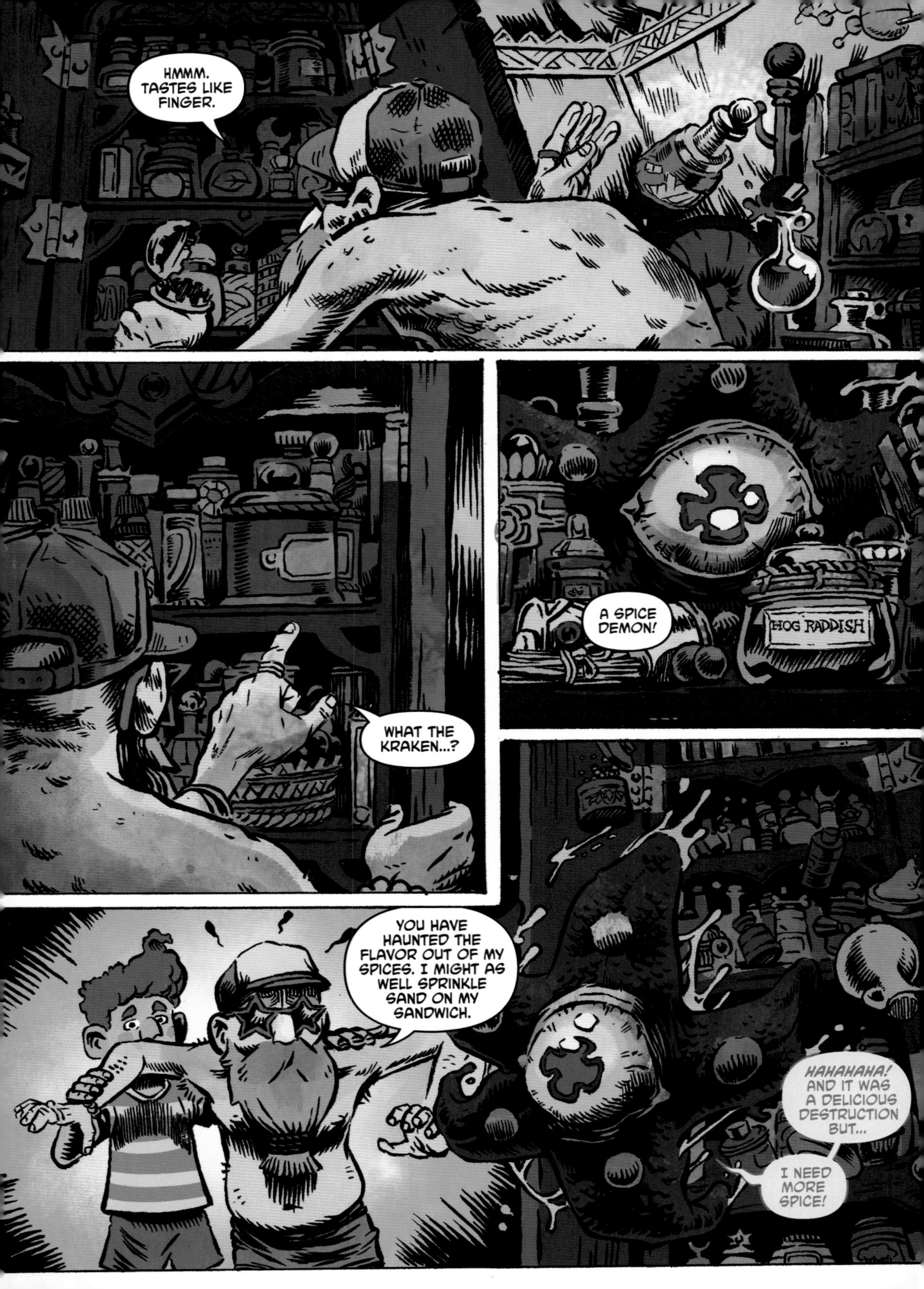
HMMM. TASTES LIKE FINGER.
WHAT THE KRAKEN...?
A SPICE DEMON!
HOG RADDISH
YOU HAVE HAUNTED THE FLAVOR OUT OF MY SPICES. I MIGHT AS WELL SPRINKLE SAND ON MY SANDWICH.
HAHAHAHA! AND IT WAS A DELICIOUS DESTRUCTION BUT...
I NEED MORE SPICE!

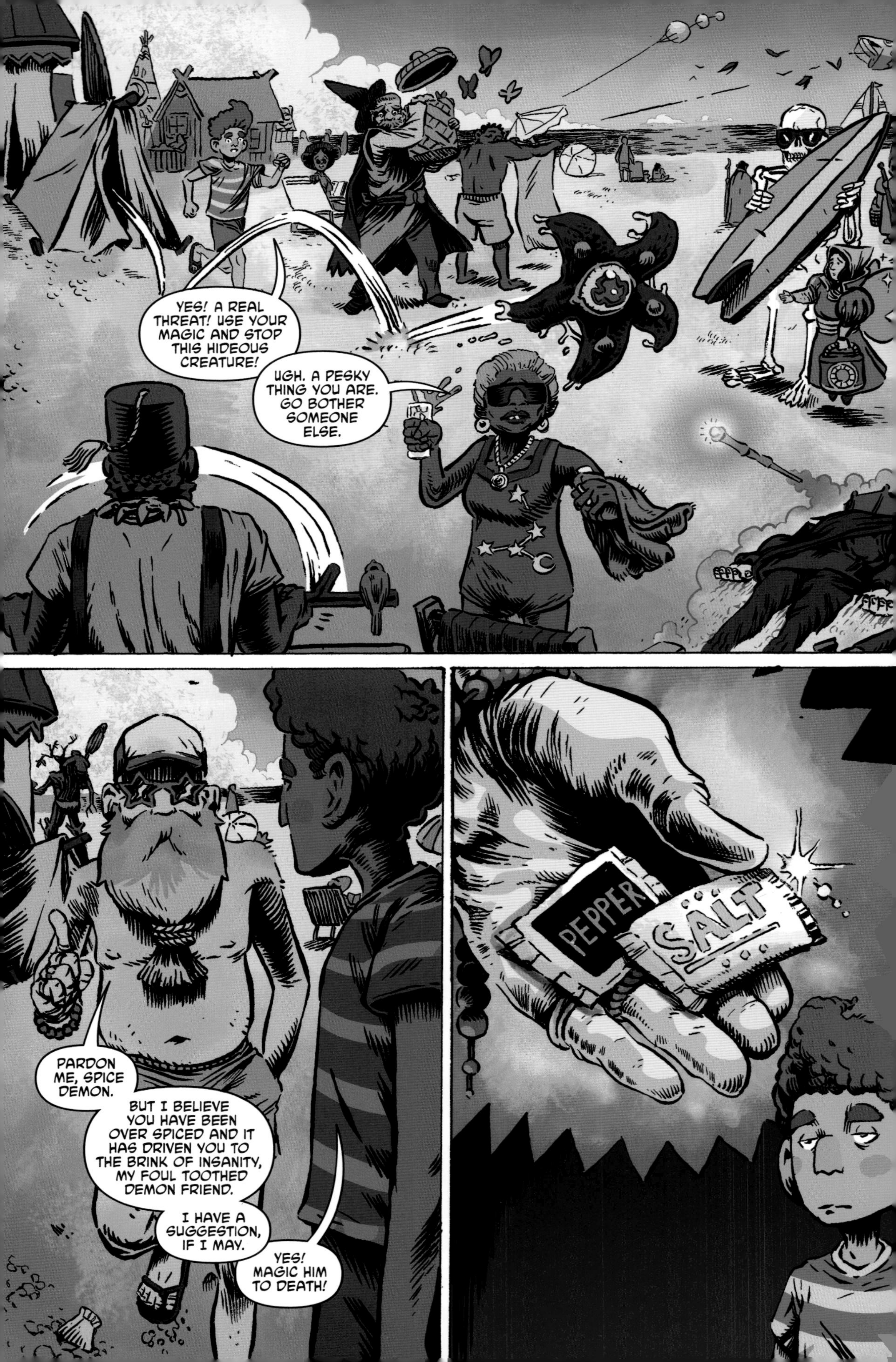
YES! A REAL THREAT! USE YOUR MAGIC AND STOP THIS HIDEOUS CREATURE!
UGH. A PESKY THING YOU ARE. GO BOTHER SOMEONE ELSE.
PARDON ME, SPICE DEMON.
BUT I BELIEVE YOU HAVE BEEN OVER SPICED AND IT HAS DRIVEN YOU TO THE BRINK OF INSANITY, MY FOUL TOOTHED DEMON FRIEND.
I HAVE A SUGGESTION, IF I MAY.
YES! MAGIC HIM TO DEATH!
PEPPER
SALT

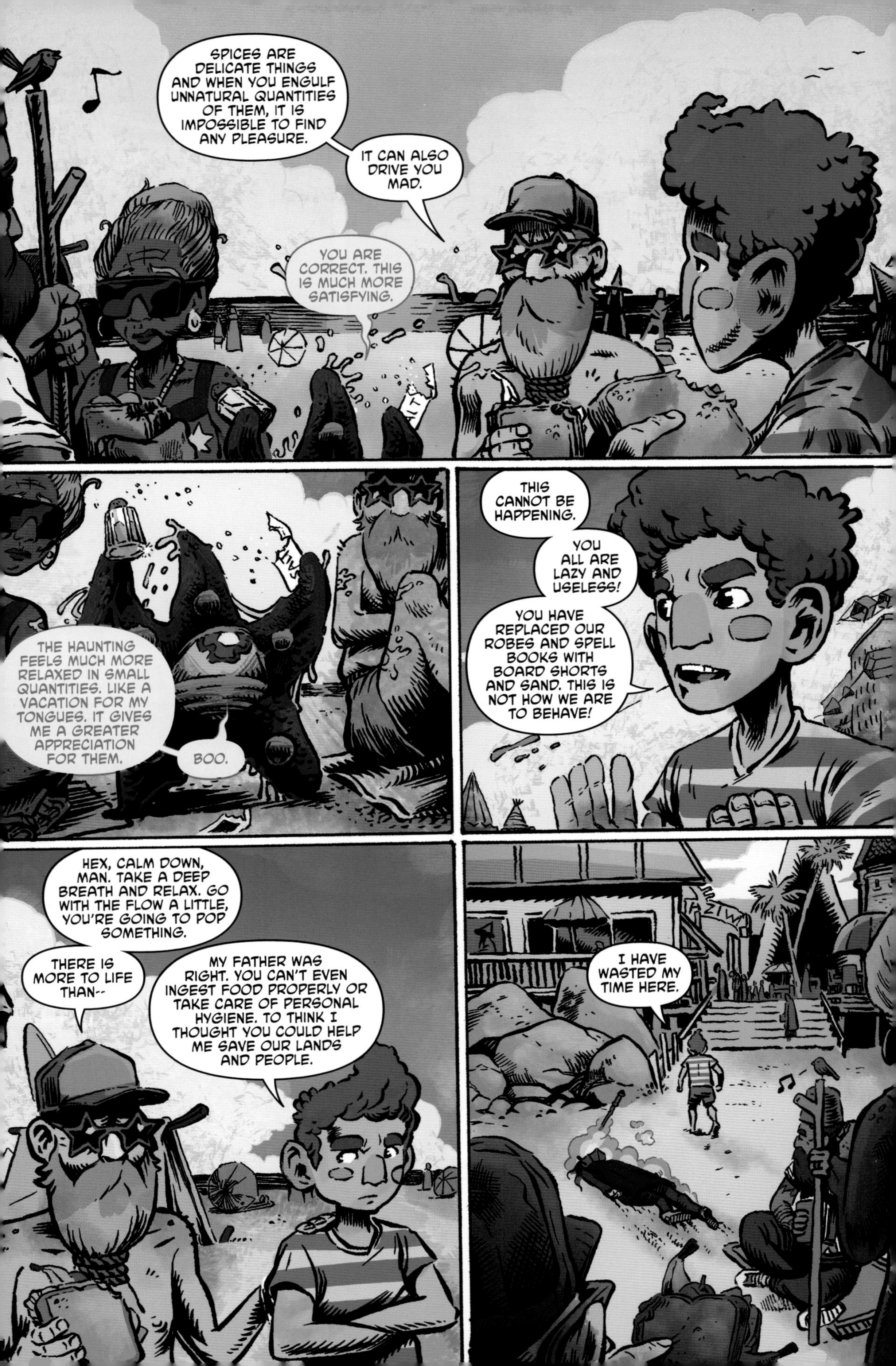

SPICES ARE DELICATE THINGS AND WHEN YOU ENGULF UNNATURAL QUANTITIES OF THEM, IT IS IMPOSSIBLE TO FIND ANY PLEASURE.
IT CAN ALSO DRIVE YOU MAD.
YOU ARE CORRECT. THIS IS MUCH MORE SATISFYING.
THE HAUNTING FEELS MUCH MORE RELAXED IN SMALL QUANTITIES. LIKE A VACATION FOR MY TONGUES. IT GIVES ME A GREATER APPRECIATION FOR THEM.
BOO.
THIS CANNOT BE HAPPENING.
YOU ALL ARE LAZY AND USELESS!
YOU HAVE REPLACED OUR ROBES AND SPELL BOOKS WITH BOARD SHORTS AND SAND. THIS IS NOT HOW WE ARE TO BEHAVE!
HEX, CALM DOWN, MAN. TAKE A DEEP BREATH AND RELAX. GO WITH THE FLOW A LITTLE, YOU'RE GOING TO POP SOMETHING.
THERE IS MORE TO LIFE THAN--
MY FATHER WAS RIGHT. YOU CAN'T EVEN INGEST FOOD PROPERLY OR TAKE CARE OF PERSONAL HYGIENE. TO THINK I THOUGHT YOU COULD HELP ME SAVE OUR LANDS AND PEOPLE.
I HAVE WASTED MY TIME HERE.

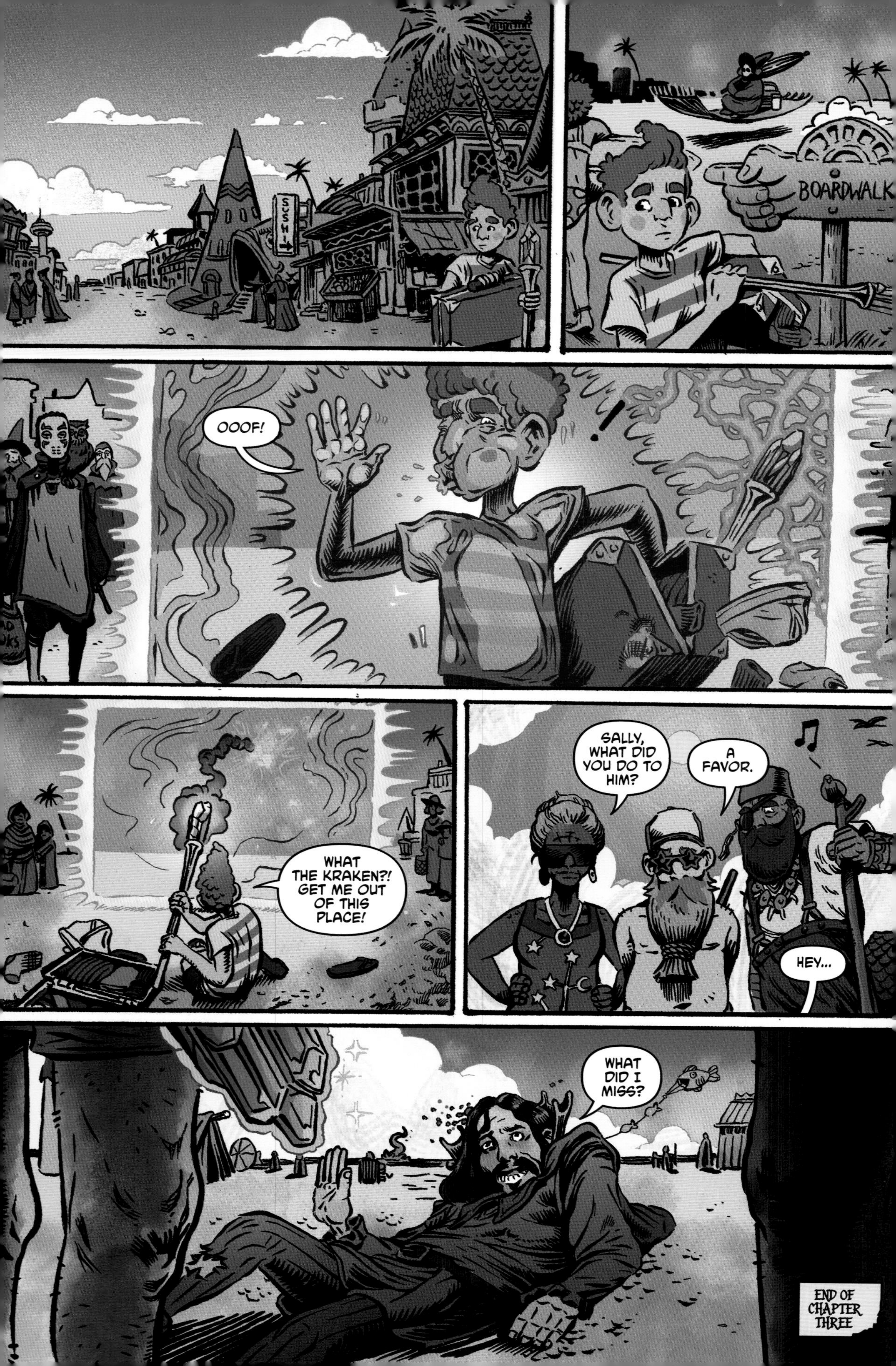
SUSHI
BOARDWALK
OOOF!
WHAT THE KRAKEN?! GET ME OUT OF THIS PLACE!
SALLY, WHAT DID YOU DO TO HIM?
A FAVOR.
HEY...
WHAT DID I MISS?
END OF CHAPTER THREE

COVER BY
CONOR NOLAN

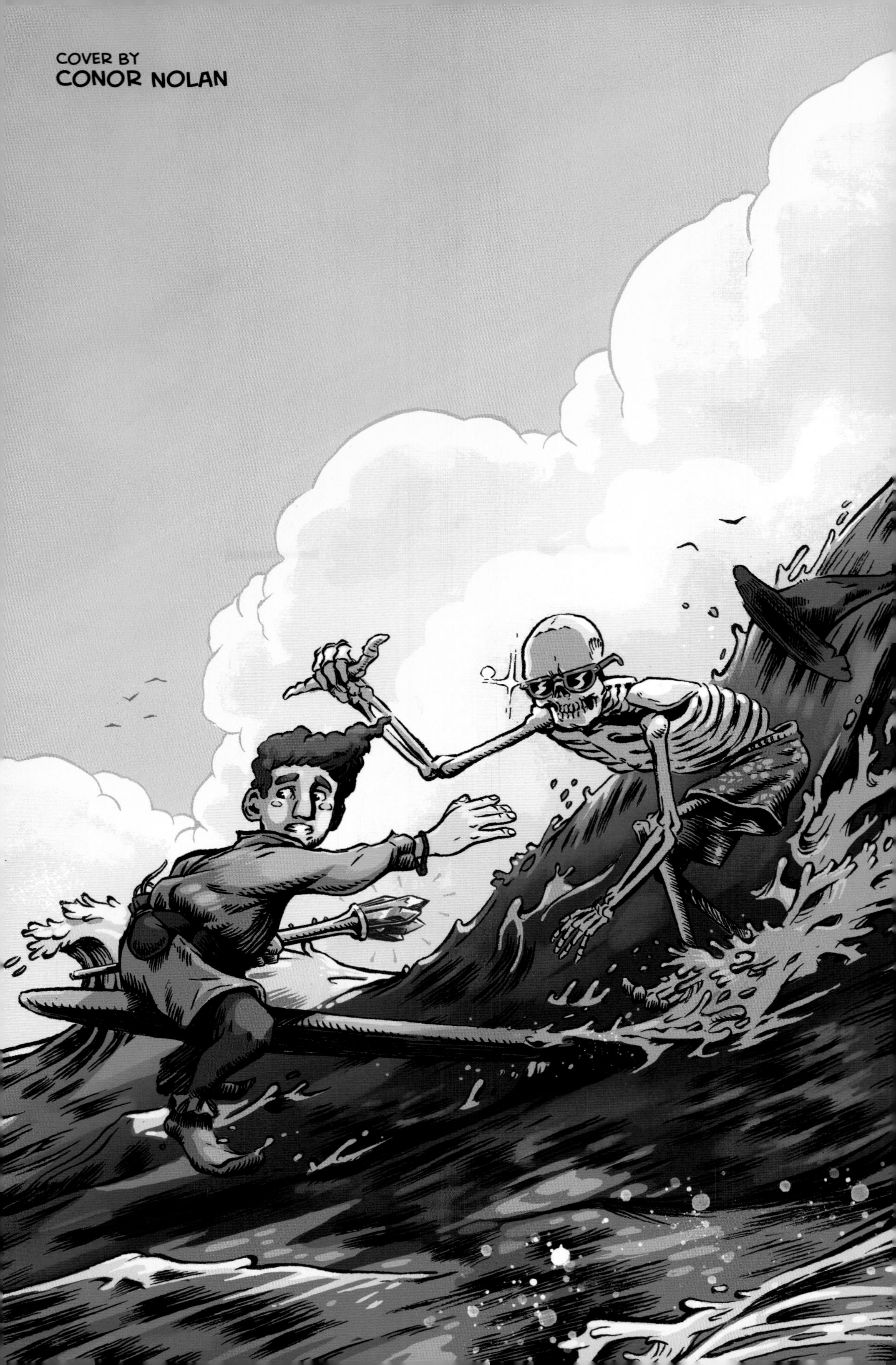

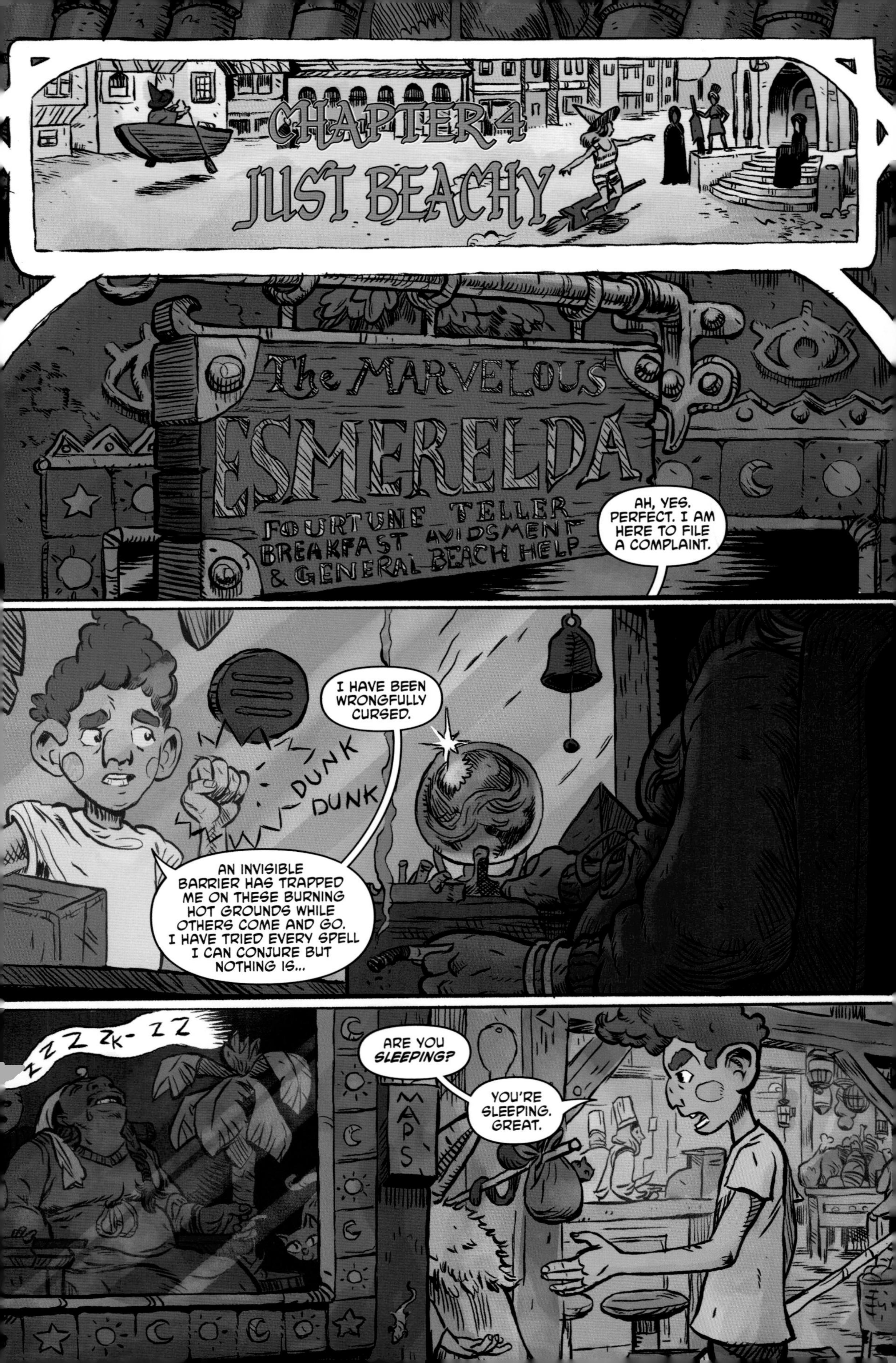
CHAPTER 4
JUST BEACHY
The MARVELOUS
ESMERELDA
FOURTUNE TELLER
BREAKFAST AVIDSMENT
& GENERAL BEACH HELP
AH, YES. PERFECT. I AM HERE TO FILE A COMPLAINT.
I HAVE BEEN WRONGFULLY CURSED.
DUNK
DUNK
AN INVISIBLE BARRIER HAS TRAPPED ME ON THESE BURNING HOT GROUNDS WHILE OTHERS COME AND GO. I HAVE TRIED EVERY SPELL I CAN CONJURE BUT NOTHING IS...
ZZZZK- ZZ
ARE YOU *SLEEPING?*
YOU'RE SLEEPING. GREAT.
MAPS

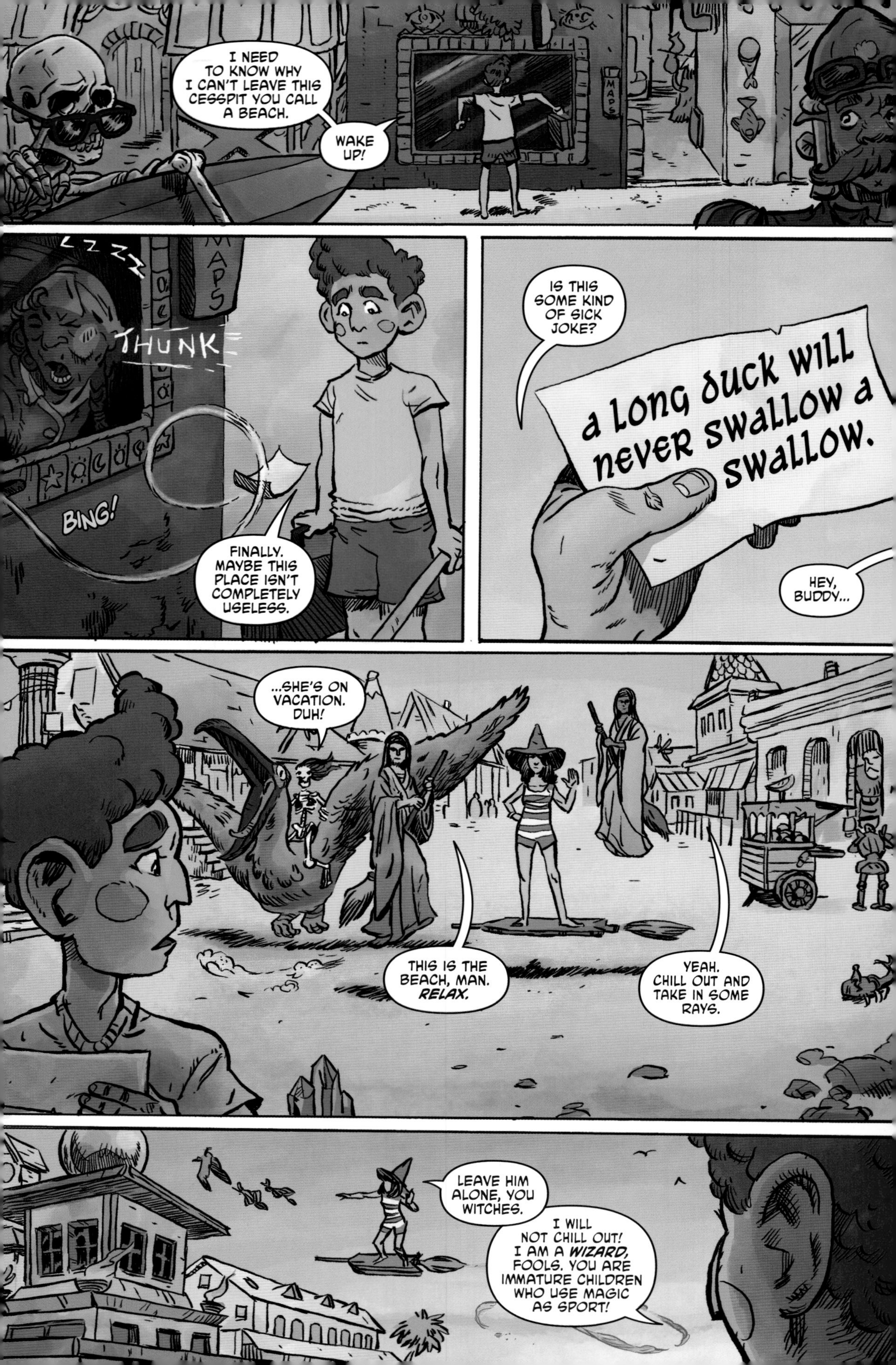
I NEED TO KNOW WHY I CAN'T LEAVE THIS CESSPIT YOU CALL A BEACH.
WAKE UP!
MAPS
ZZZZ
THUNK
BING!
FINALLY. MAYBE THIS PLACE ISN'T COMPLETELY USELESS.
IS THIS SOME KIND OF SICK JOKE?
a long duck will never swallow a swallow.
HEY, BUDDY...
...SHE'S ON VACATION. DUH!
THIS IS THE BEACH, MAN. RELAX.
YEAH. CHILL OUT AND TAKE IN SOME RAYS.
LEAVE HIM ALONE, YOU WITCHES.
I WILL NOT CHILL OUT! I AM A WIZARD, FOOLS. YOU ARE IMMATURE CHILDREN WHO USE MAGIC AS SPORT!

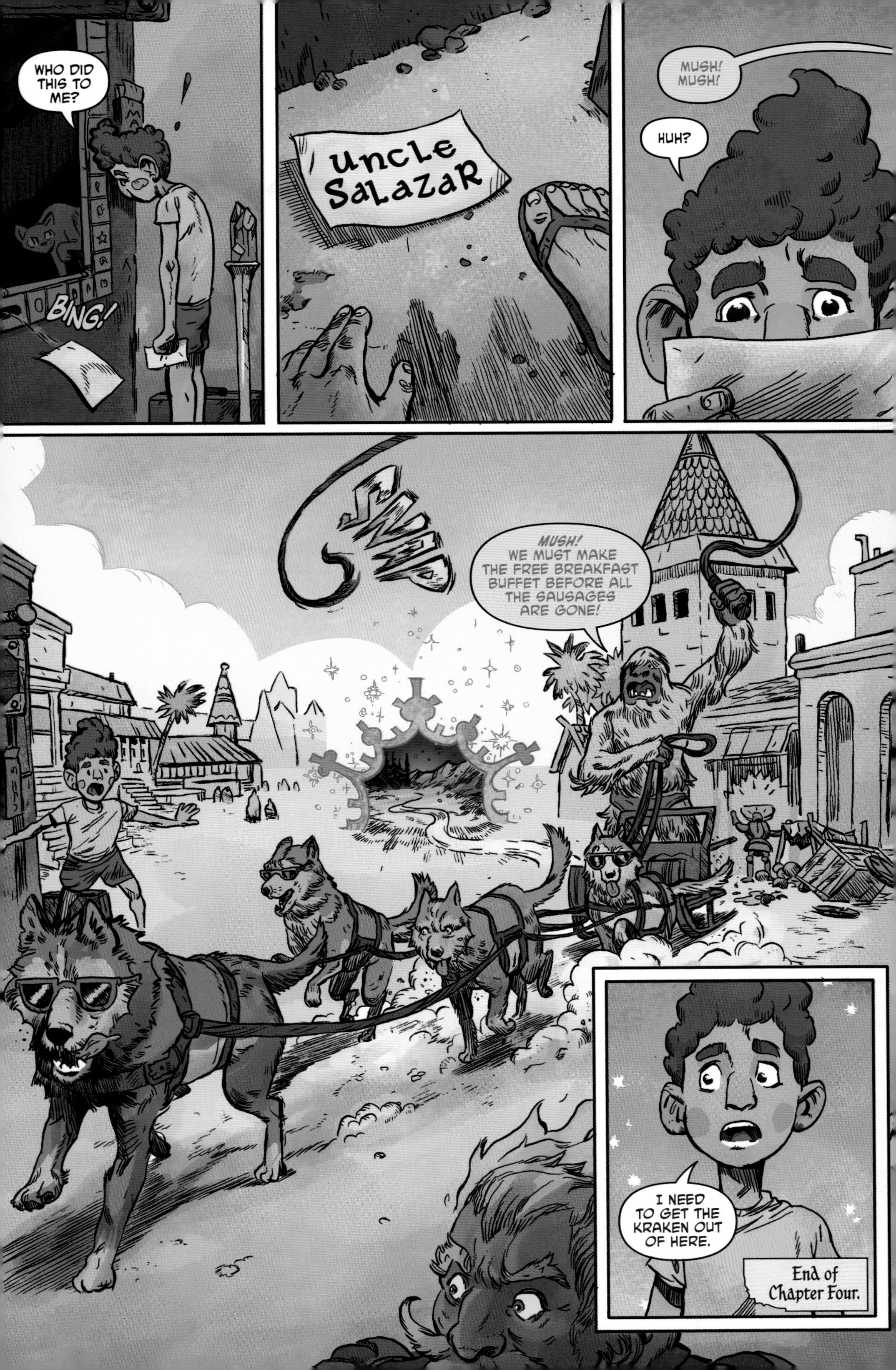
WHO DID THIS TO ME?
BING!
Uncle Salazar
MUSH! MUSH!
HUH?
MUSH! WE MUST MAKE THE FREE BREAKFAST BUFFET BEFORE ALL THE SAUSAGES ARE GONE!
I NEED TO GET THE KRAKEN OUT OF HERE.
End of Chapter Four.

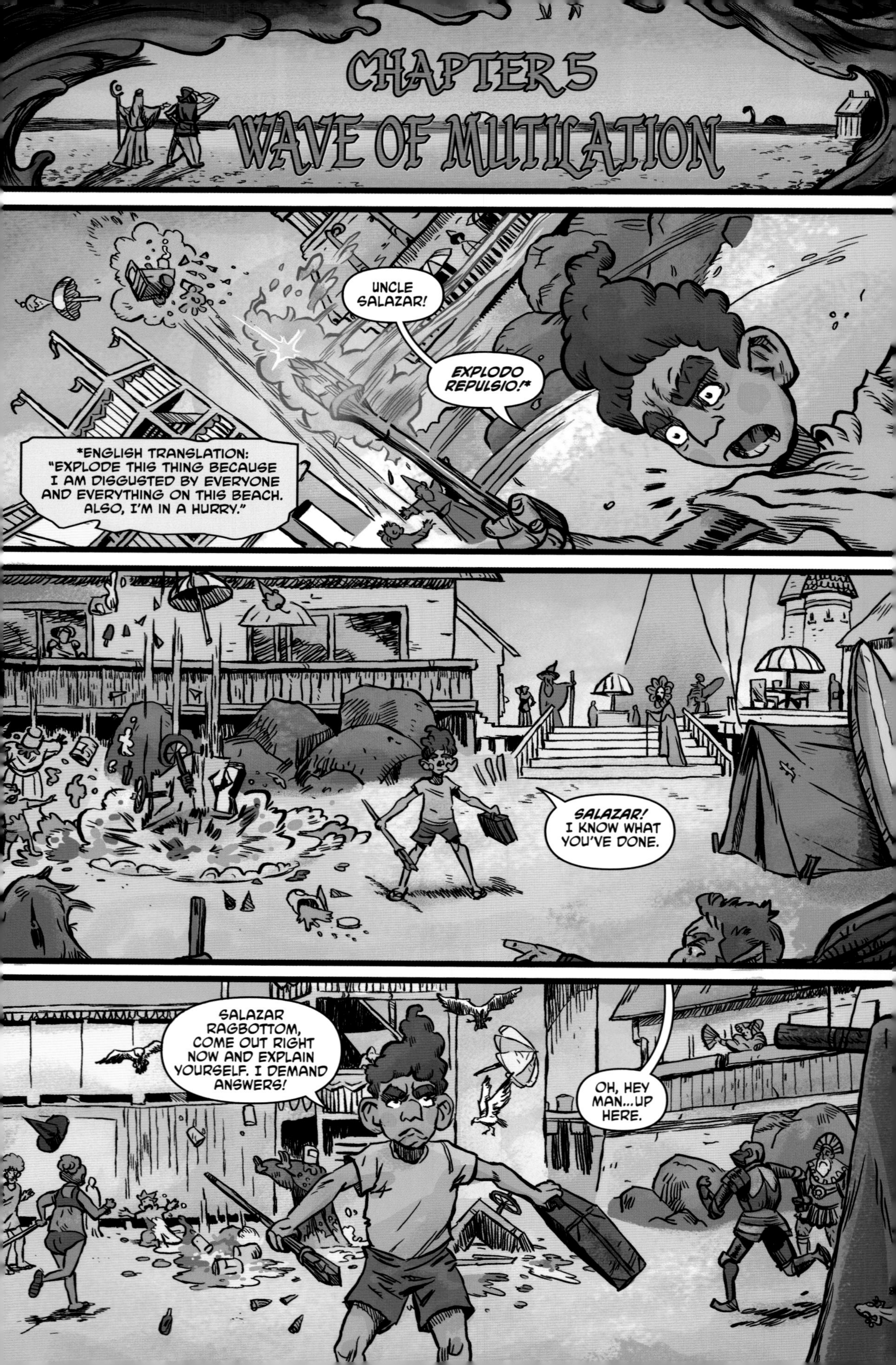
CHAPTER 5
WAVE OF MUTILATION
UNCLE SALAZAR!
EXPLODO REPULSIO!*
*ENGLISH TRANSLATION: "EXPLODE THIS THING BECAUSE I AM DISGUSTED BY EVERYONE AND EVERYTHING ON THIS BEACH. ALSO, I'M IN A HURRY."
SALAZAR! I KNOW WHAT YOU'VE DONE.
SALAZAR RAGBOTTOM, COME OUT RIGHT NOW AND EXPLAIN YOURSELF. I DEMAND ANSWERS!
OH, HEY MAN...UP HERE.

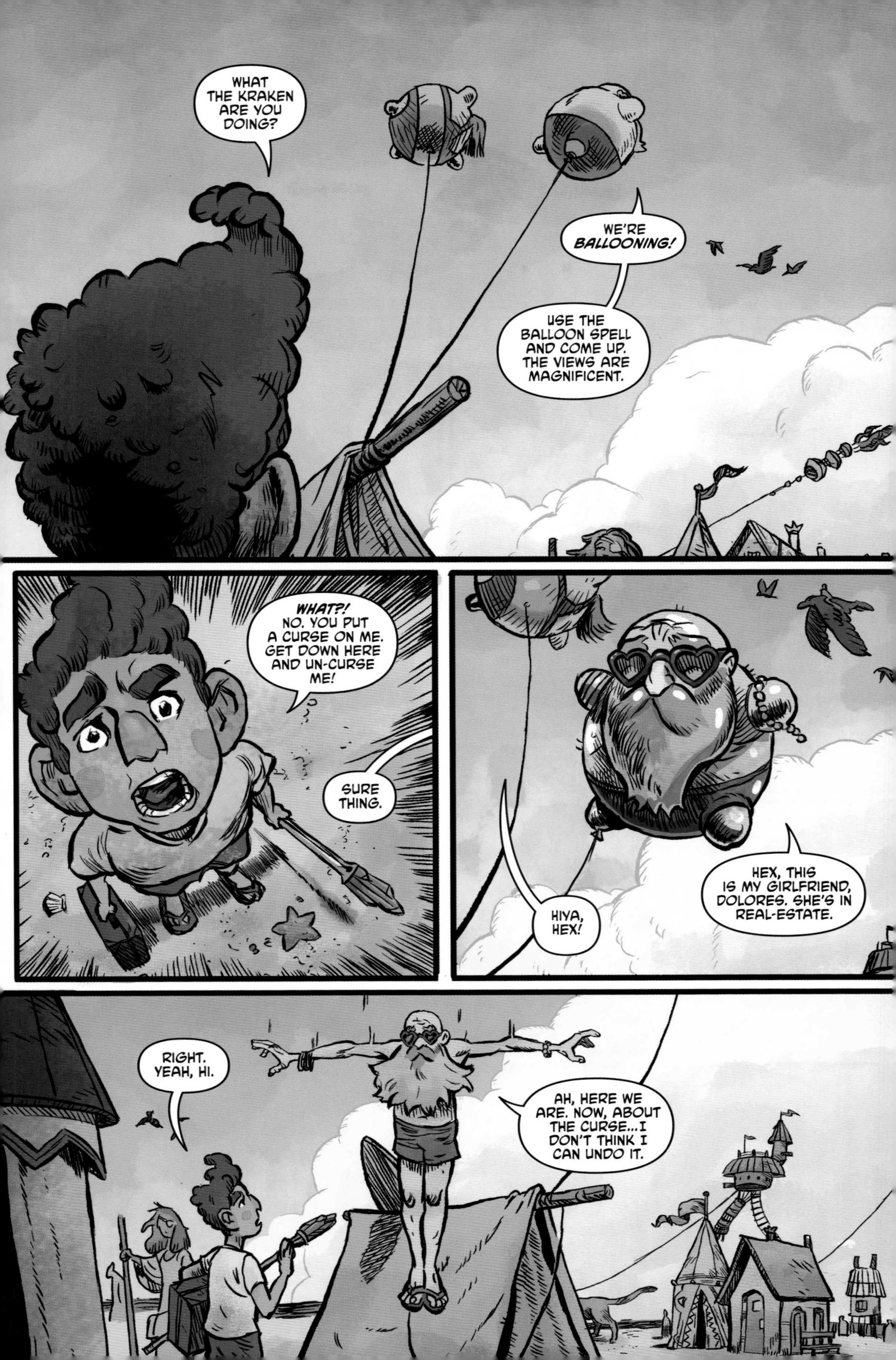
WHAT THE KRAKEN ARE YOU DOING?
WE'RE *BALLOONING!*
USE THE BALLOON SPELL AND COME UP. THE VIEWS ARE MAGNIFICENT.
WHAT?! NO. YOU PUT A CURSE ON ME. GET DOWN HERE AND UN-CURSE ME!
SURE THING.
HEX, THIS IS MY GIRLFRIEND, DOLORES. SHE'S IN REAL-ESTATE.
HIYA, HEX!
RIGHT. YEAH, HI.
AH, HERE WE ARE. NOW, ABOUT THE CURSE... I DON'T THINK I CAN UNDO IT.

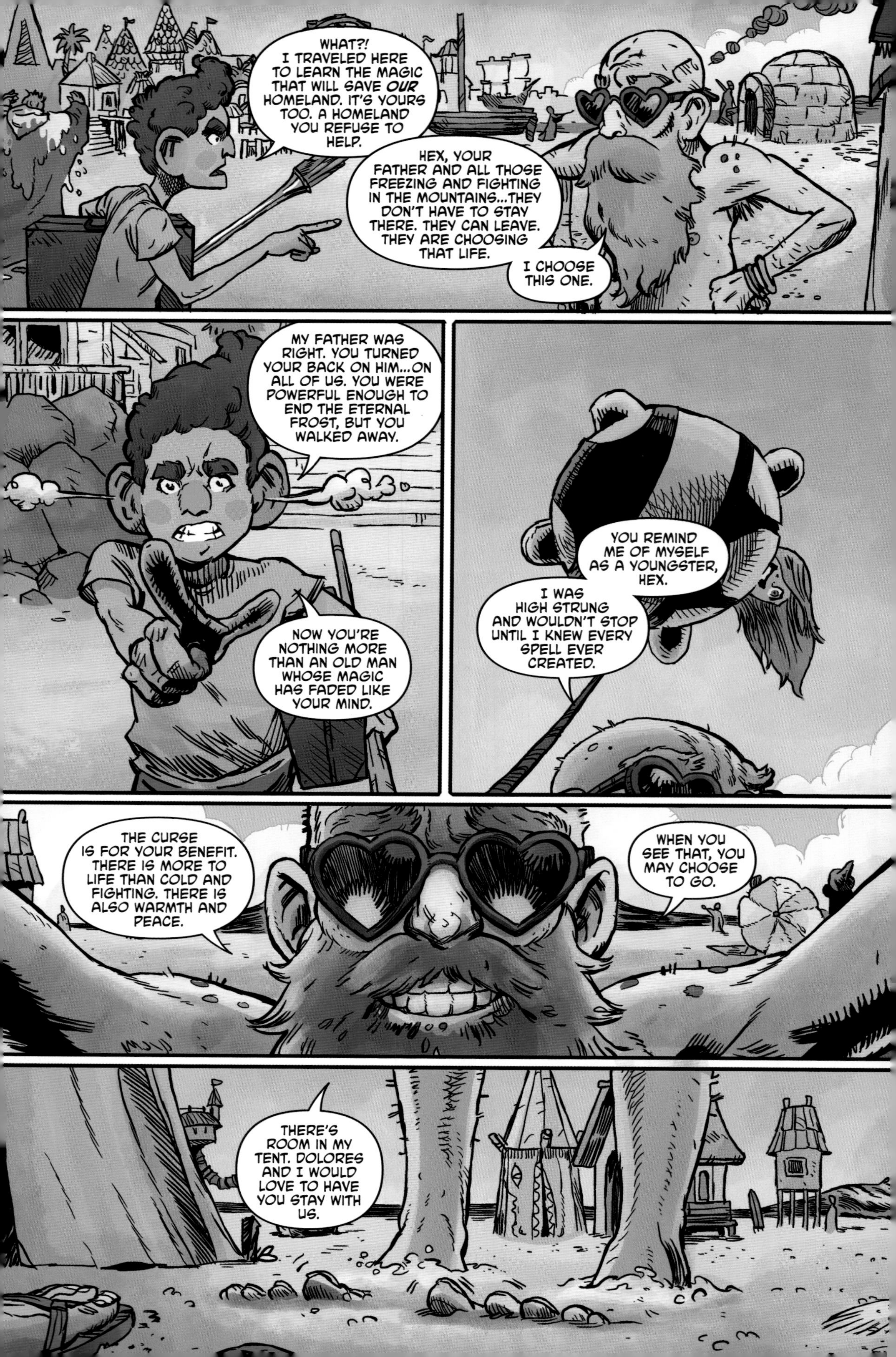
WHAT?! I TRAVELED HERE TO LEARN THE MAGIC THAT WILL SAVE *OUR* HOMELAND. IT'S YOURS TOO. A HOMELAND YOU REFUSE TO HELP.
HEX, YOUR FATHER AND ALL THOSE FREEZING AND FIGHTING IN THE MOUNTAINS...THEY DON'T HAVE TO STAY THERE. THEY CAN LEAVE. THEY ARE CHOOSING THAT LIFE.
I CHOOSE THIS ONE.
MY FATHER WAS RIGHT. YOU TURNED YOUR BACK ON HIM...ON ALL OF US. YOU WERE POWERFUL ENOUGH TO END THE ETERNAL FROST, BUT YOU WALKED AWAY.
NOW YOU'RE NOTHING MORE THAN AN OLD MAN WHOSE MAGIC HAS FADED LIKE YOUR MIND.
YOU REMIND ME OF MYSELF AS A YOUNGSTER, HEX.
I WAS HIGH STRUNG AND WOULDN'T STOP UNTIL I KNEW EVERY SPELL EVER CREATED.
THE CURSE IS FOR YOUR BENEFIT. THERE IS MORE TO LIFE THAN COLD AND FIGHTING. THERE IS ALSO WARMTH AND PEACE.
WHEN YOU SEE THAT, YOU MAY CHOOSE TO GO.
THERE'S ROOM IN MY TENT. DOLORES AND I WOULD LOVE TO HAVE YOU STAY WITH US.

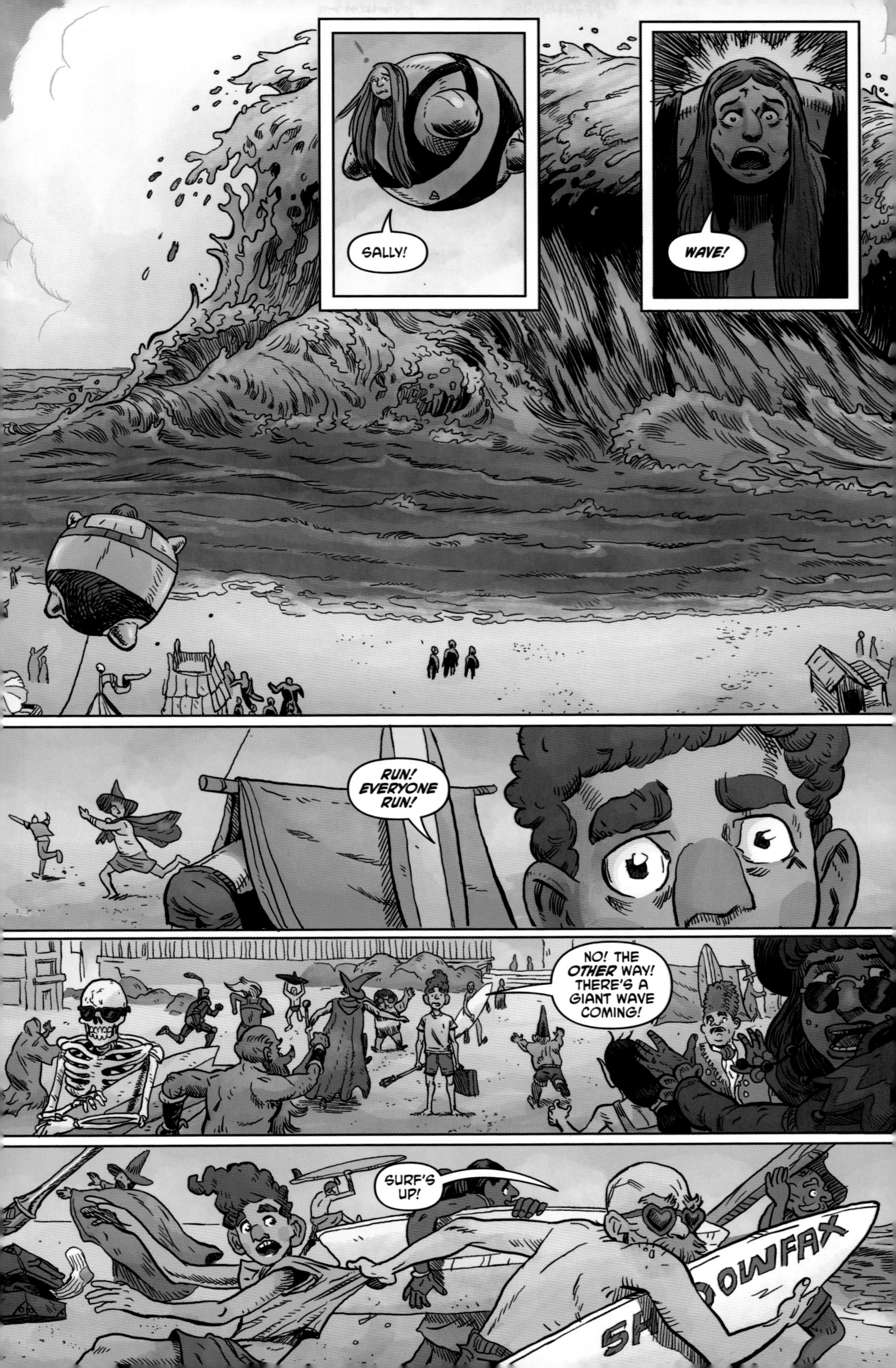
SALLY!
WAVE!
RUN! EVERYONE RUN!
NO! THE OTHER WAY! THERE'S A GIANT WAVE COMING!
SURF'S UP!

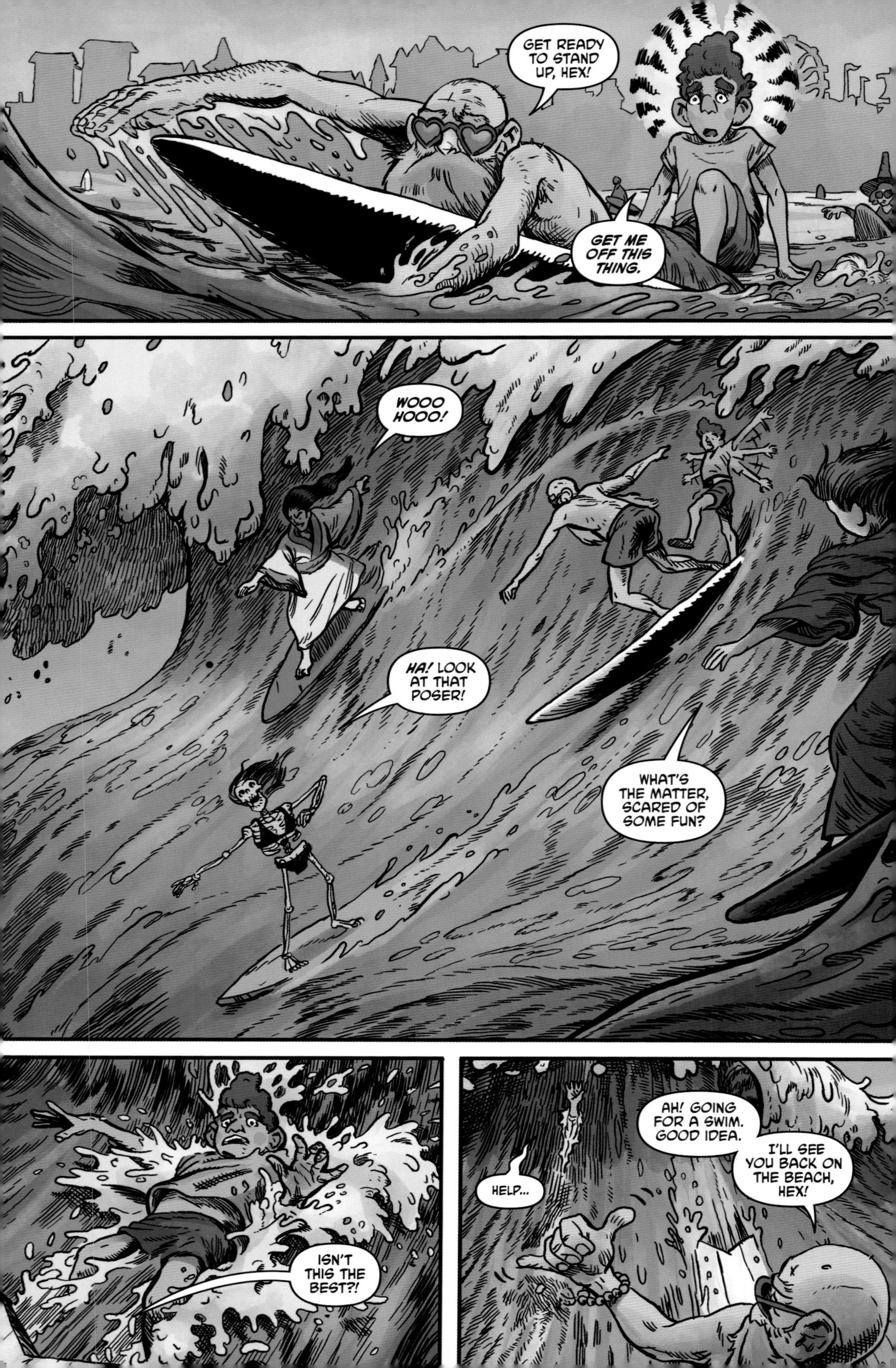
GET READY TO STAND UP, HEX!
GET ME OFF THIS THING.
WOOO HOOO!
HA! LOOK AT THAT POSER!
WHAT'S THE MATTER, SCARED OF SOME FUN?
ISN'T THIS THE BEST?!
AH! GOING FOR A SWIM. GOOD IDEA.
HELP...
I'LL SEE YOU BACK ON THE BEACH, HEX!

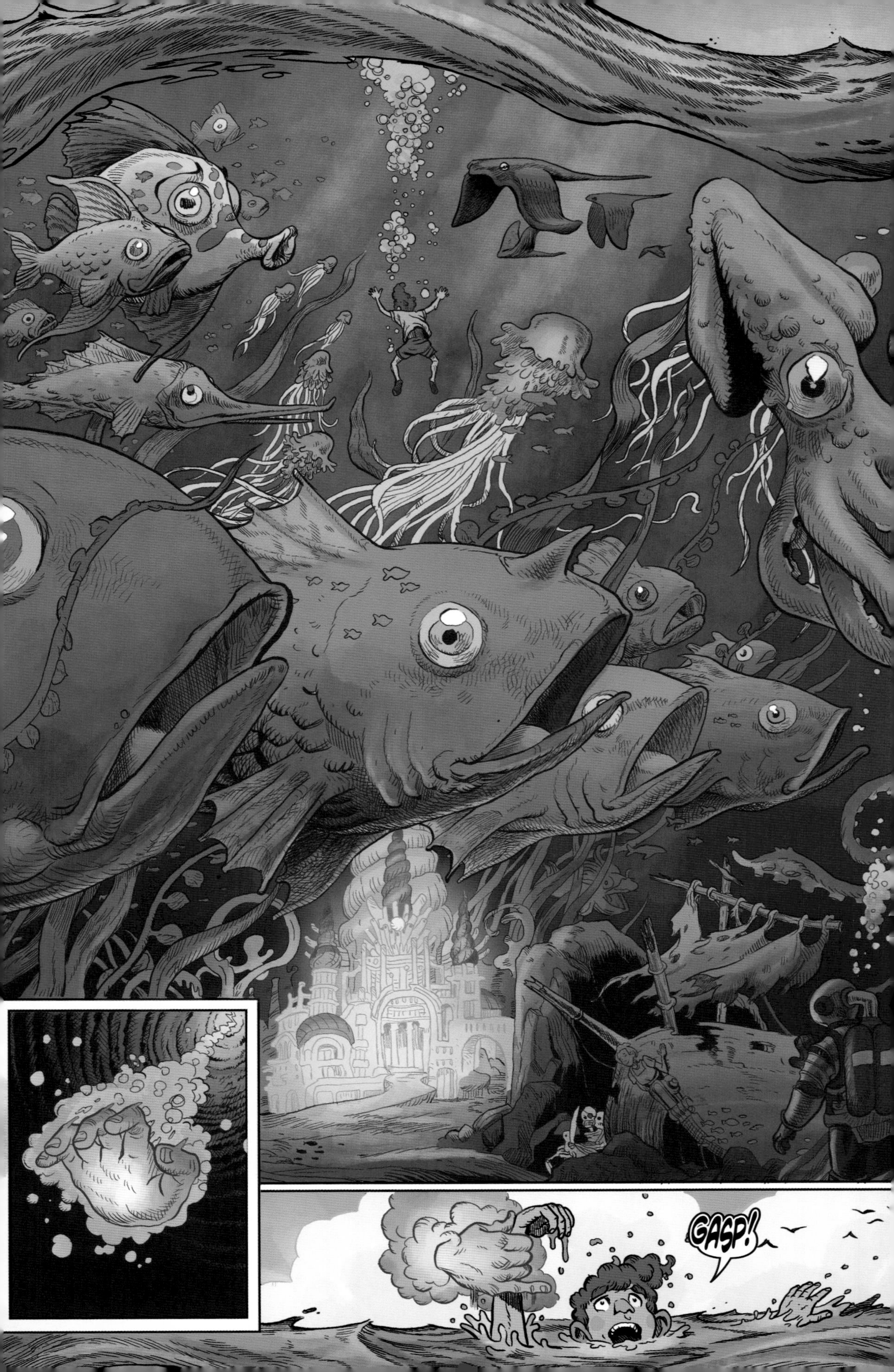
GASP!

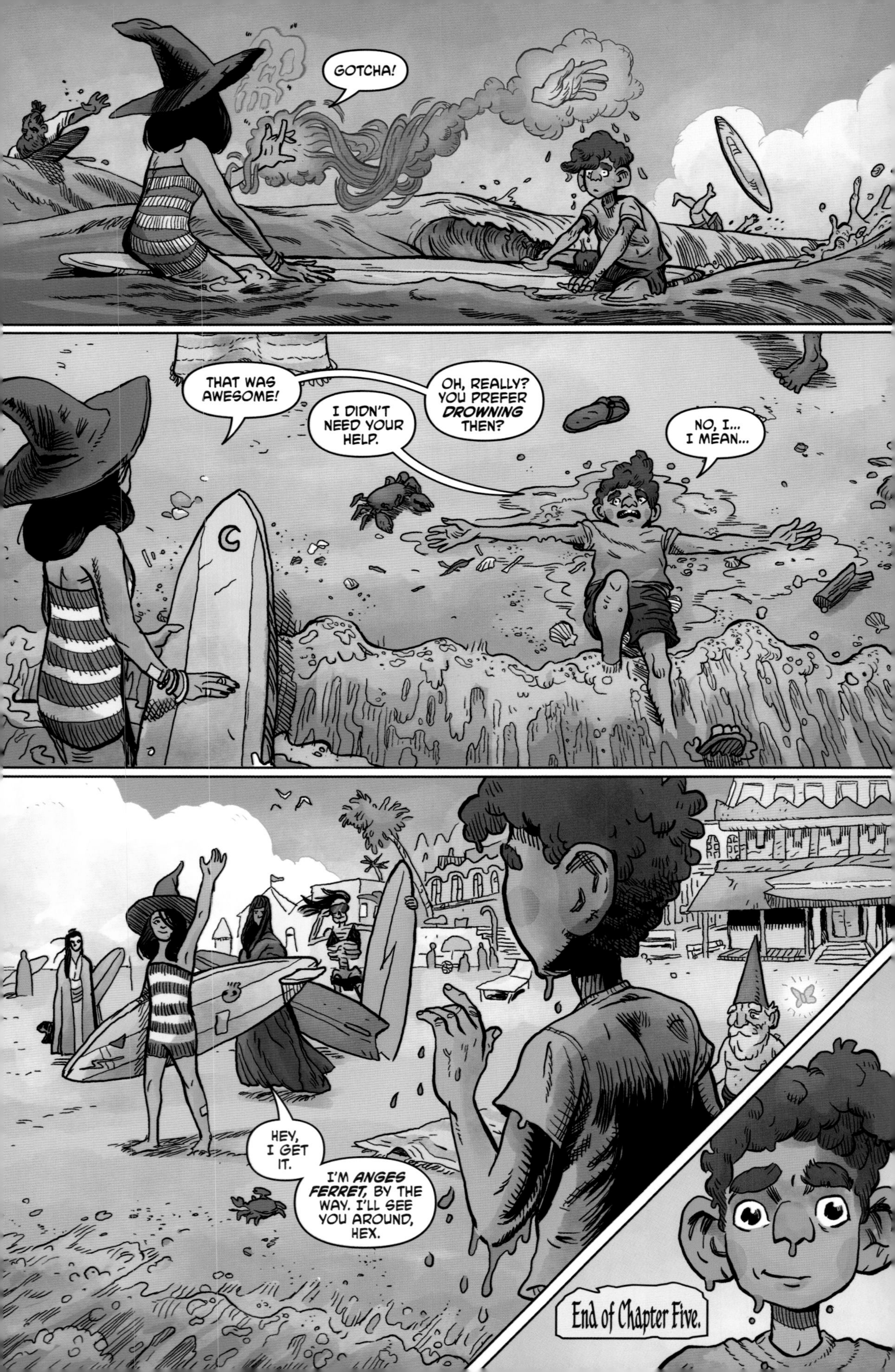
GOTCHA!
THAT WAS AWESOME!
I DIDN'T NEED YOUR HELP.
OH, REALLY? YOU PREFER DROWNING THEN?
NO, I... I MEAN...
HEY, I GET IT.
I'M ANGES FERRET, BY THE WAY. I'LL SEE YOU AROUND, HEX.
End of Chapter Five.

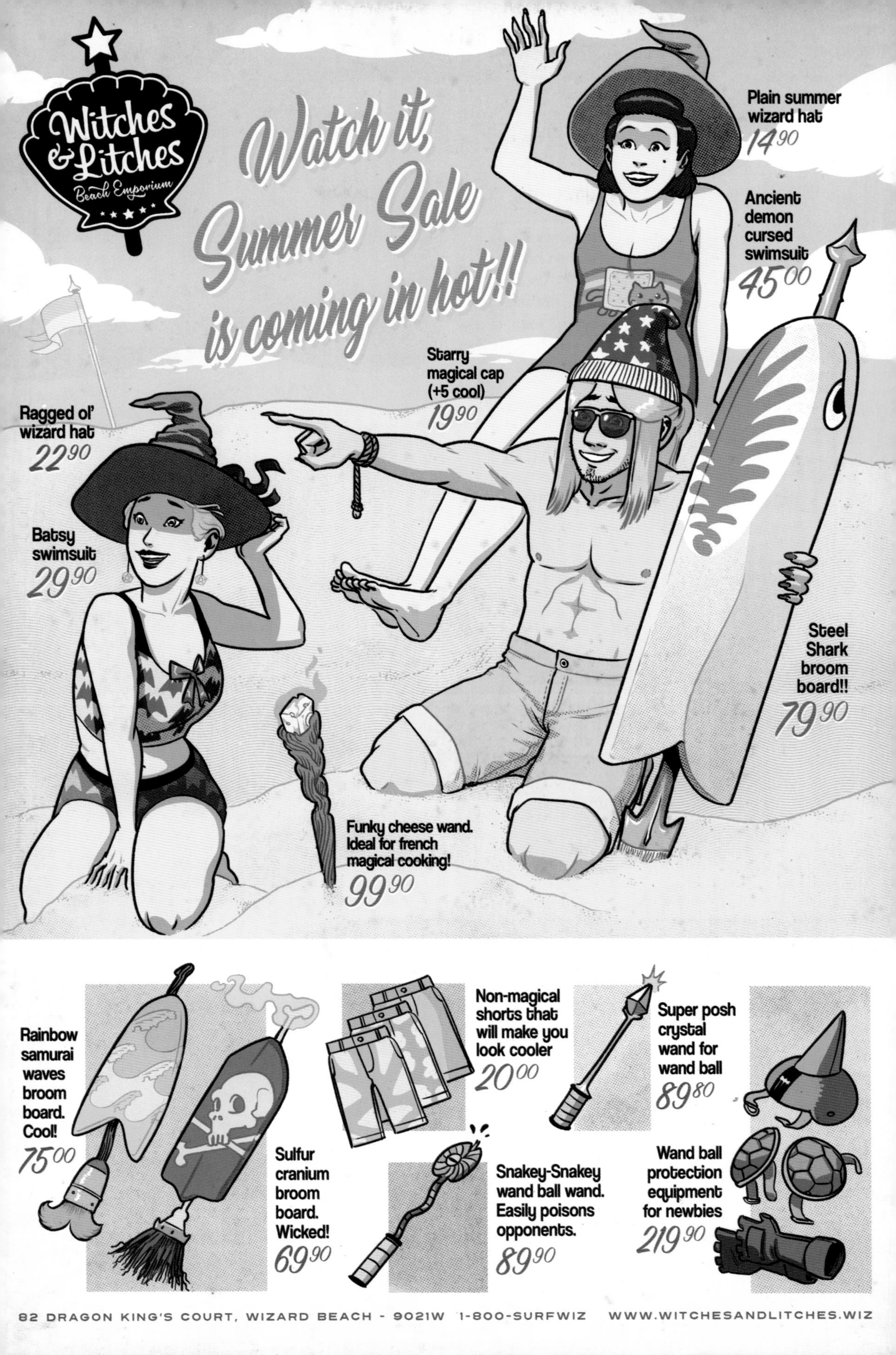

Witches & Litches
Beach Emporium
Watch it, Summer Sale is coming in hot!!
Plain summer wizard hat 14 90
Ancient demon cursed swimsuit 45 00
Starry magical cap (+5 cool) 19 90
Ragged ol' wizard hat 22 90
Batsy swimsuit 29 90
Steel Shark broom board!! 79 90
Funky cheese wand. Ideal for french magical cooking! 99 90
Rainbow samurai waves broom board. Cool! 75 00
Sulfur cranium broom board. Wicked! 69 90
Non-magical shorts that will make you look cooler 20 00
Snakey-Snakey wand ball wand. Easily poisons opponents. 89 90
Super posh crystal wand for wand ball 89 80
Wand ball protection equipment for newbies 219 90
82 DRAGON KING'S COURT, WIZARD BEACH - 9021W 1-800-SURFWIZ WWW.WITCHESANDLITCHES.WIZ

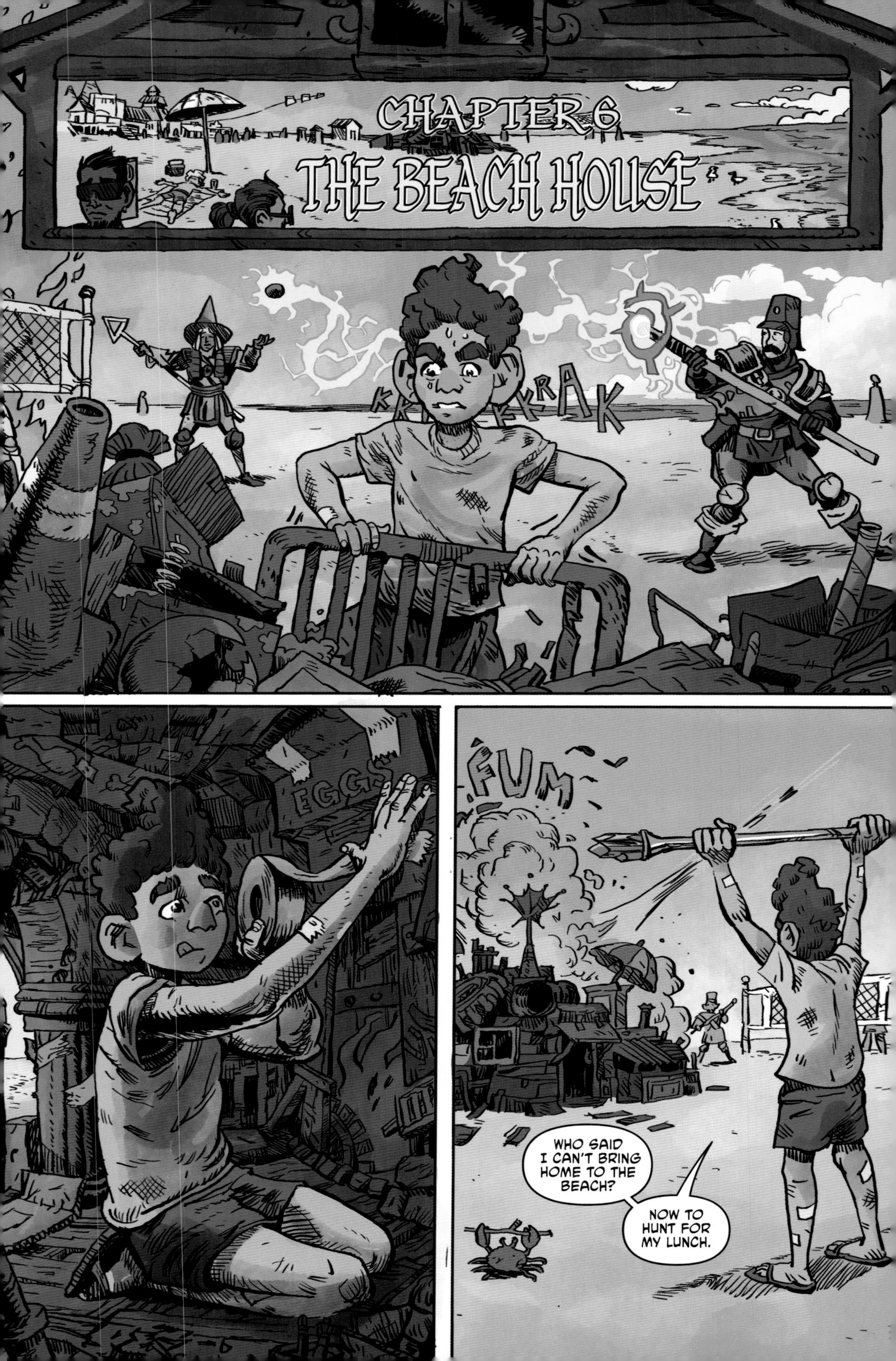
CHAPTER 6
THE BEACH HOUSE
KRAK KRAK
EGGS
FUM
WHO SAID I CAN'T BRING HOME TO THE BEACH?
NOW TO HUNT FOR MY LUNCH.

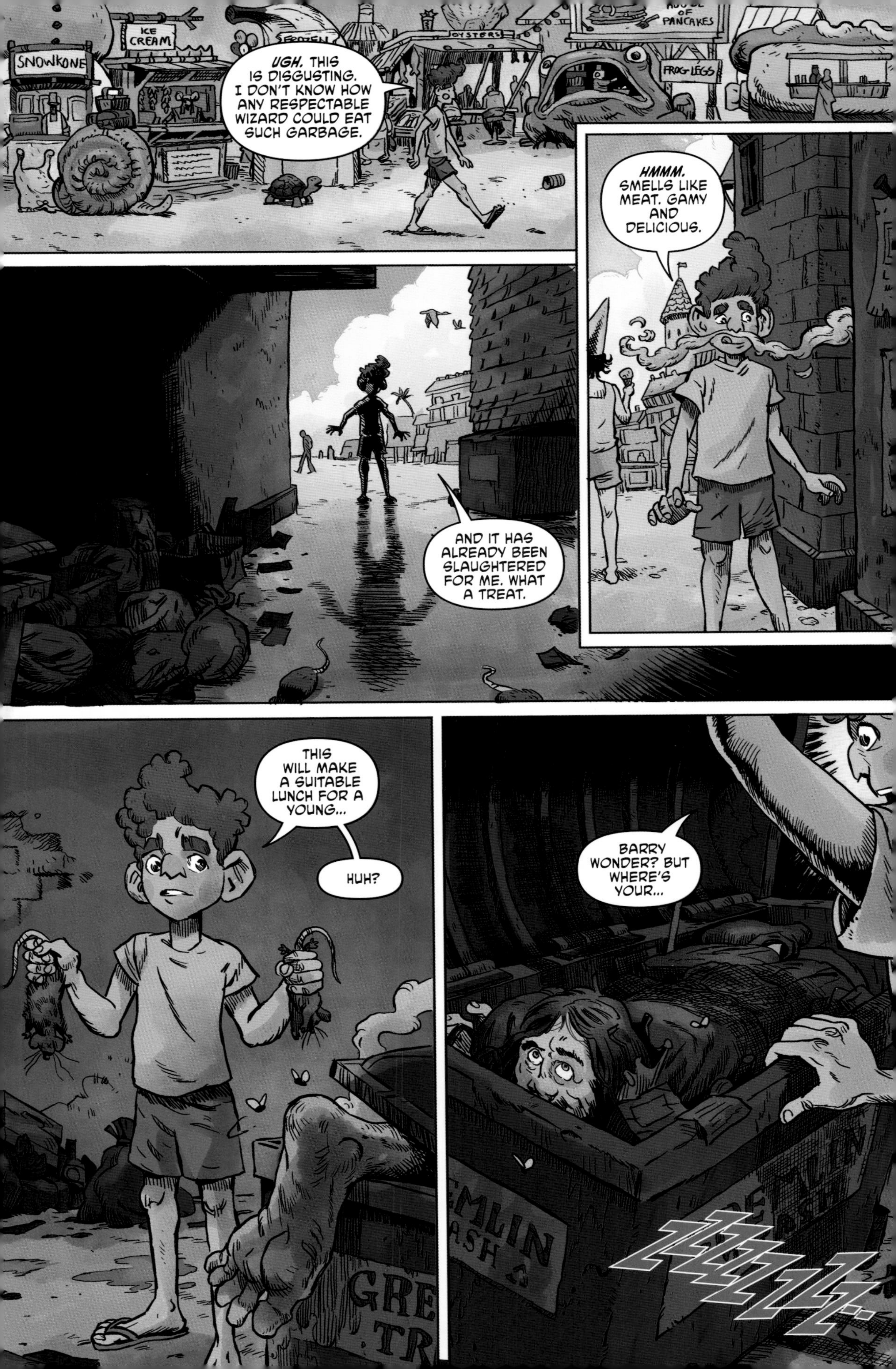
SNOWKONE
ICE CREAM
OYSTERS
HOUSE OF PANCAKES
FROG-LEGS
UGH. THIS IS DISGUSTING. I DON'T KNOW HOW ANY RESPECTABLE WIZARD COULD EAT SUCH GARBAGE.
HMMM. SMELLS LIKE MEAT. GAMY AND DELICIOUS.
AND IT HAS ALREADY BEEN SLAUGHTERED FOR ME. WHAT A TREAT.
THIS WILL MAKE A SUITABLE LUNCH FOR A YOUNG...
HUH?
BARRY WONDER? BUT WHERE'S YOUR...
ZZZZZZ.

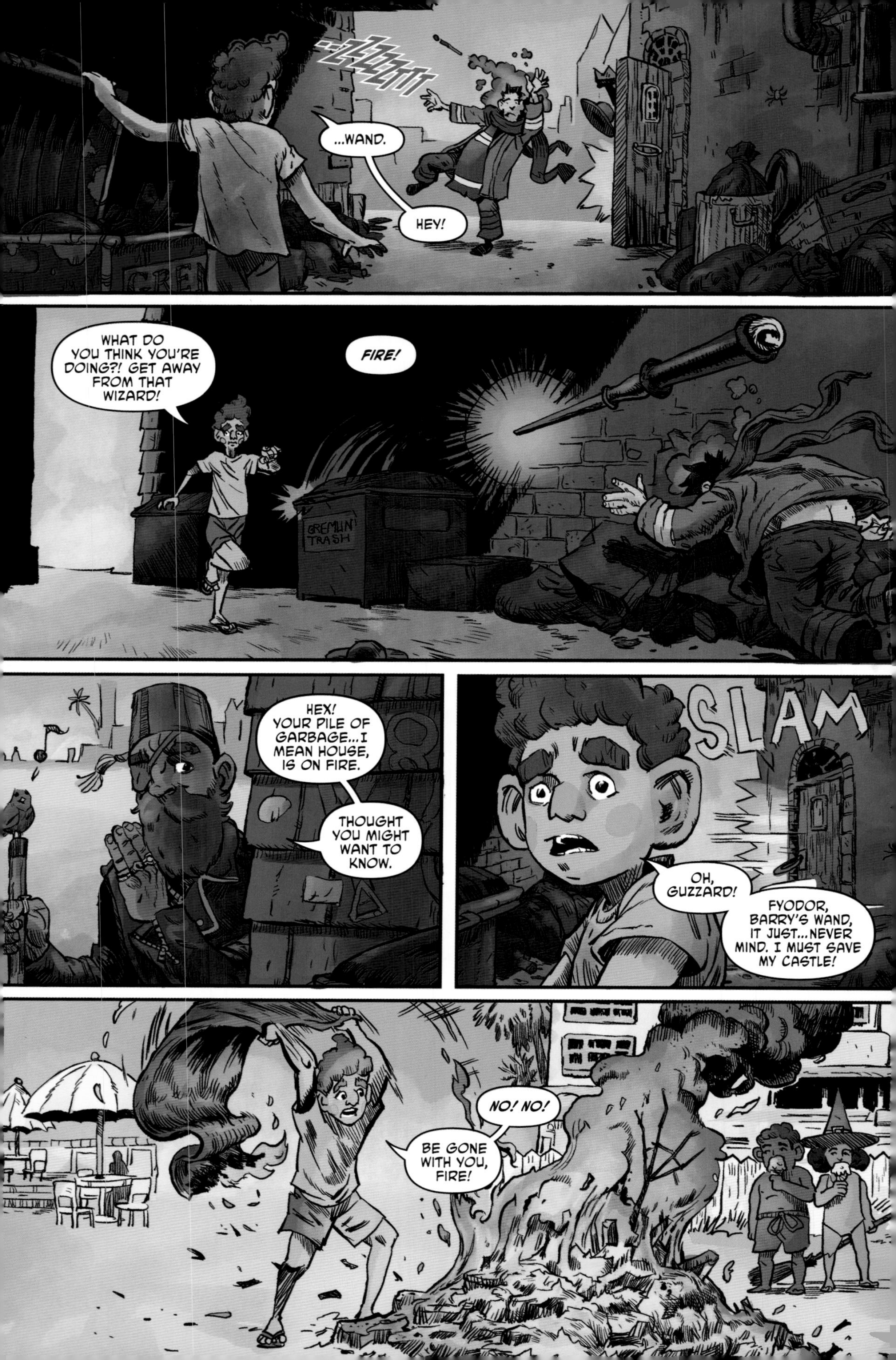
ZZZZZTTT
...WAND.
HEY!
WHAT DO YOU THINK YOU'RE DOING?! GET AWAY FROM THAT WIZARD!
FIRE!
GREMLIN TRASH
HEX! YOUR PILE OF GARBAGE...I MEAN HOUSE, IS ON FIRE.
THOUGHT YOU MIGHT WANT TO KNOW.
SLAM
OH, GUZZARD!
FYODOR, BARRY'S WAND, IT JUST...NEVER MIND. I MUST SAVE MY CASTLE!
NO! NO!
BE GONE WITH YOU, FIRE!

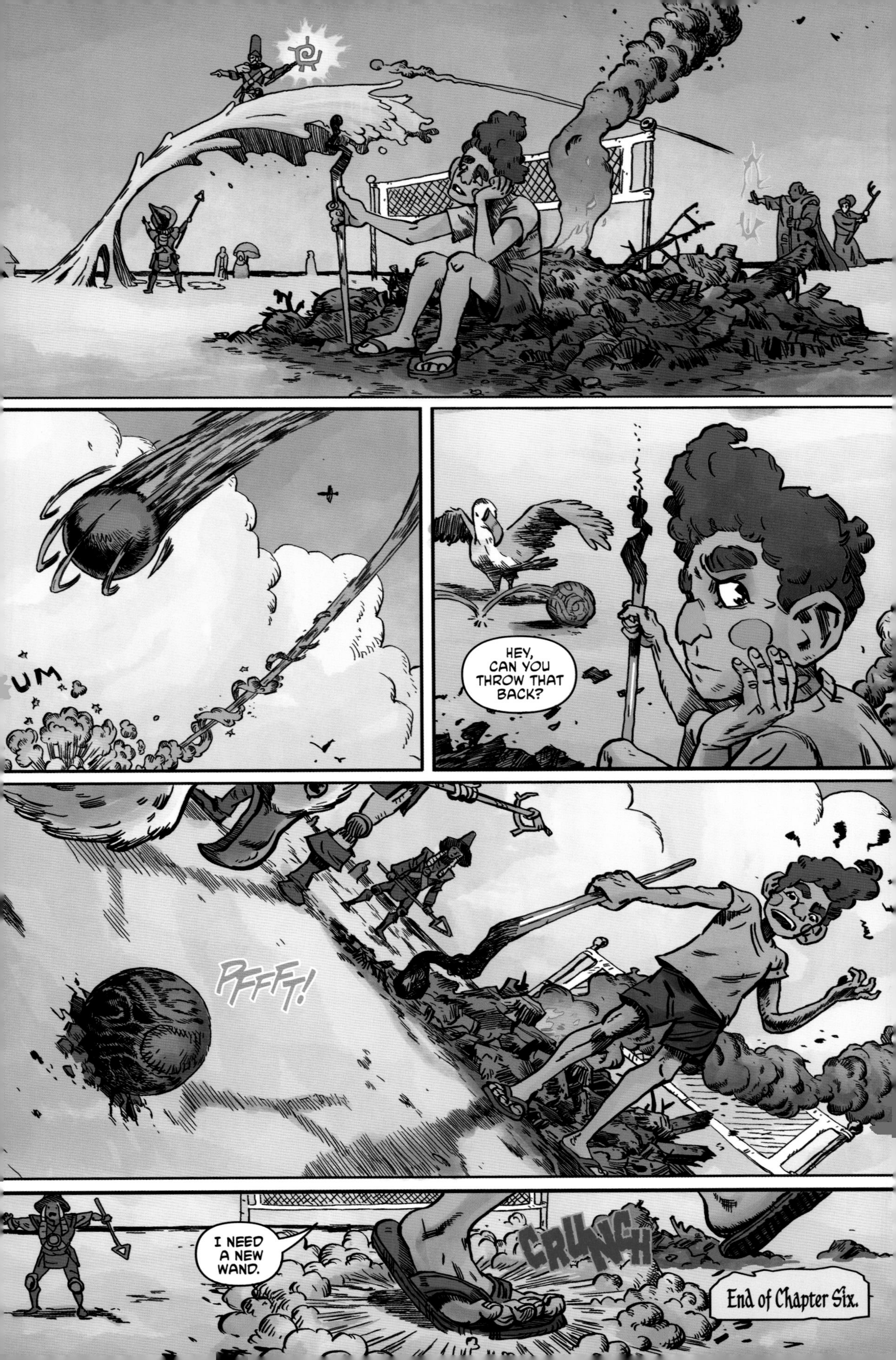
UM
HEY, CAN YOU THROW THAT BACK?
PFFFT!
I NEED A NEW WAND.
CRUNCH
End of Chapter Six.

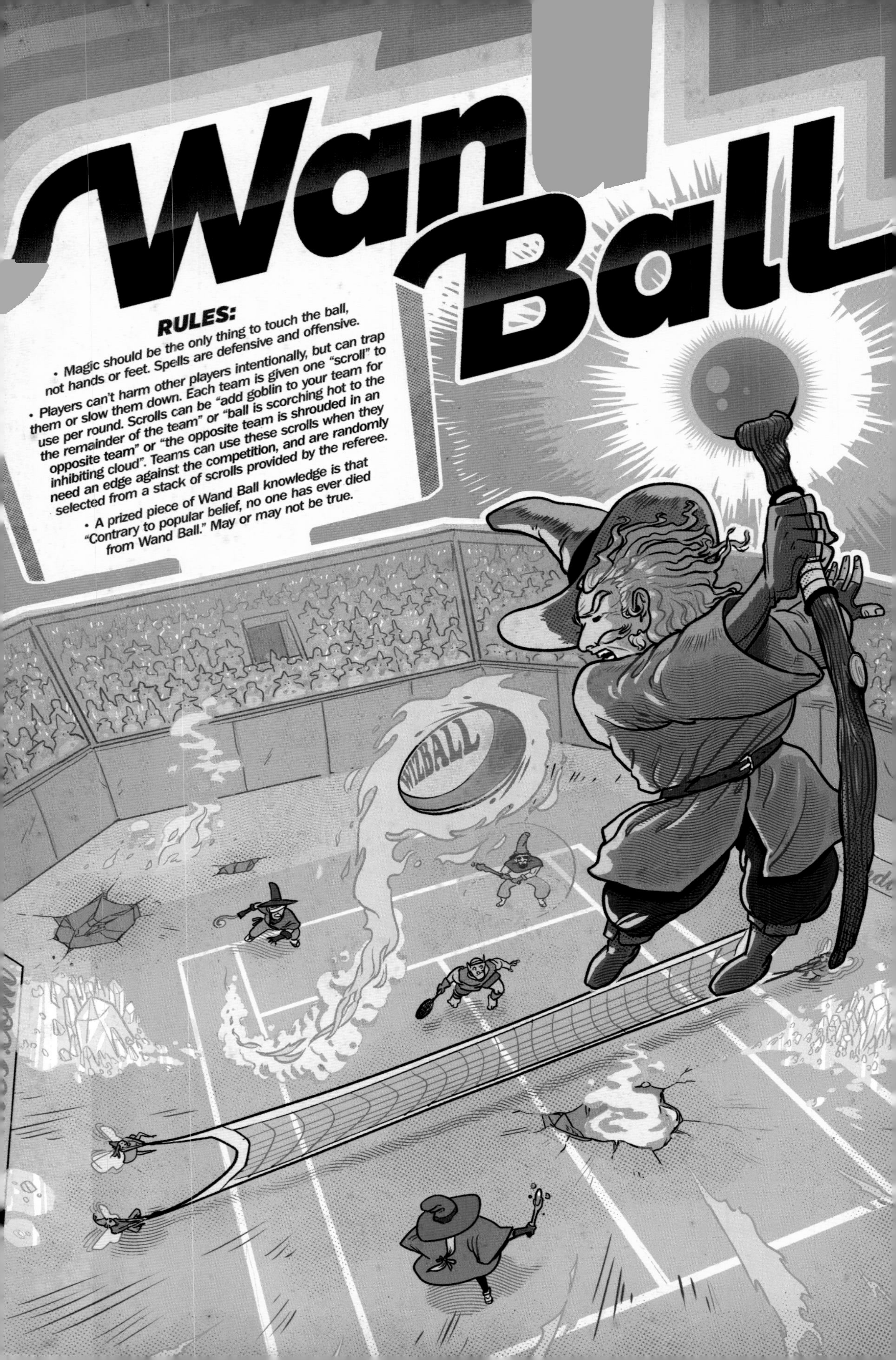
Wan Ball
RULES:
• Magic should be the only thing to touch the ball, not hands or feet. Spells are defensive and offensive.
• Players can't harm other players intentionally, but can trap them or slow them down. Each team is given one "scroll" to use per round. Scrolls can be "add goblin to your team for the remainder of the team" or "ball is scorching hot to the opposite team" or "the opposite team is shrouded in an inhibiting cloud". Teams can use these scrolls when they need an edge against the competition, and are randomly selected from a stack of scrolls provided by the referee.
• A prized piece of Wand Ball knowledge is that "Contrary to popular belief, no one has ever died from Wand Ball." May or may not be true.
WIZBALL

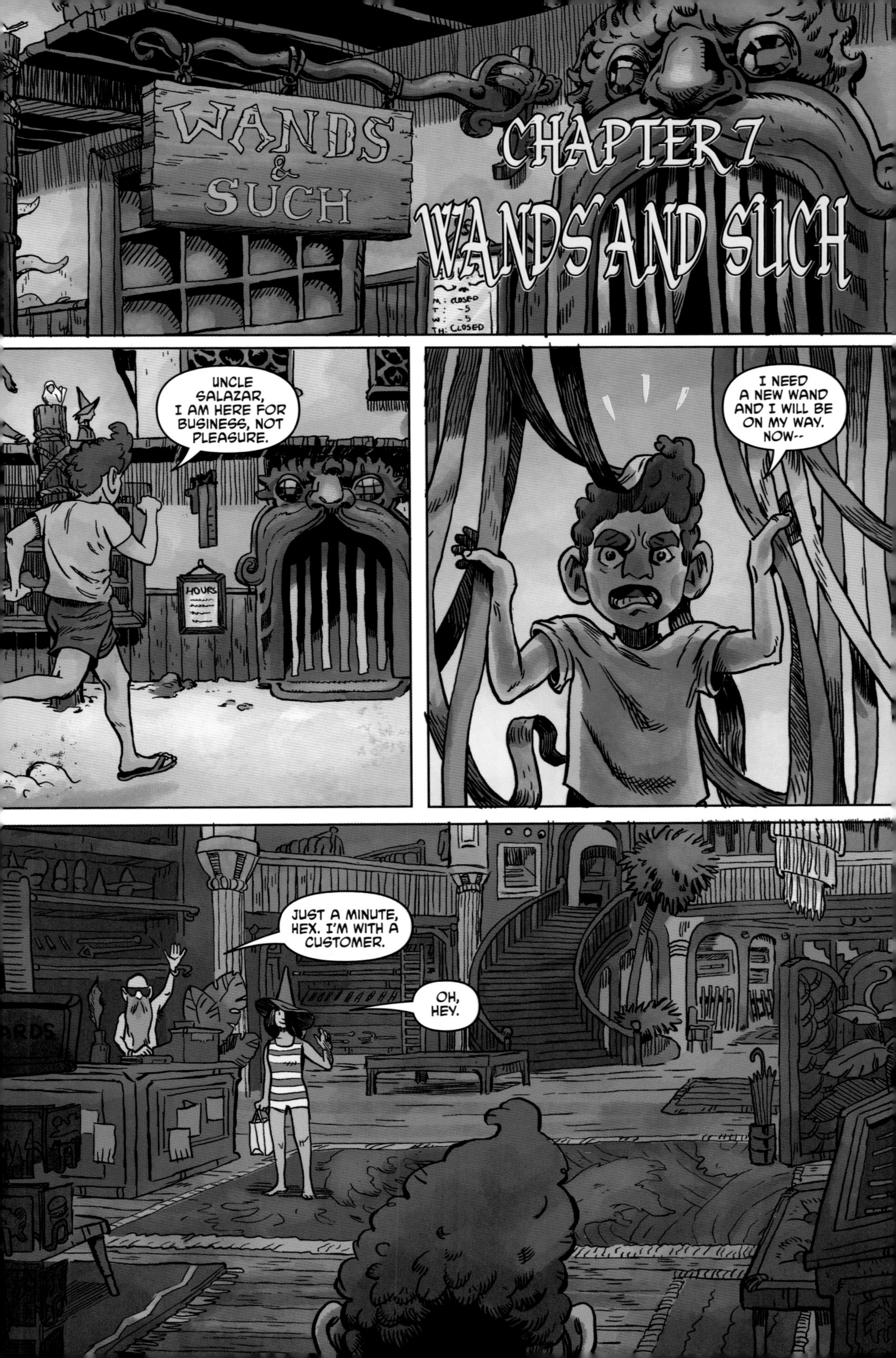
WANDS & SUCH
CHAPTER 7
WANDS AND SUCH
M: CLOSED
T: -5
W: -5
TH: CLOSED
UNCLE SALAZAR, I AM HERE FOR BUSINESS, NOT PLEASURE.
HOURS
I NEED A NEW WAND AND I WILL BE ON MY WAY. NOW--
JUST A MINUTE, HEX. I'M WITH A CUSTOMER.
OH, HEY.

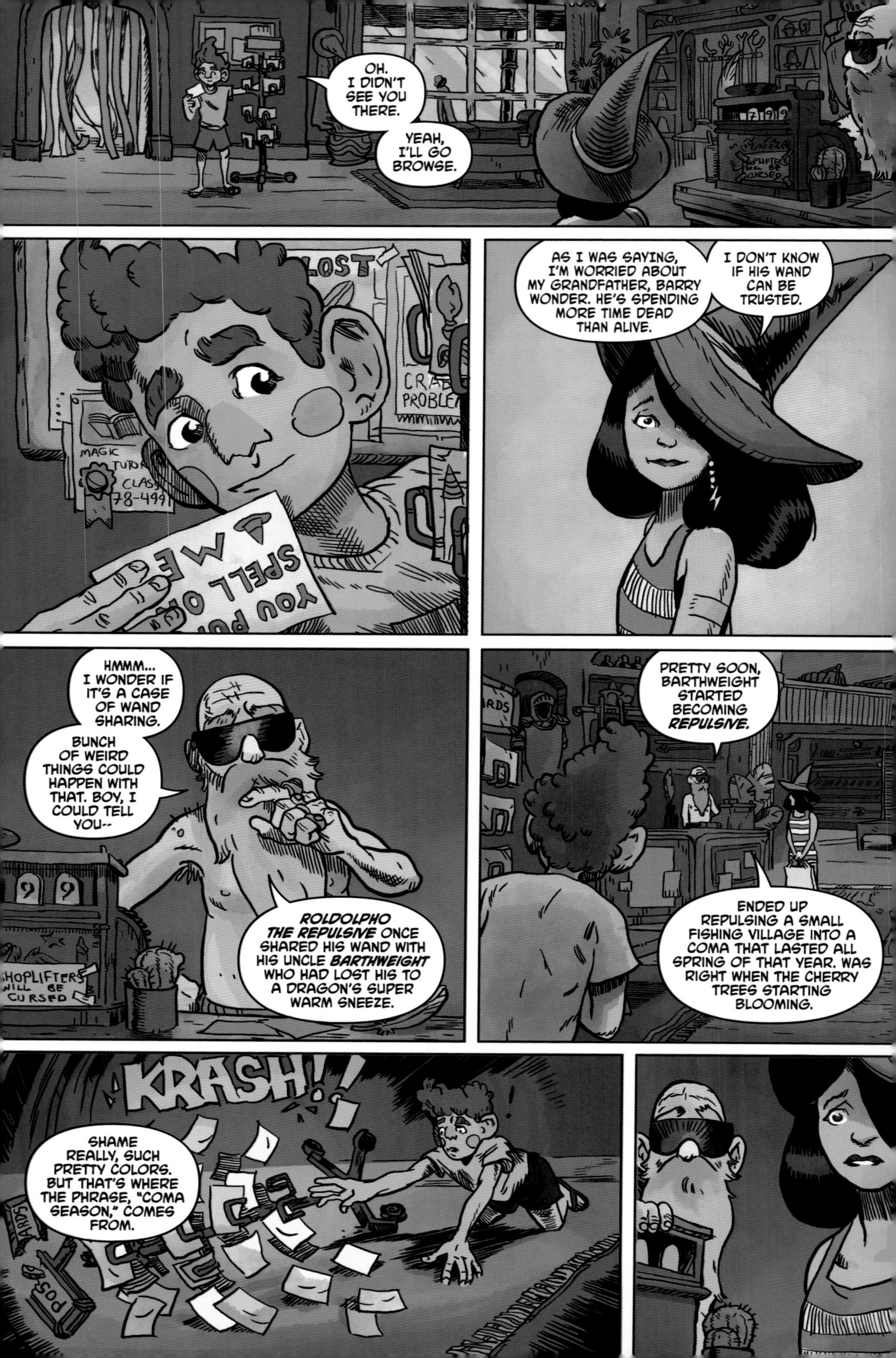
OH. I DIDN'T SEE YOU THERE.
YEAH, I'LL GO BROWSE.
SHOPLIFTERS WILL BE CURSED
LOST
MAGIC TUTOR CLASS 78-499
CRAB PROBLE
YOU PUT A SPELL ON ME
AS I WAS SAYING, I'M WORRIED ABOUT MY GRANDFATHER, BARRY WONDER. HE'S SPENDING MORE TIME DEAD THAN ALIVE.
I DON'T KNOW IF HIS WAND CAN BE TRUSTED.
HMMM... I WONDER IF IT'S A CASE OF WAND SHARING.
BUNCH OF WEIRD THINGS COULD HAPPEN WITH THAT. BOY, I COULD TELL YOU--
ROLDOLPHO THE REPULSIVE ONCE SHARED HIS WAND WITH HIS UNCLE BARTHWEIGHT WHO HAD LOST HIS TO A DRAGON'S SUPER WARM SNEEZE.
SHOPLIFTERS WILL BE CURSED
PRETTY SOON, BARTHWEIGHT STARTED BECOMING REPULSIVE.
ENDED UP REPULSING A SMALL FISHING VILLAGE INTO A COMA THAT LASTED ALL SPRING OF THAT YEAR. WAS RIGHT WHEN THE CHERRY TREES STARTING BLOOMING.
KRASH!!
SHAME REALLY, SUCH PRETTY COLORS. BUT THAT'S WHERE THE PHRASE, "COMA SEASON," COMES FROM.

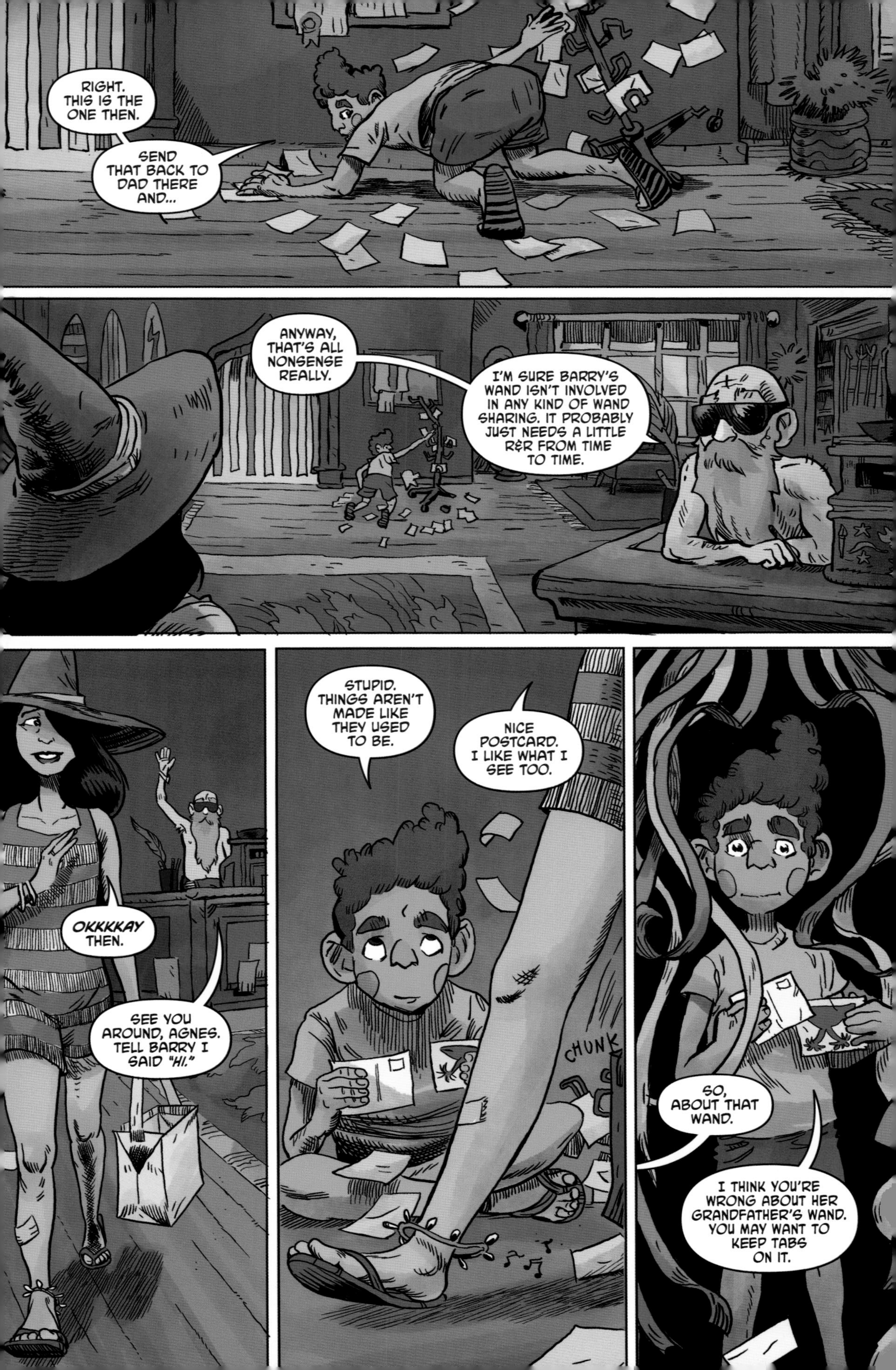
RIGHT. THIS IS THE ONE THEN.
SEND THAT BACK TO DAD THERE AND...
ANYWAY, THAT'S ALL NONSENSE REALLY.
I'M SURE BARRY'S WAND ISN'T INVOLVED IN ANY KIND OF WAND SHARING. IT PROBABLY JUST NEEDS A LITTLE R&R FROM TIME TO TIME.
OKKKKAY THEN.
SEE YOU AROUND, AGNES. TELL BARRY I SAID *"HI."*
STUPID. THINGS AREN'T MADE LIKE THEY USED TO BE.
NICE POSTCARD. I LIKE WHAT I SEE TOO.
CHUNK
SO, ABOUT THAT WAND.
I THINK YOU'RE WRONG ABOUT HER GRANDFATHER'S WAND. YOU MAY WANT TO KEEP TABS ON IT.

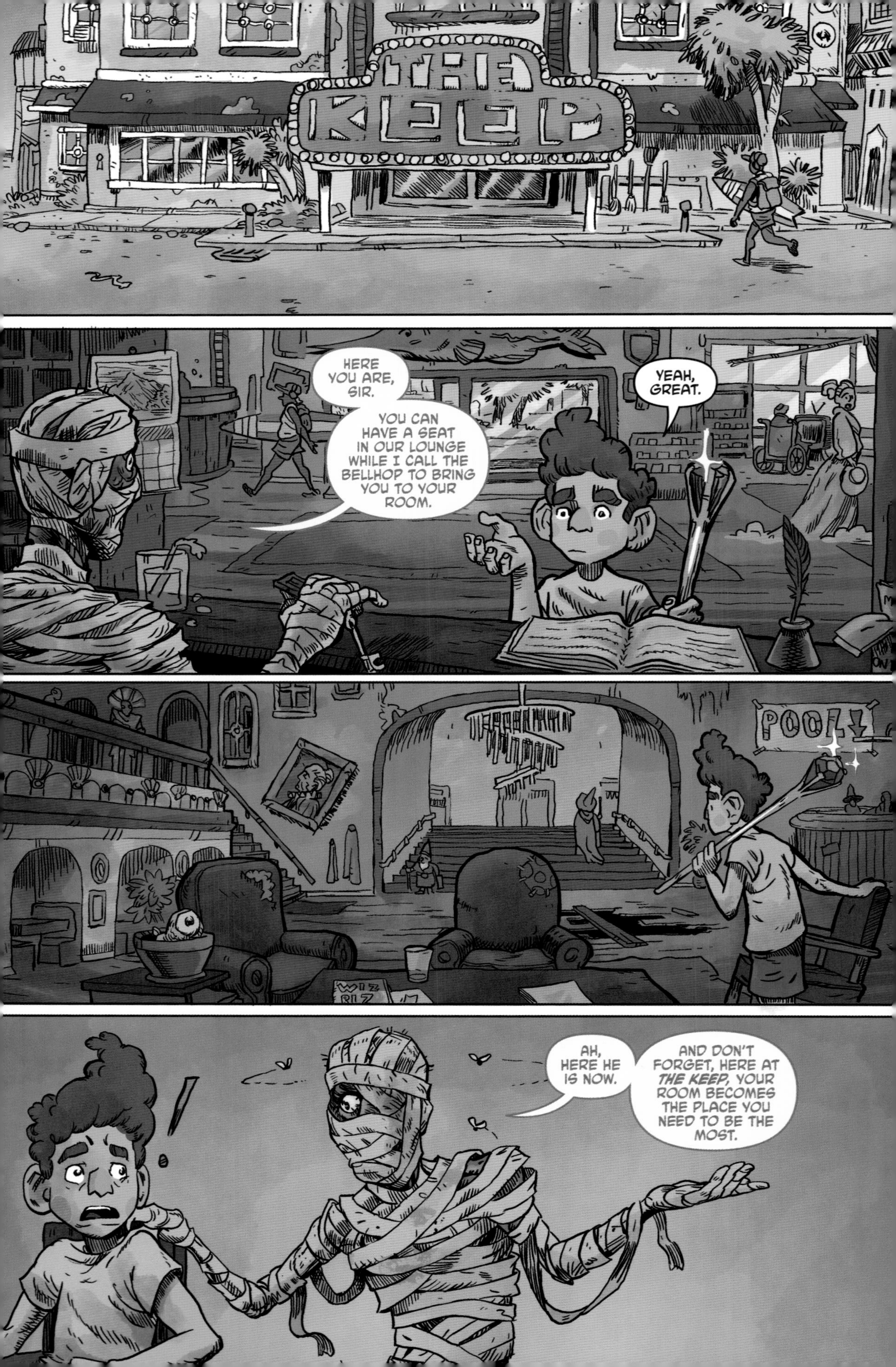
THE KEEP
HERE YOU ARE, SIR.
YOU CAN HAVE A SEAT IN OUR LOUNGE WHILE I CALL THE BELLHOP TO BRING YOU TO YOUR ROOM.
YEAH, GREAT.
POOL
AH, HERE HE IS NOW.
AND DON'T FORGET, HERE AT *THE KEEP,* YOUR ROOM BECOMES THE PLACE YOU NEED TO BE THE MOST.

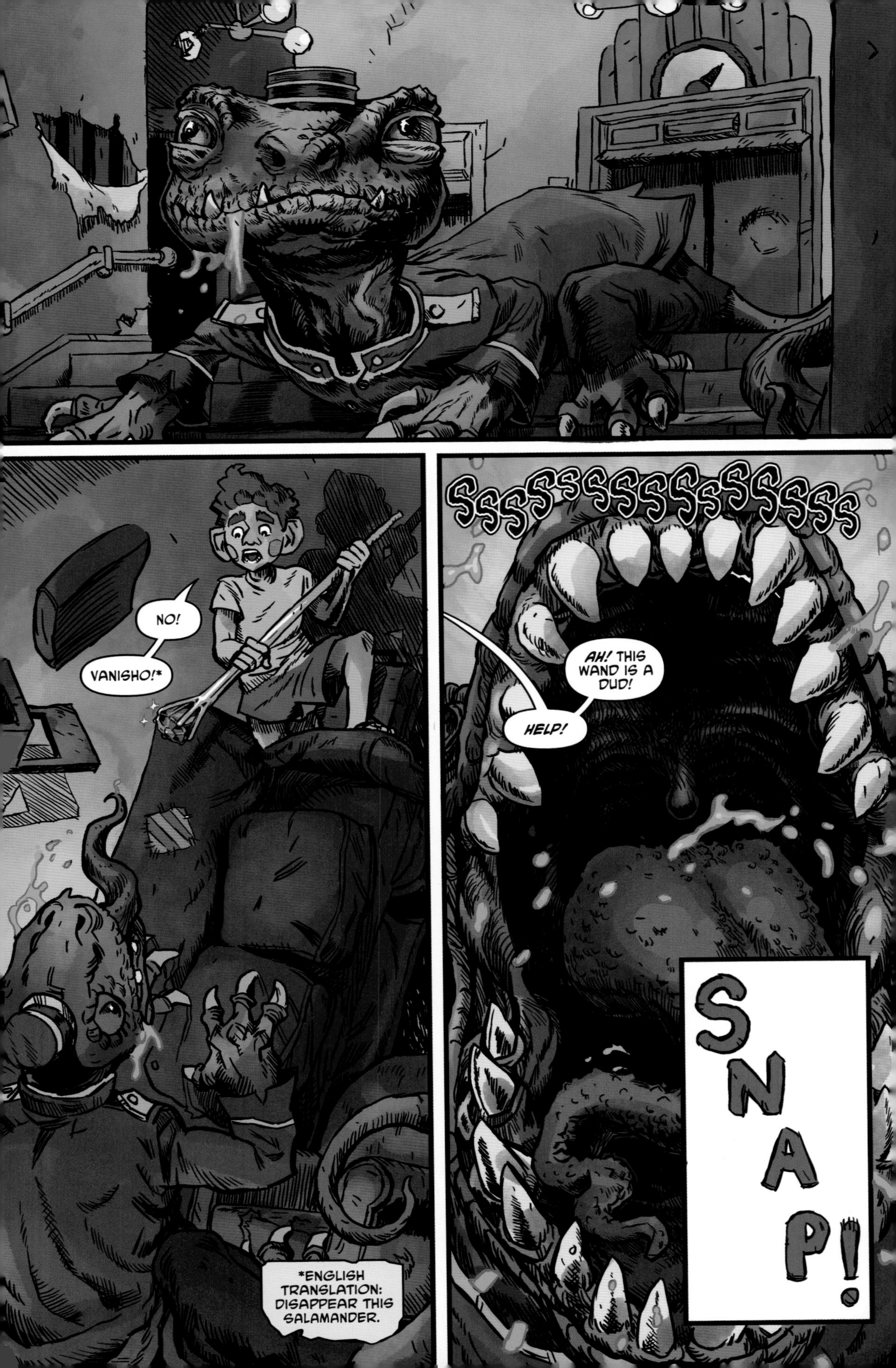
NO!
VANISHO!*
*ENGLISH TRANSLATION: DISAPPEAR THIS SALAMANDER.
SSSSSSSSSSSSSSSSSS
AH! THIS WAND IS A DUD!
HELP!
SNAP!

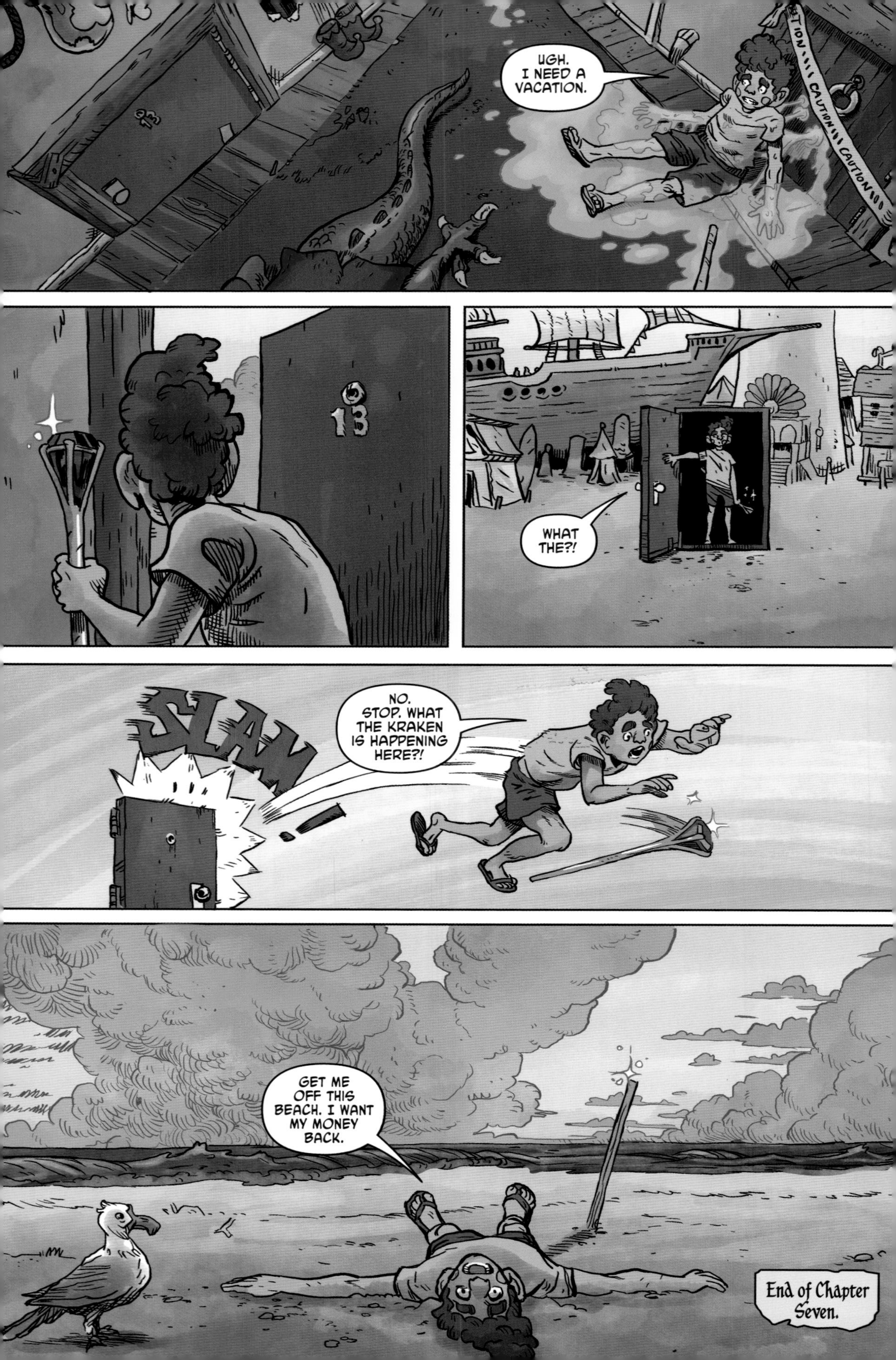
CAUTION
UGH. I NEED A VACATION.
13
WHAT THE?!
SLAM
NO. STOP. WHAT THE KRAKEN IS HAPPENING HERE?!
GET ME OFF THIS BEACH. I WANT MY MONEY BACK.
End of Chapter Seven.

COVER BY
GEORGE SCHALL

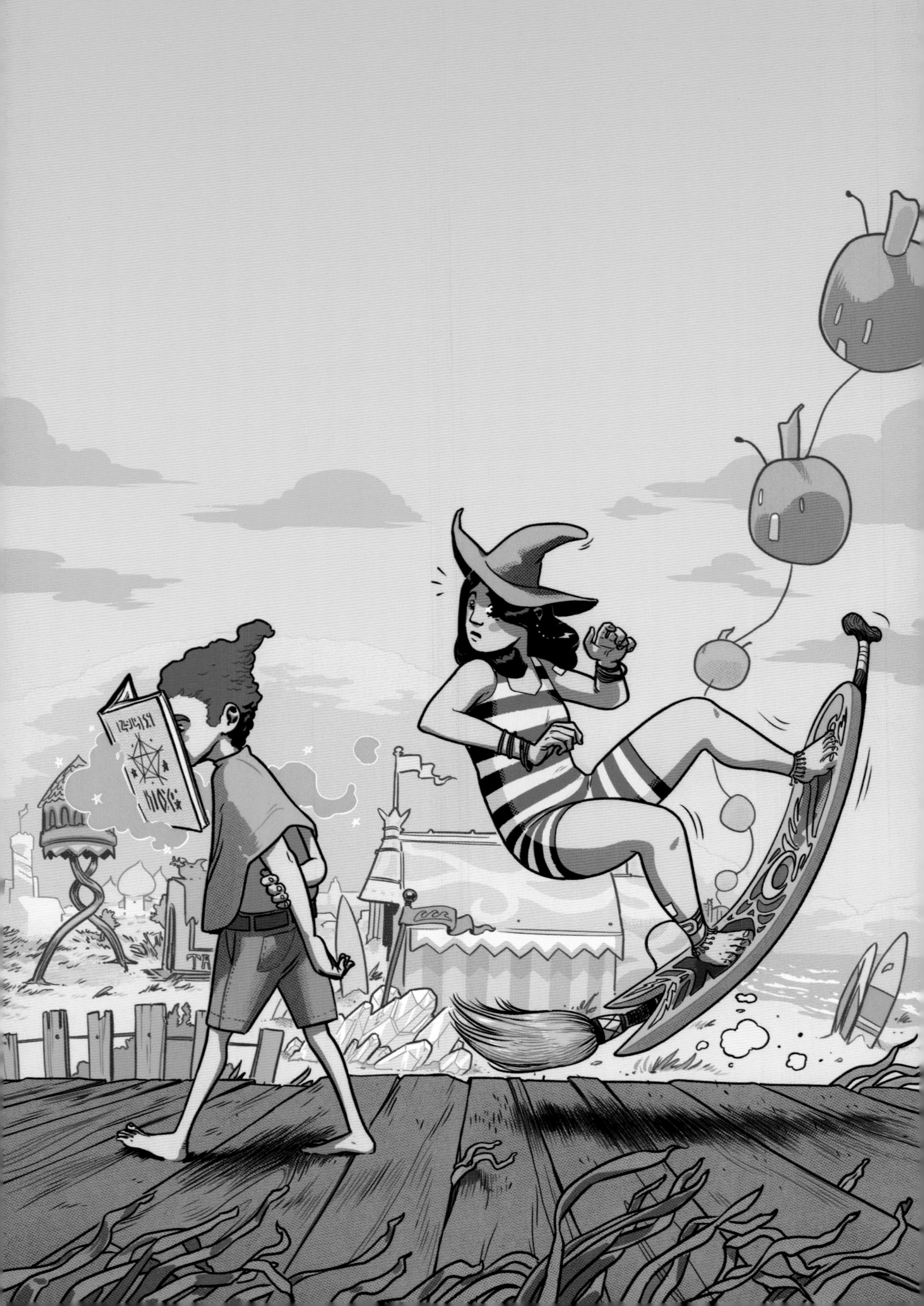

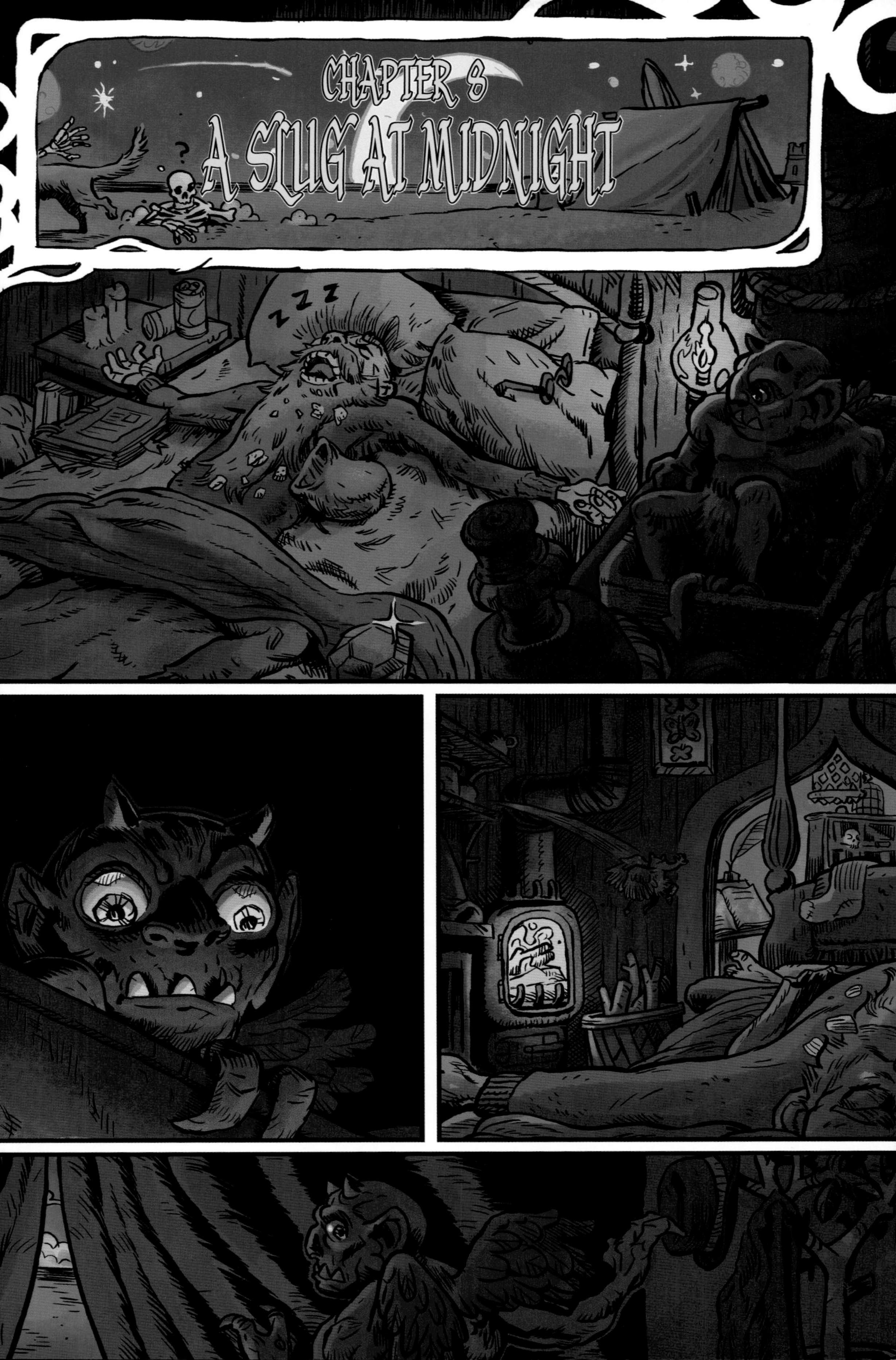
CHAPTER 8
A SLUG AT MIDNIGHT
?
Z Z Z

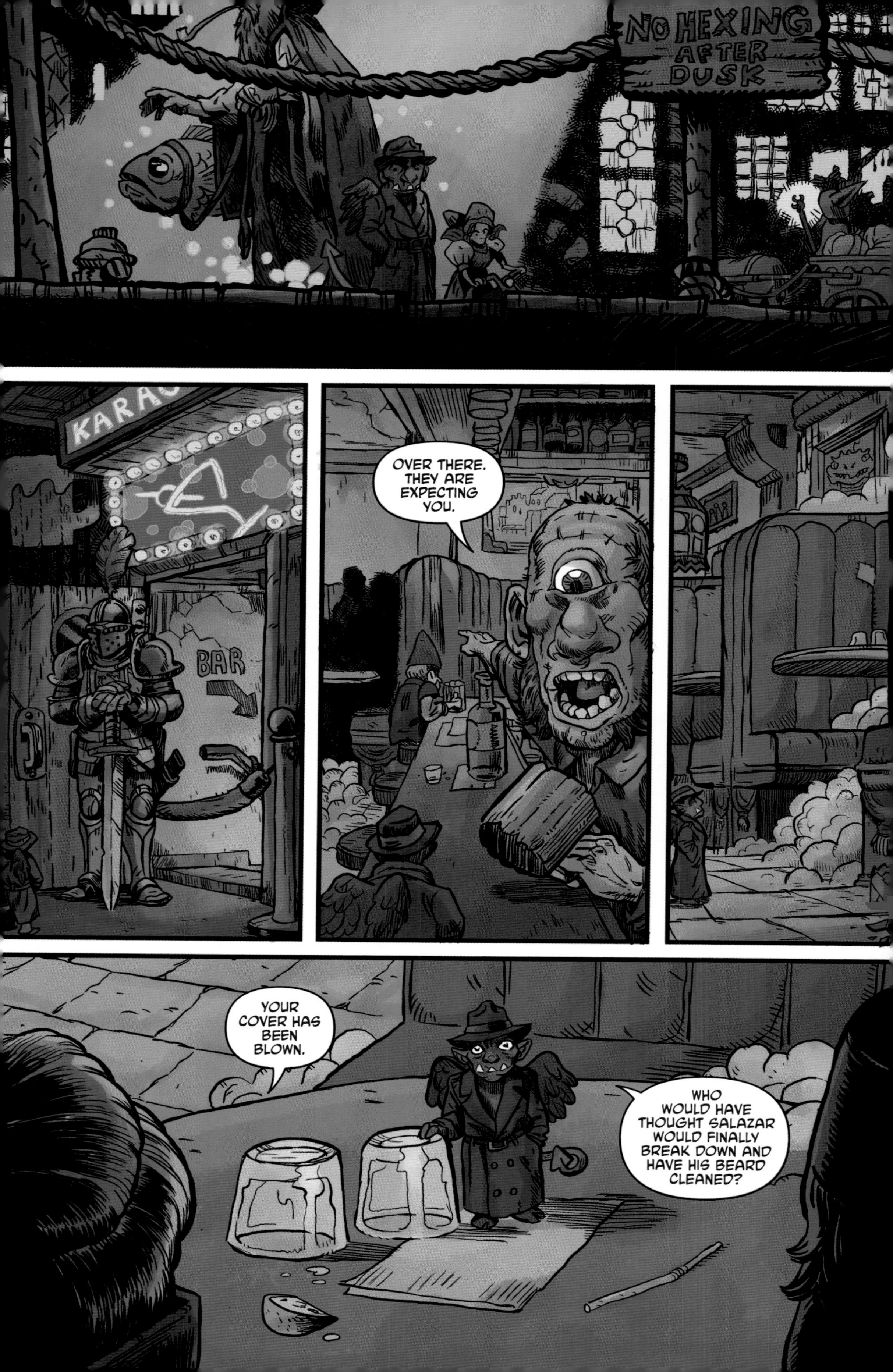
NO HEXING AFTER DUSK
KARA
BAR
OVER THERE. THEY ARE EXPECTING YOU.
YOUR COVER HAS BEEN BLOWN.
WHO WOULD HAVE THOUGHT SALAZAR WOULD FINALLY BREAK DOWN AND HAVE HIS BEARD CLEANED?

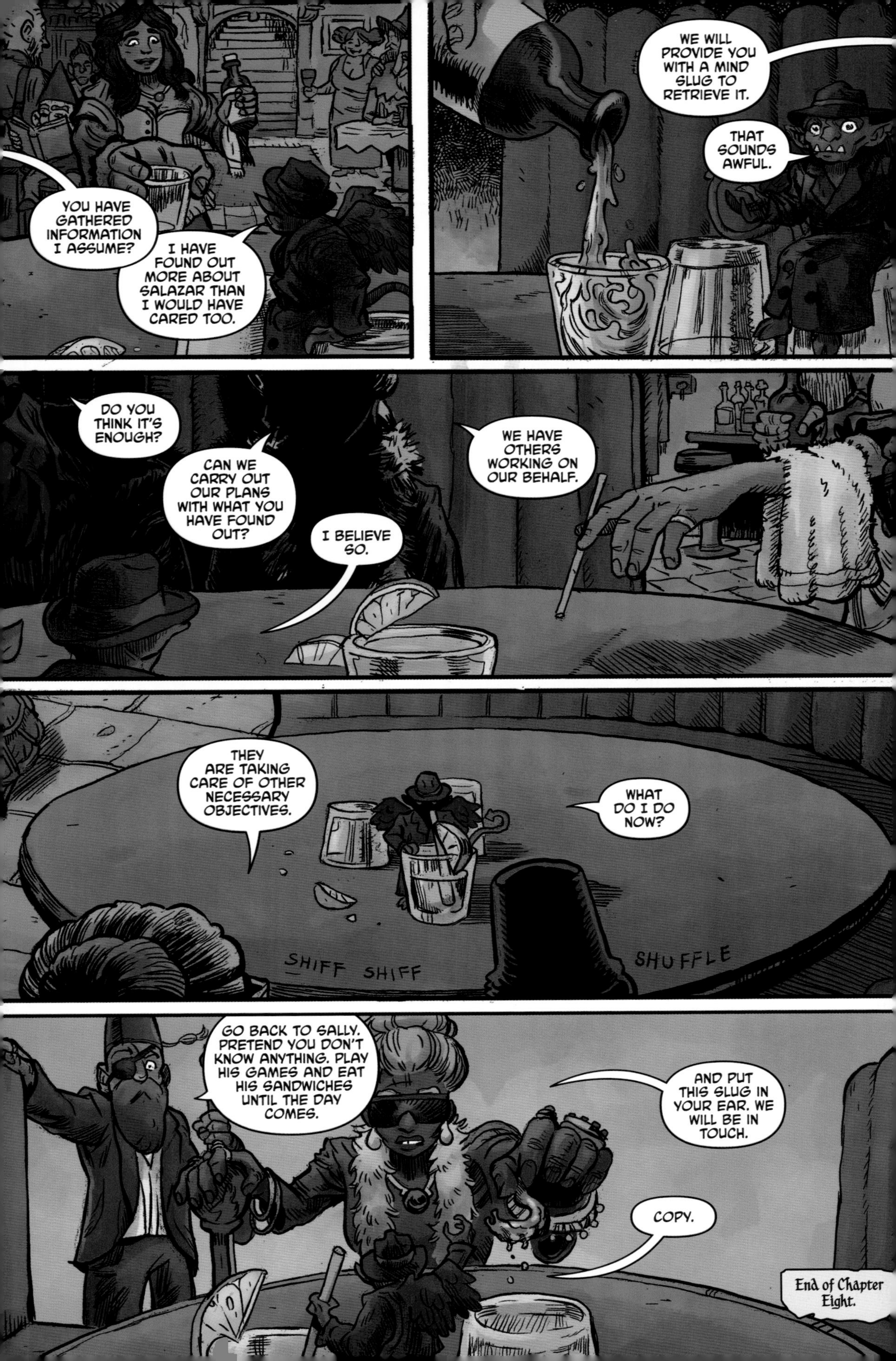
YOU HAVE GATHERED INFORMATION I ASSUME?
I HAVE FOUND OUT MORE ABOUT SALAZAR THAN I WOULD HAVE CARED TOO.
WE WILL PROVIDE YOU WITH A MIND SLUG TO RETRIEVE IT.
THAT SOUNDS AWFUL.
DO YOU THINK IT'S ENOUGH?
CAN WE CARRY OUT OUR PLANS WITH WHAT YOU HAVE FOUND OUT?
I BELIEVE SO.
WE HAVE OTHERS WORKING ON OUR BEHALF.
THEY ARE TAKING CARE OF OTHER NECESSARY OBJECTIVES.
WHAT DO I DO NOW?
SHIFF SHIFF
SHUFFLE
GO BACK TO SALLY. PRETEND YOU DON'T KNOW ANYTHING. PLAY HIS GAMES AND EAT HIS SANDWICHES UNTIL THE DAY COMES.
AND PUT THIS SLUG IN YOUR EAR. WE WILL BE IN TOUCH.
COPY.
End of Chapter Eight.

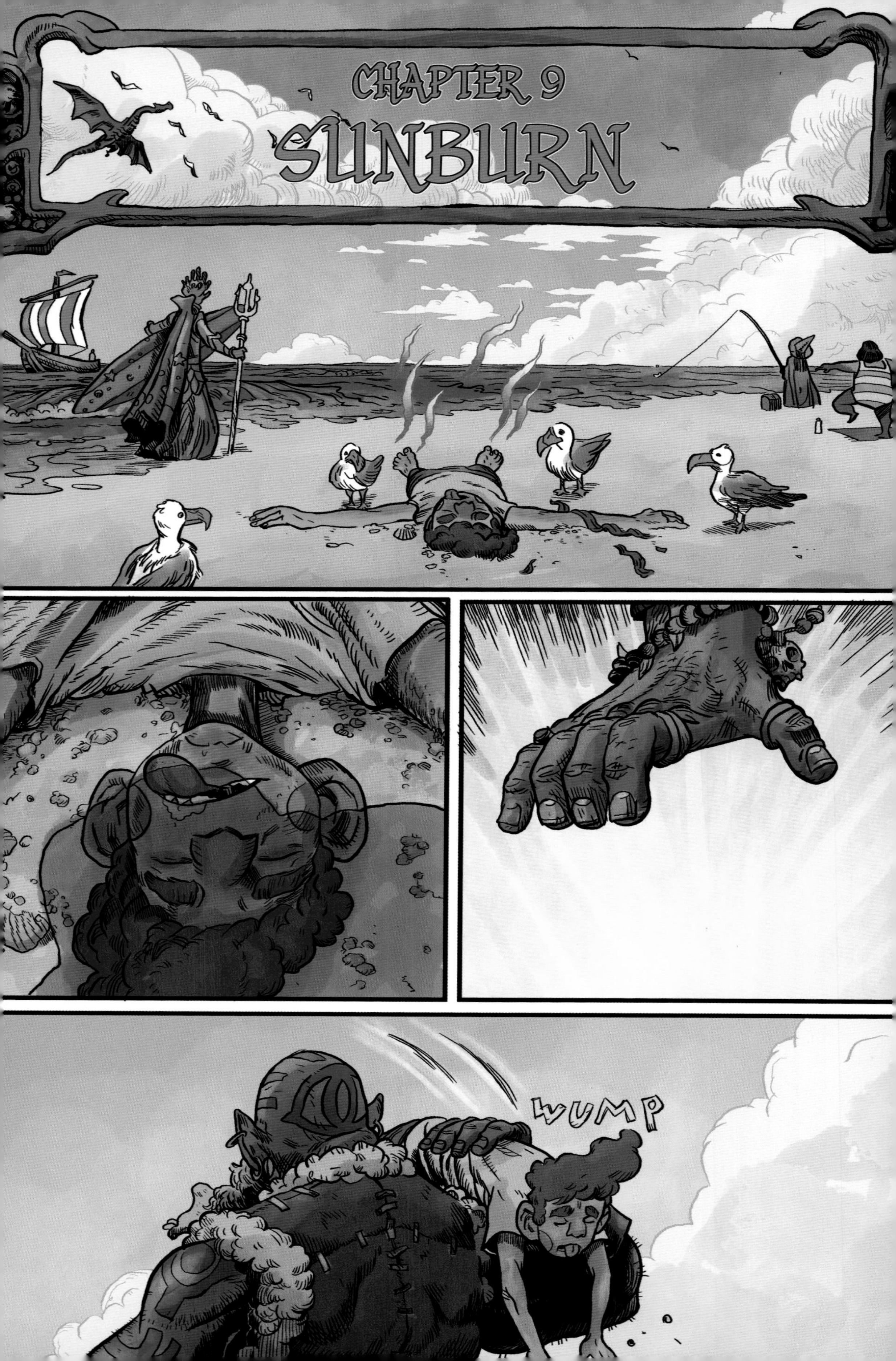
CHAPTER 9
SUNBURN
WUMP

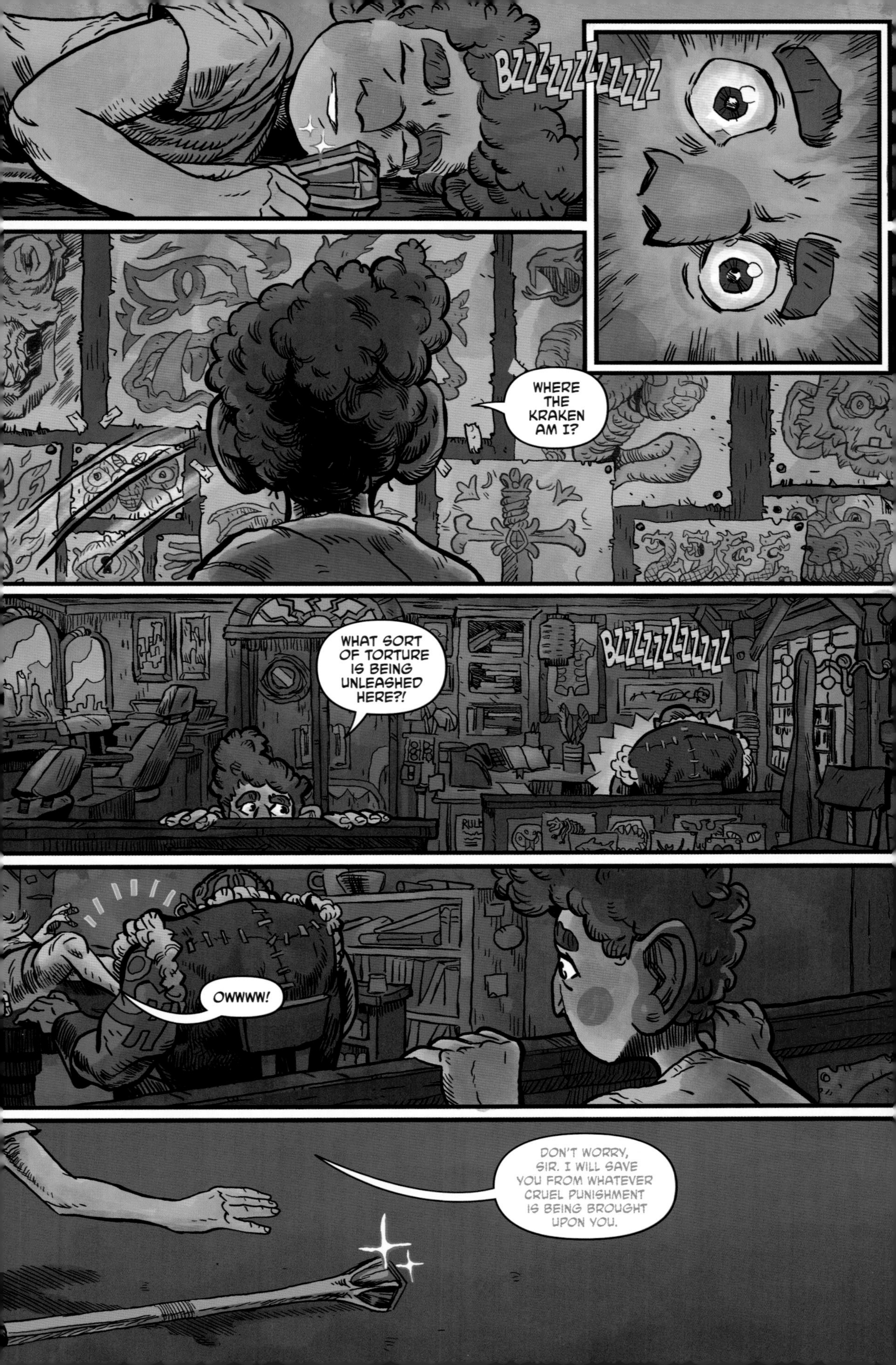
BZZZZZZZZZZZZ
WHERE THE KRAKEN AM I?
WHAT SORT OF TORTURE IS BEING UNLEASHED HERE?!
BZZZZZZZZZZZZ
OWWWW!
DON'T WORRY, SIR. I WILL SAVE YOU FROM WHATEVER CRUEL PUNISHMENT IS BEING BROUGHT UPON YOU.

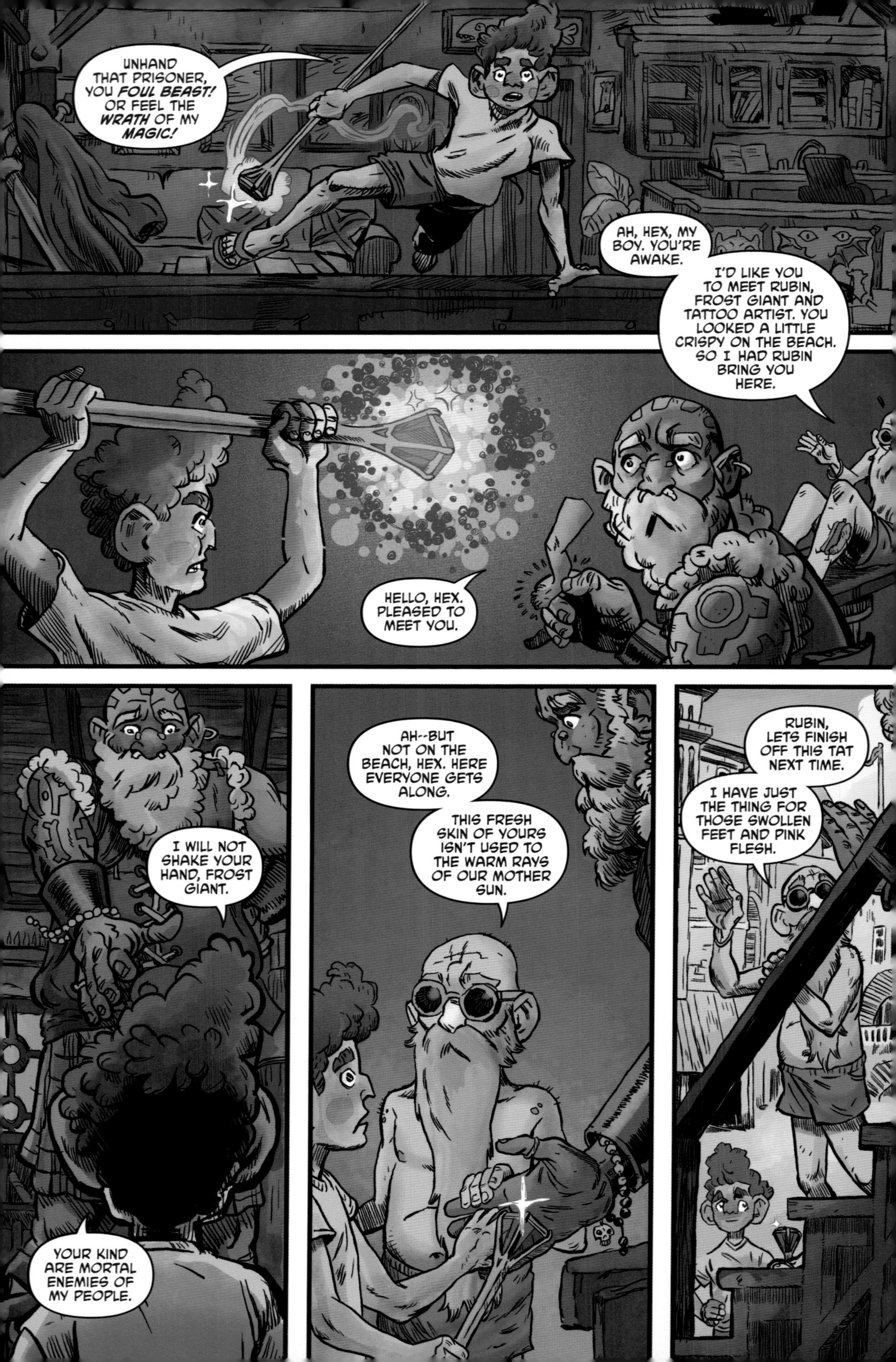
UNHAND THAT PRISONER, YOU FOUL BEAST! OR FEEL THE WRATH OF MY MAGIC!
AH, HEX, MY BOY. YOU'RE AWAKE.
I'D LIKE YOU TO MEET RUBIN, FROST GIANT AND TATTOO ARTIST. YOU LOOKED A LITTLE CRISPY ON THE BEACH. SO I HAD RUBIN BRING YOU HERE.
HELLO, HEX. PLEASED TO MEET YOU.
I WILL NOT SHAKE YOUR HAND, FROST GIANT.
YOUR KIND ARE MORTAL ENEMIES OF MY PEOPLE.
AH--BUT NOT ON THE BEACH, HEX. HERE EVERYONE GETS ALONG.
THIS FRESH SKIN OF YOURS ISN'T USED TO THE WARM RAYS OF OUR MOTHER SUN.
RUBIN, LETS FINISH OFF THIS TAT NEXT TIME.
I HAVE JUST THE THING FOR THOSE SWOLLEN FEET AND PINK FLESH.

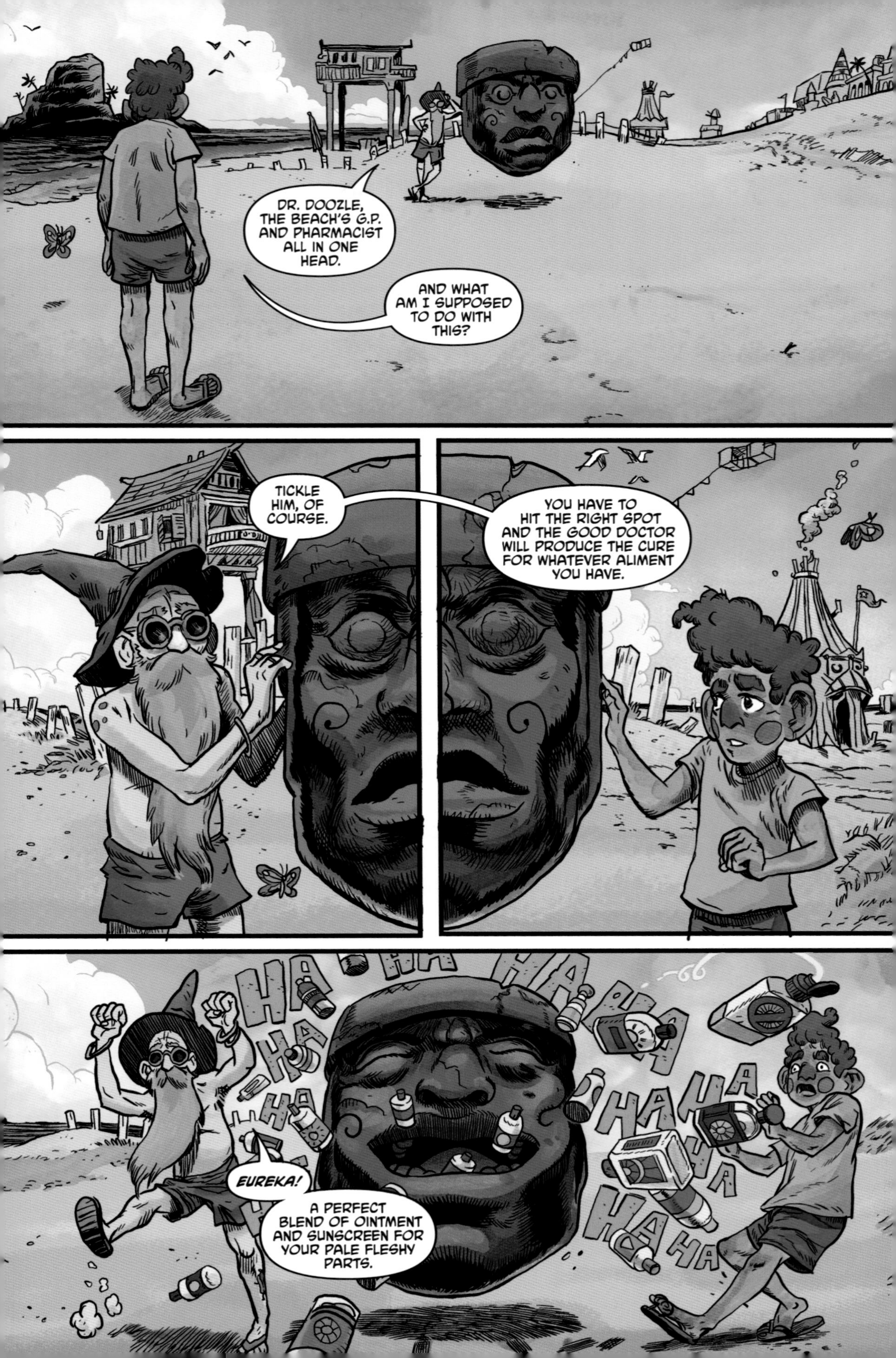

DR. DOOZLE, THE BEACH'S G.P. AND PHARMACIST ALL IN ONE HEAD.
AND WHAT AM I SUPPOSED TO DO WITH THIS?
TICKLE HIM, OF COURSE.
YOU HAVE TO HIT THE RIGHT SPOT AND THE GOOD DOCTOR WILL PRODUCE THE CURE FOR WHATEVER ALIMENT YOU HAVE.
HA HA HA HA HA HA HA HA HA HA HA HA HA HA HA
EUREKA!
A PERFECT BLEND OF OINTMENT AND SUNSCREEN FOR YOUR PALE FLESHY PARTS.

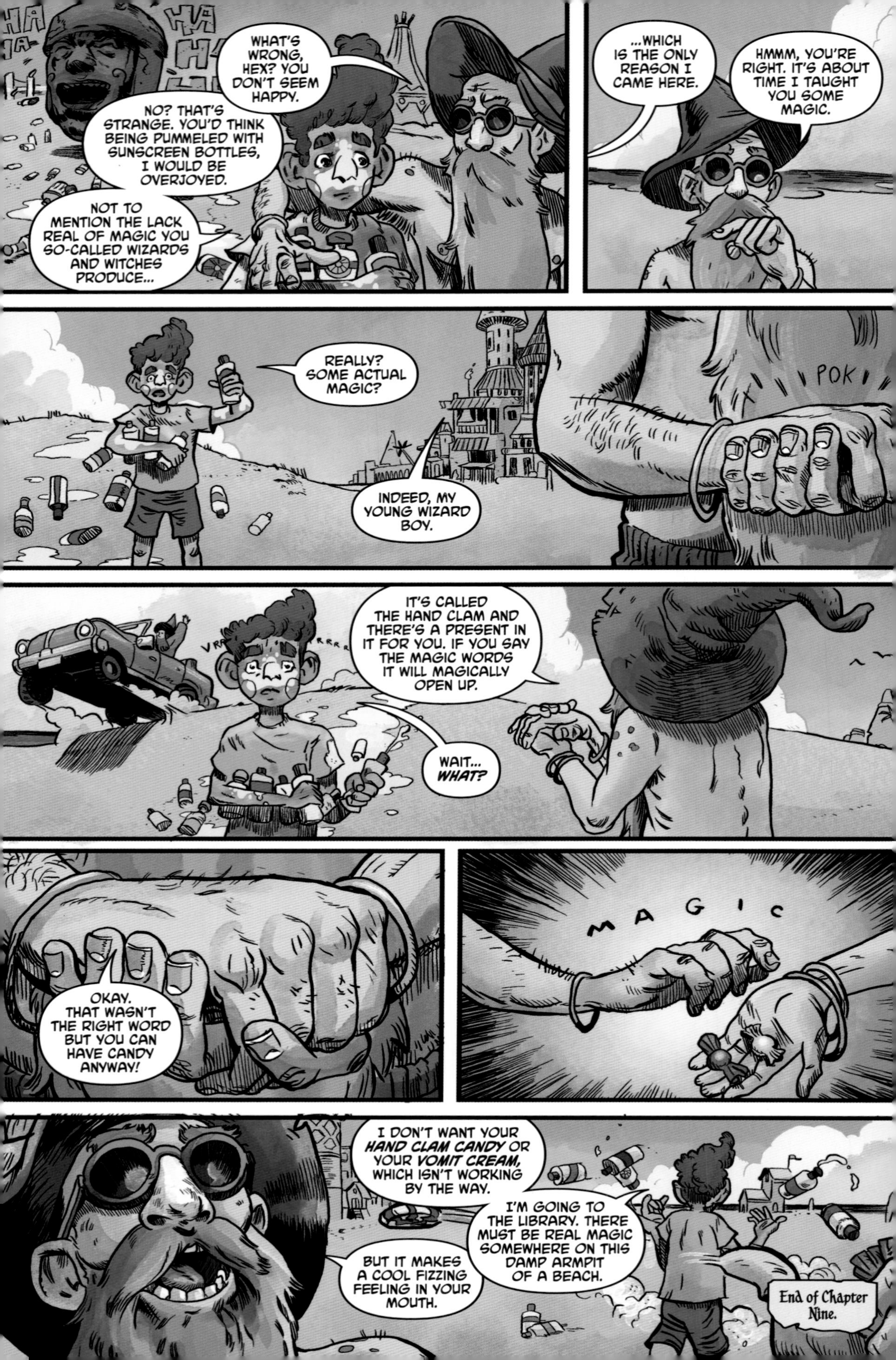
HA HA HA HA HA
WHAT'S WRONG, HEX? YOU DON'T SEEM HAPPY.
NO? THAT'S STRANGE. YOU'D THINK BEING PUMMELED WITH SUNSCREEN BOTTLES, I WOULD BE OVERJOYED.
NOT TO MENTION THE LACK REAL OF MAGIC YOU SO-CALLED WIZARDS AND WITCHES PRODUCE...
...WHICH IS THE ONLY REASON I CAME HERE.
HMMM, YOU'RE RIGHT. IT'S ABOUT TIME I TAUGHT YOU SOME MAGIC.
POK
REALLY? SOME ACTUAL MAGIC?
INDEED, MY YOUNG WIZARD BOY.
VRRRRRR
IT'S CALLED THE HAND CLAM AND THERE'S A PRESENT IN IT FOR YOU. IF YOU SAY THE MAGIC WORDS IT WILL MAGICALLY OPEN UP.
WAIT... *WHAT?*
OKAY. THAT WASN'T THE RIGHT WORD BUT YOU CAN HAVE CANDY ANYWAY!
MAGIC
I DON'T WANT YOUR *HAND CLAM CANDY* OR YOUR *VOMIT CREAM,* WHICH ISN'T WORKING BY THE WAY.
I'M GOING TO THE LIBRARY. THERE MUST BE REAL MAGIC SOMEWHERE ON THIS DAMP ARMPIT OF A BEACH.
BUT IT MAKES A COOL FIZZING FEELING IN YOUR MOUTH.
End of Chapter Nine.

INSTRUCTIONS ON HOW TO PERFORM THE HAND CLAM

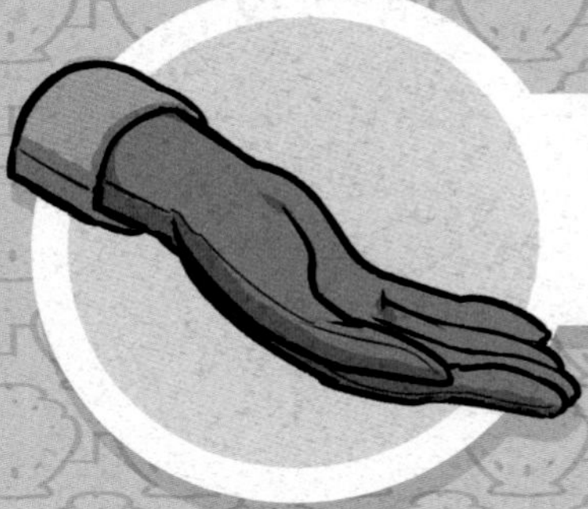

STEP 1:

CUP ONE OF YOUR HANDS. MAKE SURE THE CUP IS DEEP ENOUGH TO HOLD A SMALL TRINKET.

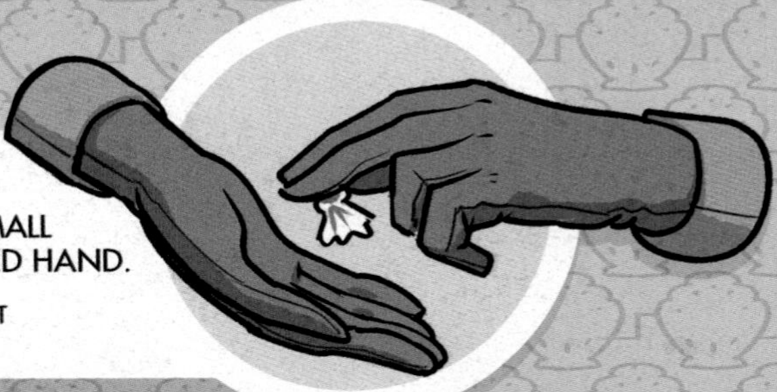

STEP 2:

WITH YOUR OTHER HAND, PLACE A SMALL TRINKET OR TREASURE INSIDE OF THE CUPPED HAND.

*NOTE. MAKE SURE THE SMALL PRIZE IS NOT TOO LARGE TO FIT IN YOUR PALM."

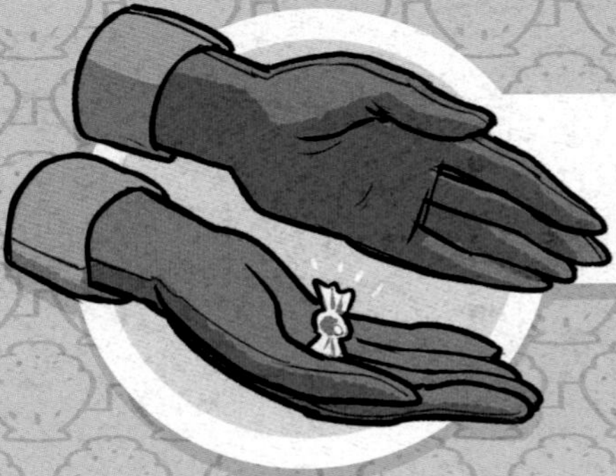

STEP 3:

NOW, CUP YOUR OTHER HAND AND PLACE IT OVER THE FIRST HAND AND TRINKET.

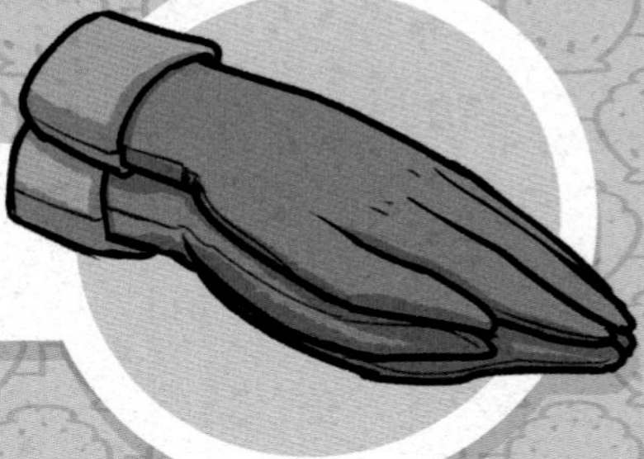

STEP 4:

CONGRATULATIONS!
YOU NOW HAVE A CLOSED HAND CLAM.

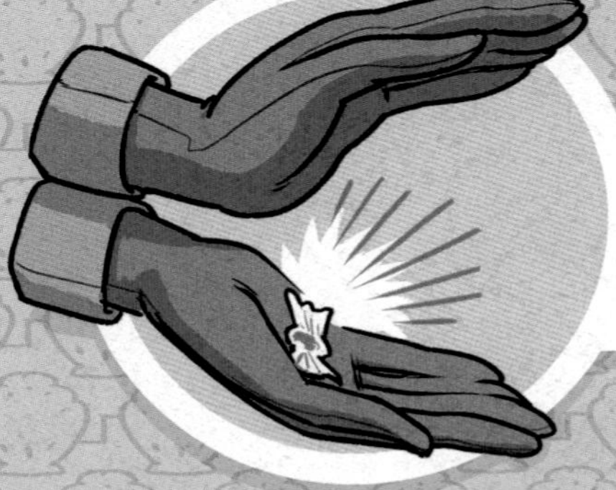

STEP 5:

TO REVEAL, LIFT THE FINGERS ON THE TOP HAND WHILE KEEPING THE BOTTOM PALM TIGHTLY PRESSED ON THE LOWER HAND.

THE HAND CLAM IS GREAT FOR BIRTHDAY PARTIES, GRADUATIONS, OR ANY OCCASION WHERE A LITTLE JOY AND HAPPINESS IS NEEDED.

ENJOY THE HAND CLAM!

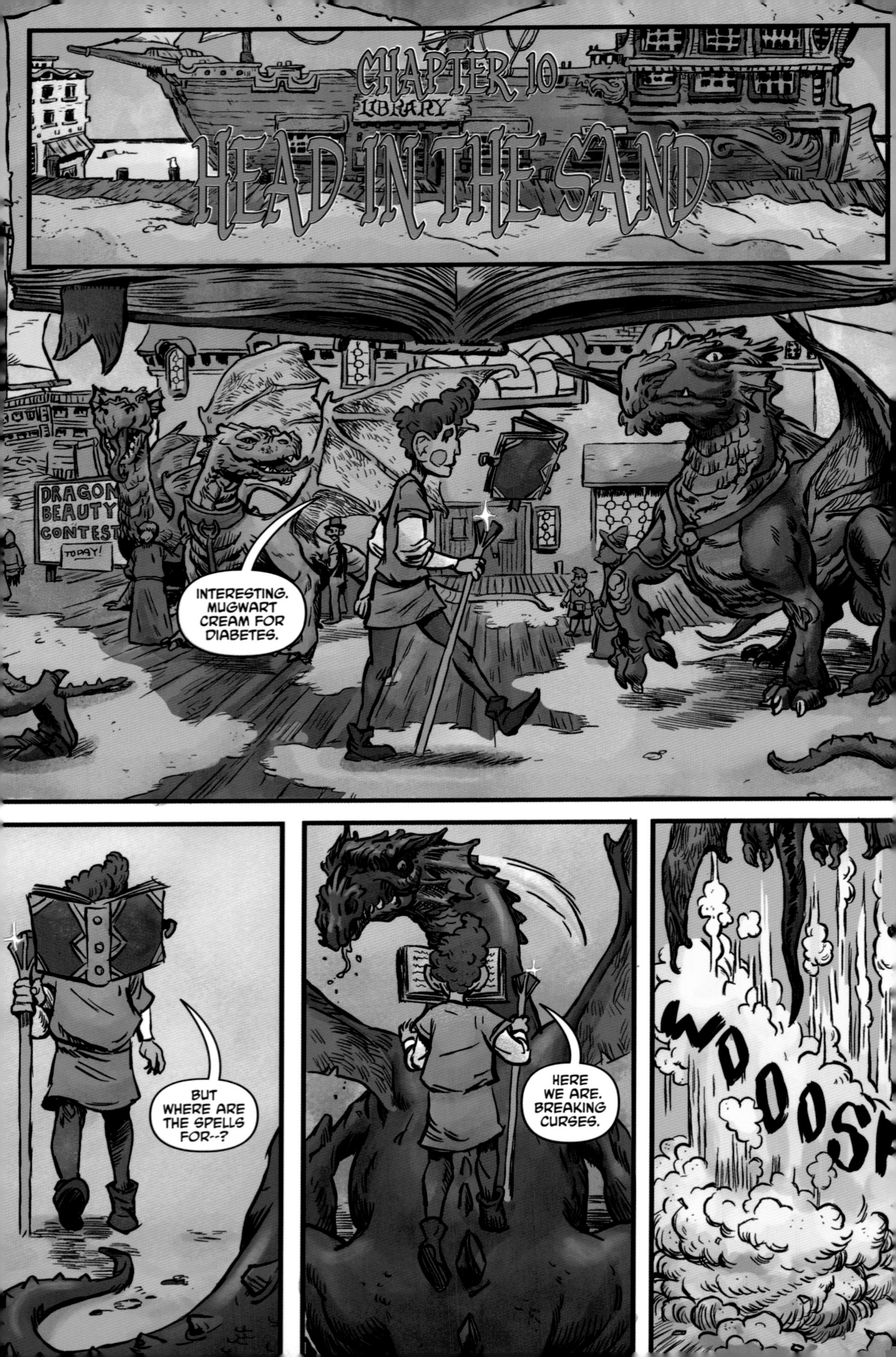
CHAPTER 10
LIBRARY
HEAD IN THE SAND
DRAGON BEAUTY CONTEST
TODAY!
INTERESTING. MUGWART CREAM FOR DIABETES.
BUT WHERE ARE THE SPELLS FOR--?
HERE WE ARE. BREAKING CURSES.
WDOOSH

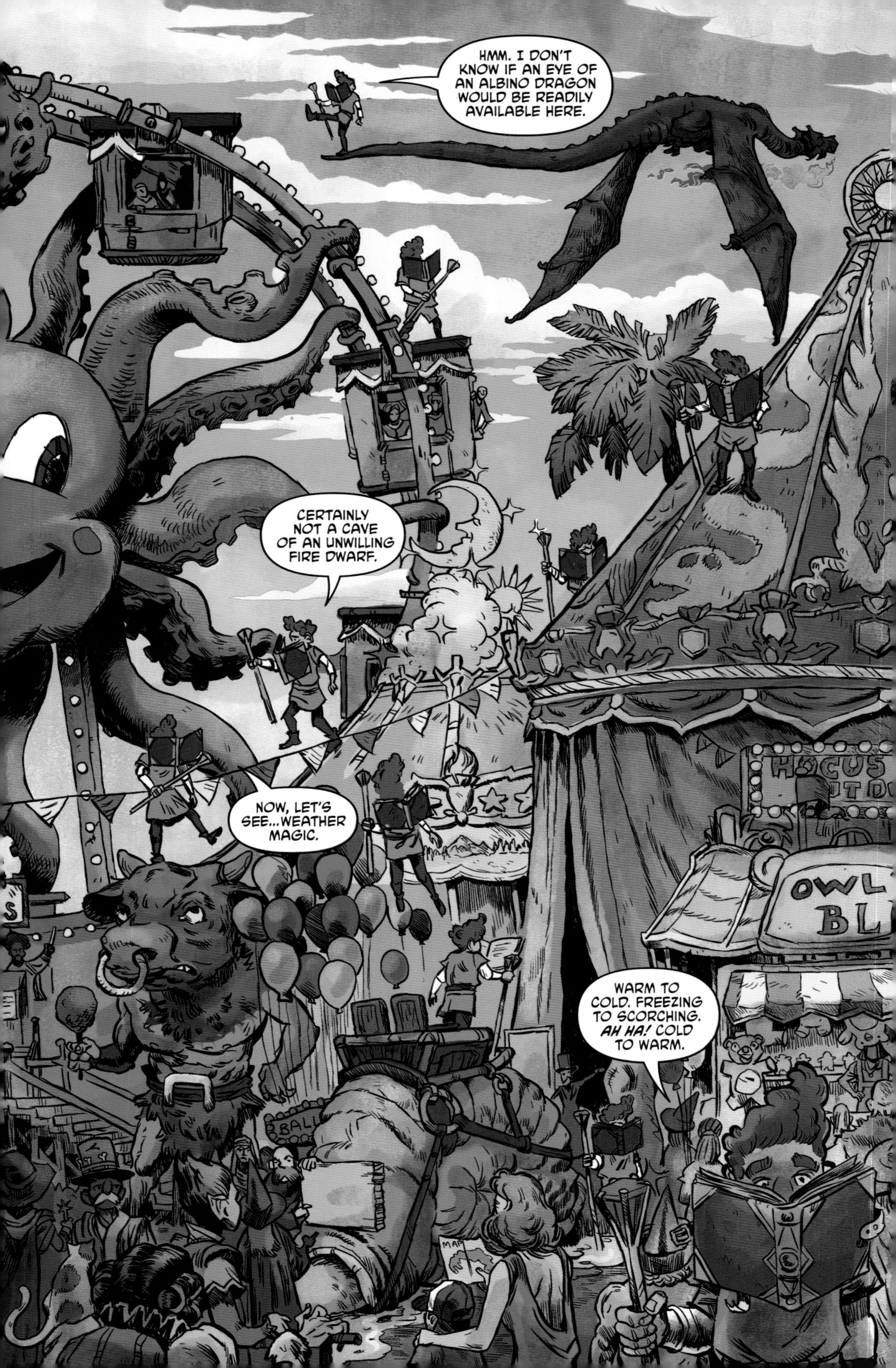
HMM. I DON'T KNOW IF AN EYE OF AN ALBINO DRAGON WOULD BE READILY AVAILABLE HERE.
CERTAINLY NOT A CAVE OF AN UNWILLING FIRE DWARF.
NOW, LET'S SEE...WEATHER MAGIC.
WARM TO COLD. FREEZING TO SCORCHING. *AH HA!* COLD TO WARM.

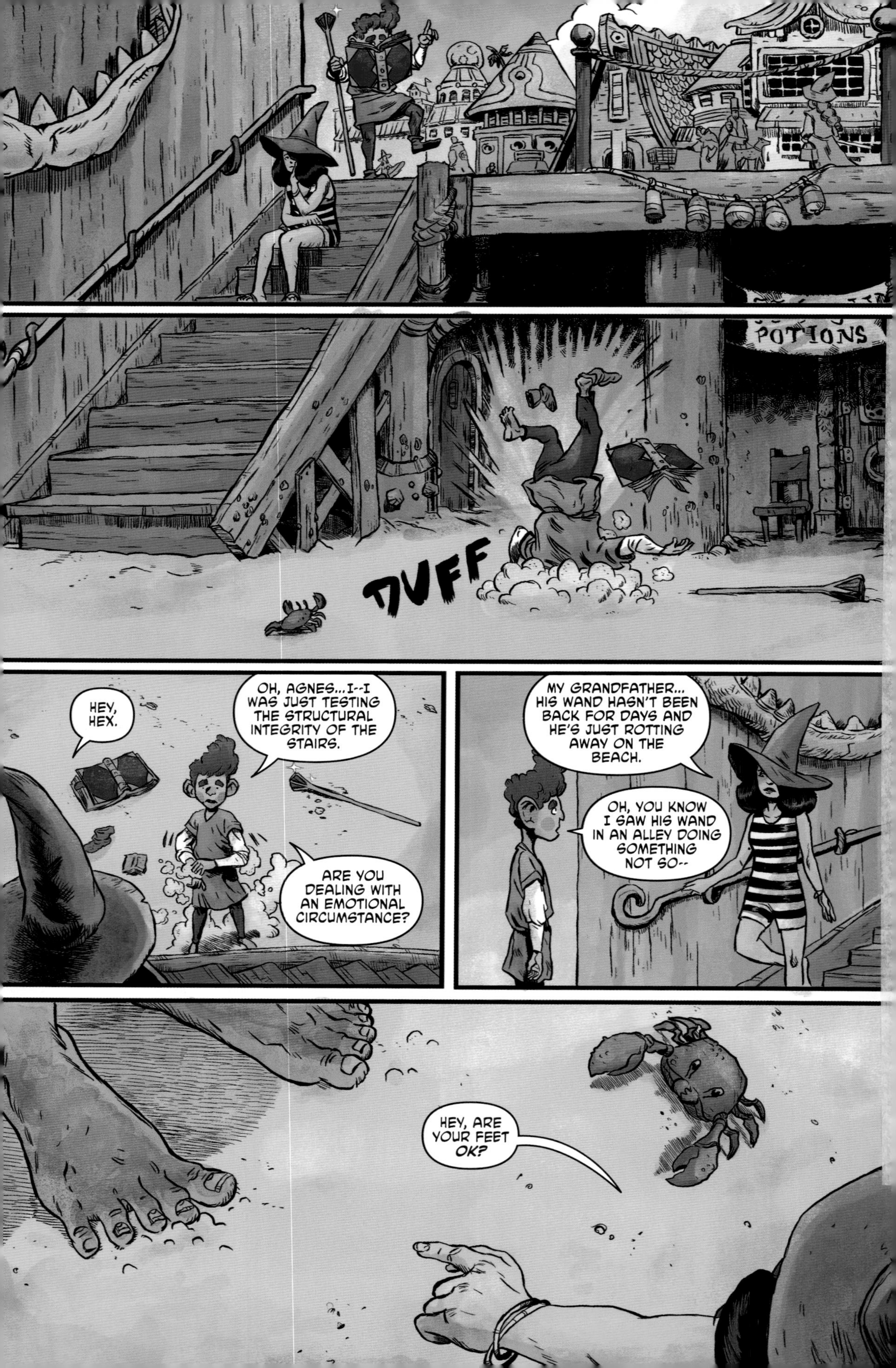

POTIONS
DUFF
HEY, HEX.
OH, AGNES...I--I WAS JUST TESTING THE STRUCTURAL INTEGRITY OF THE STAIRS.
ARE YOU DEALING WITH AN EMOTIONAL CIRCUMSTANCE?
MY GRANDFATHER... HIS WAND HASN'T BEEN BACK FOR DAYS AND HE'S JUST ROTTING AWAY ON THE BEACH.
OH, YOU KNOW I SAW HIS WAND IN AN ALLEY DOING SOMETHING NOT SO--
HEY, ARE YOUR FEET *OK?*

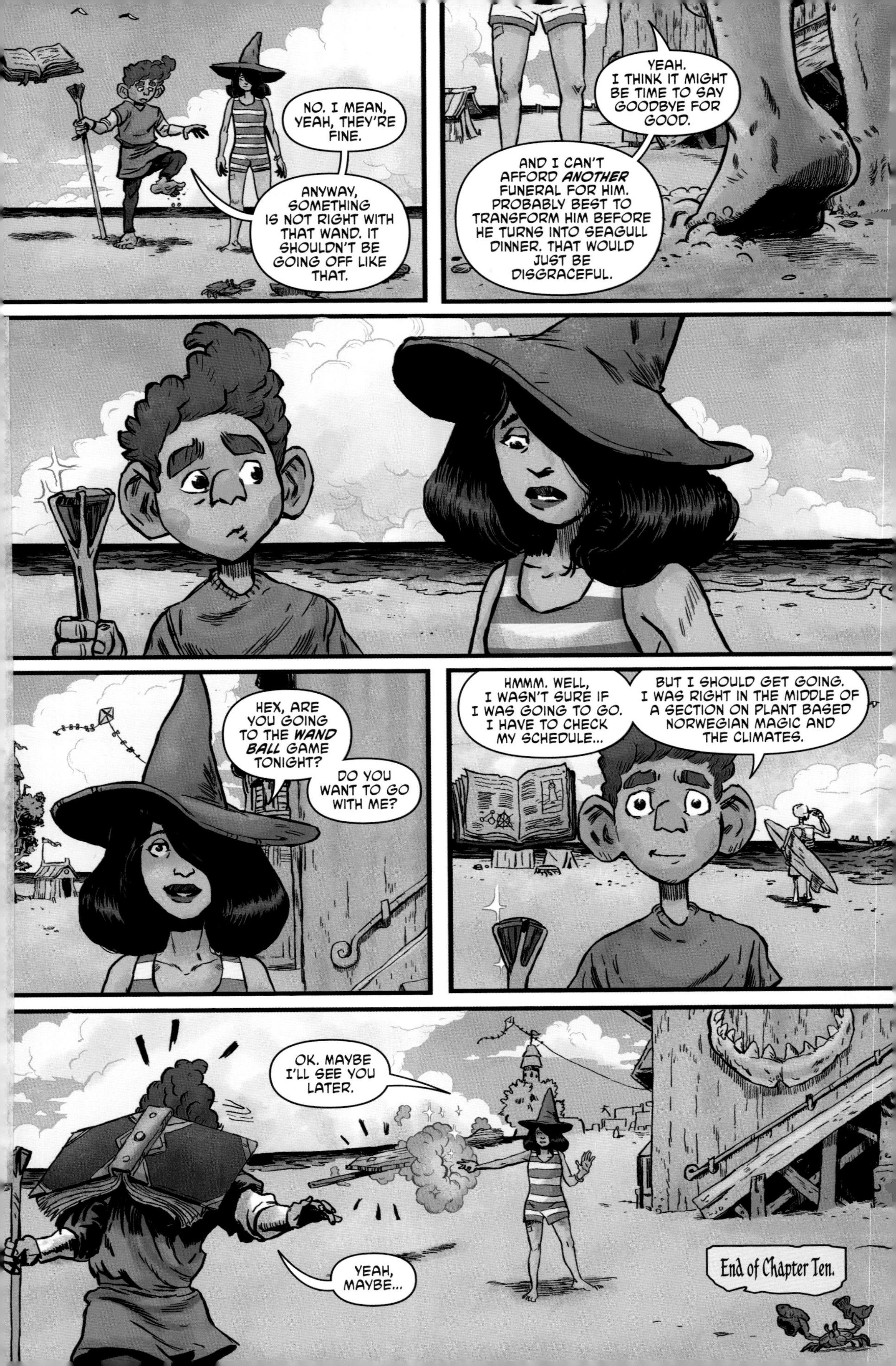
NO. I MEAN, YEAH, THEY'RE FINE.
ANYWAY, SOMETHING IS NOT RIGHT WITH THAT WAND. IT SHOULDN'T BE GOING OFF LIKE THAT.
YEAH. I THINK IT MIGHT BE TIME TO SAY GOODBYE FOR GOOD.
AND I CAN'T AFFORD ANOTHER FUNERAL FOR HIM. PROBABLY BEST TO TRANSFORM HIM BEFORE HE TURNS INTO SEAGULL DINNER. THAT WOULD JUST BE DISGRACEFUL.
HEX, ARE YOU GOING TO THE WAND BALL GAME TONIGHT?
DO YOU WANT TO GO WITH ME?
HMMM. WELL, I WASN'T SURE IF I WAS GOING TO GO. I HAVE TO CHECK MY SCHEDULE...
BUT I SHOULD GET GOING. I WAS RIGHT IN THE MIDDLE OF A SECTION ON PLANT BASED NORWEGIAN MAGIC AND THE CLIMATES.
OK. MAYBE I'LL SEE YOU LATER.
YEAH, MAYBE...
End of Chapter Ten.

The Wizardverse

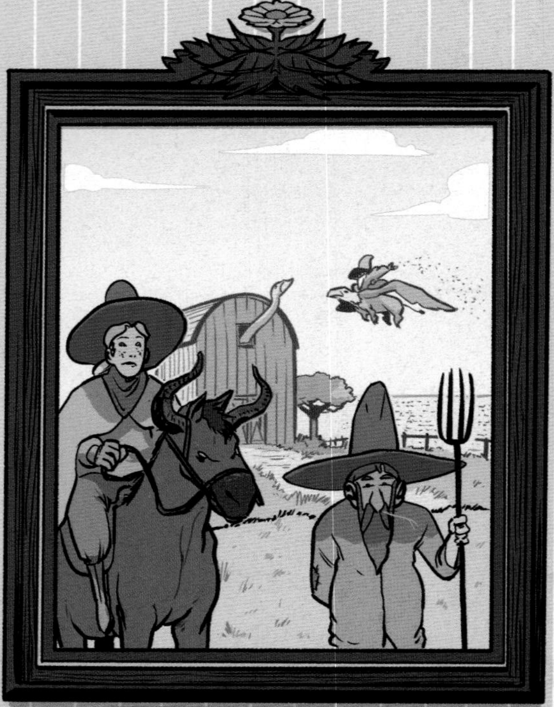

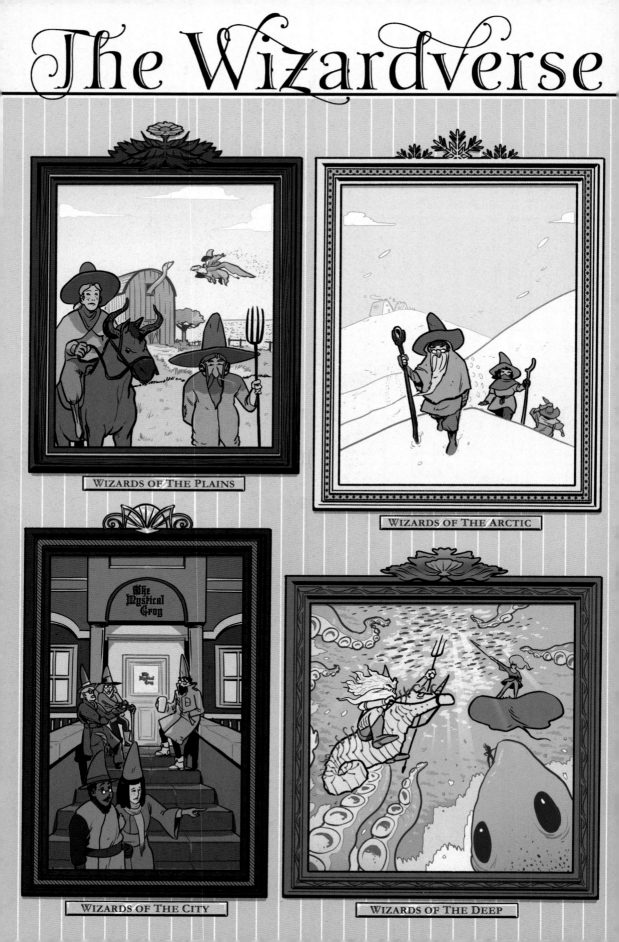

WIZARDS OF THE PLAINS

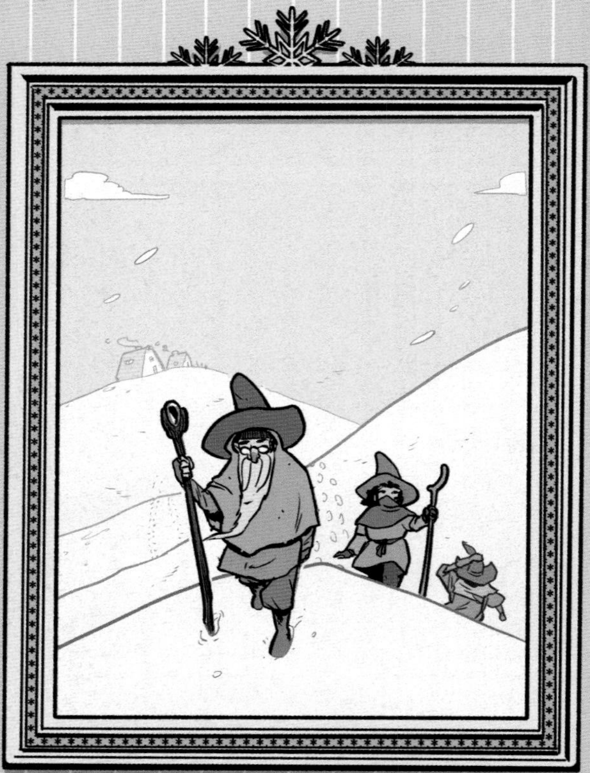

WIZARDS OF THE ARCTIC

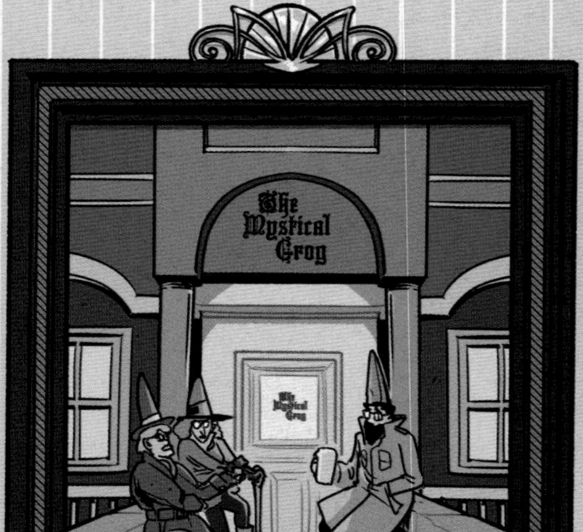
The Mystical Grog

WIZARDS OF THE CITY

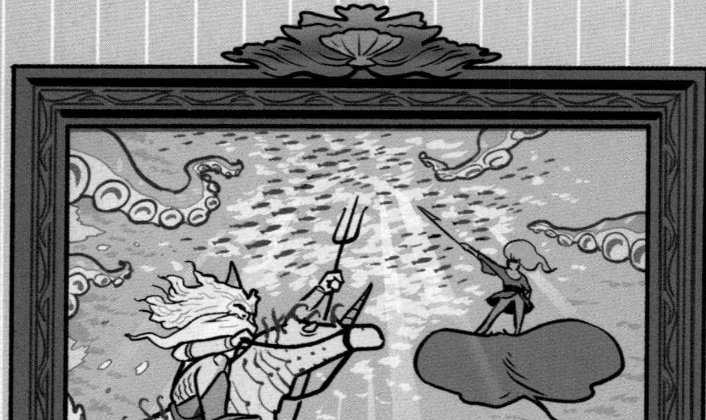

WIZARDS OF THE DEEP

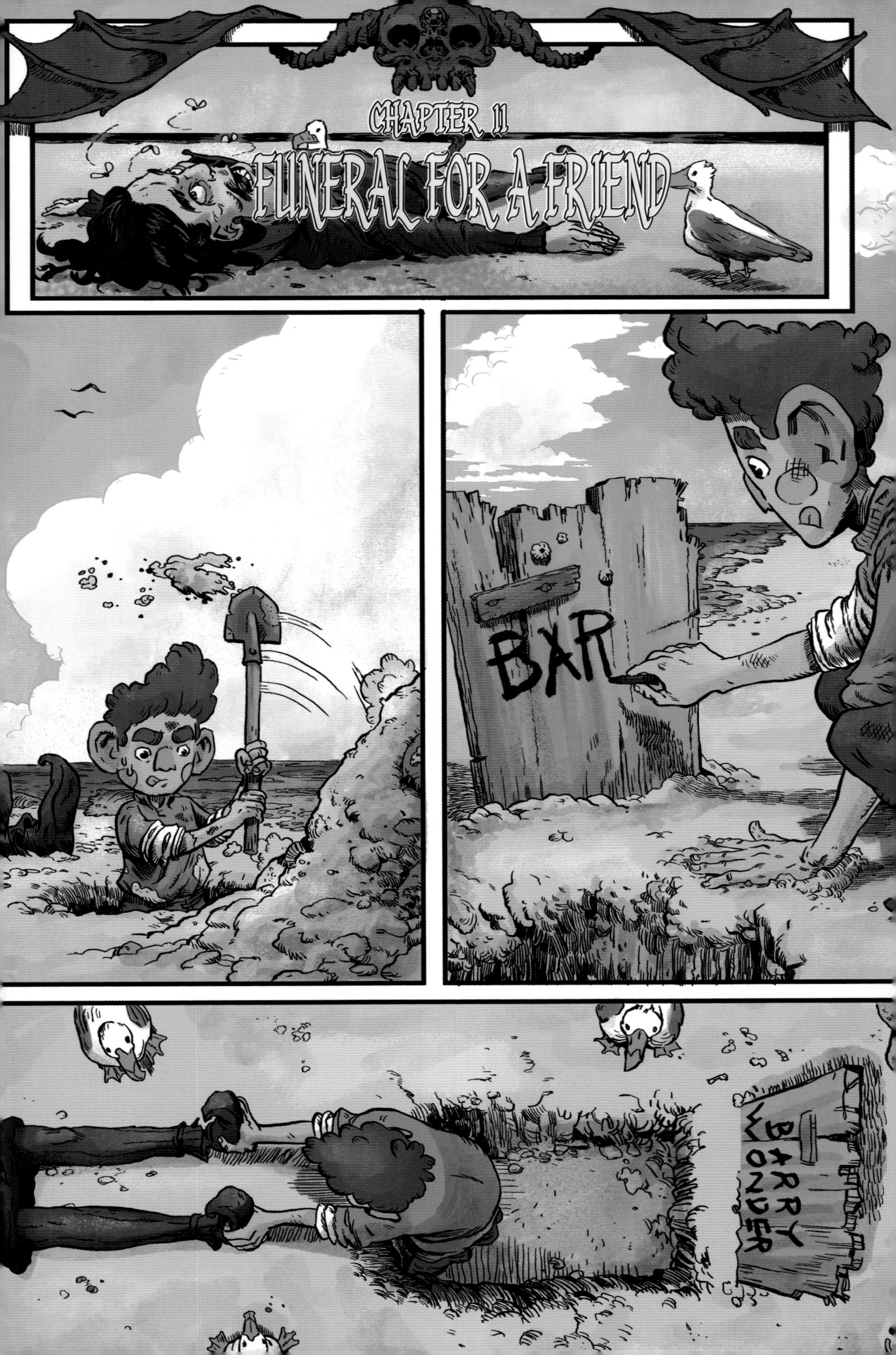
CHAPTER 11
FUNERAL FOR A FRIEND
BAR
BARRY WONDER

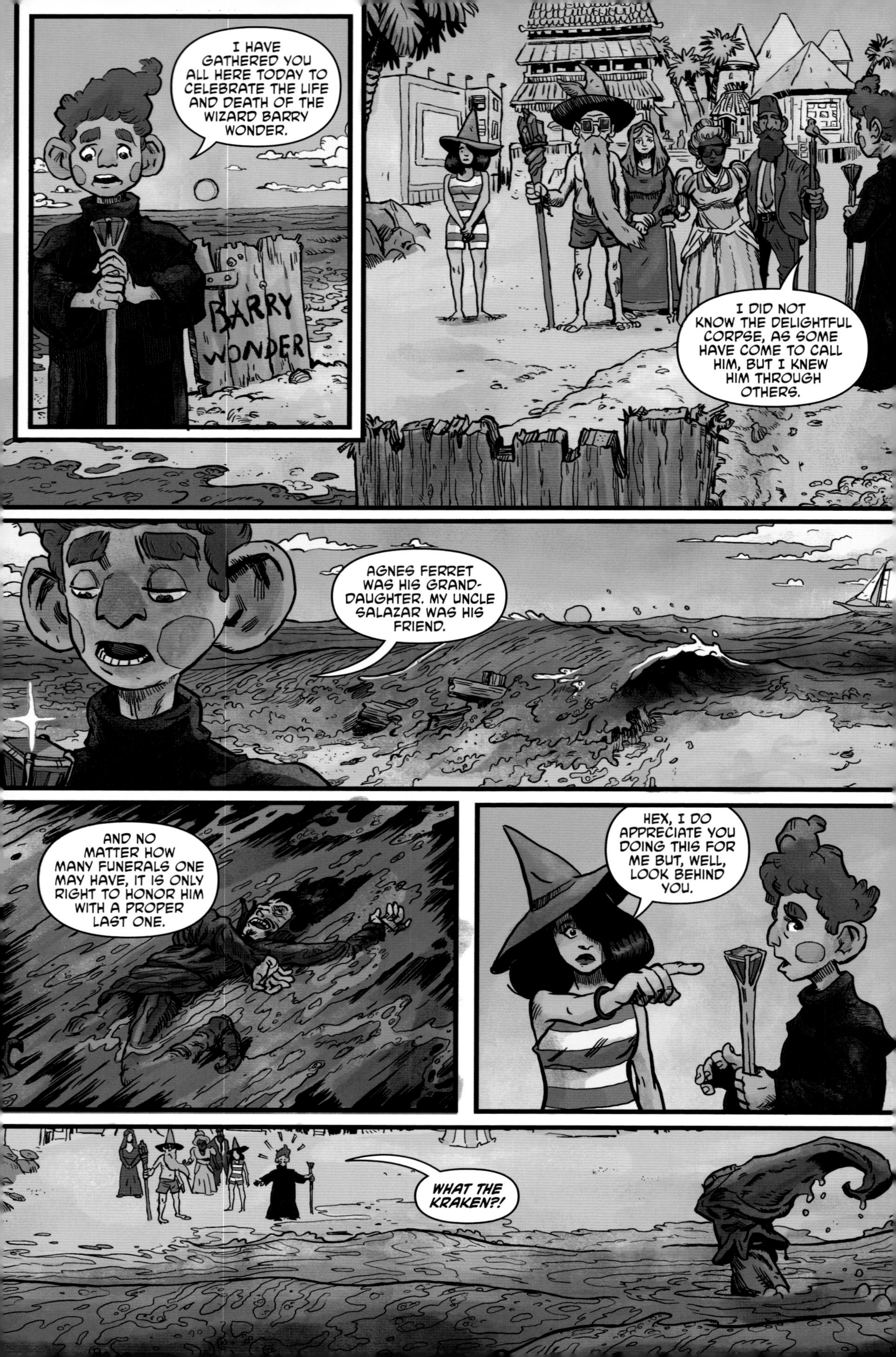
I HAVE GATHERED YOU ALL HERE TODAY TO CELEBRATE THE LIFE AND DEATH OF THE WIZARD BARRY WONDER.
BARRY WONDER
I DID NOT KNOW THE DELIGHTFUL CORPSE, AS SOME HAVE COME TO CALL HIM, BUT I KNEW HIM THROUGH OTHERS.
AGNES FERRET WAS HIS GRAND-DAUGHTER. MY UNCLE SALAZAR WAS HIS FRIEND.
AND NO MATTER HOW MANY FUNERALS ONE MAY HAVE, IT IS ONLY RIGHT TO HONOR HIM WITH A PROPER LAST ONE.
HEX, I DO APPRECIATE YOU DOING THIS FOR ME BUT, WELL, LOOK BEHIND YOU.
WHAT THE KRAKEN?!

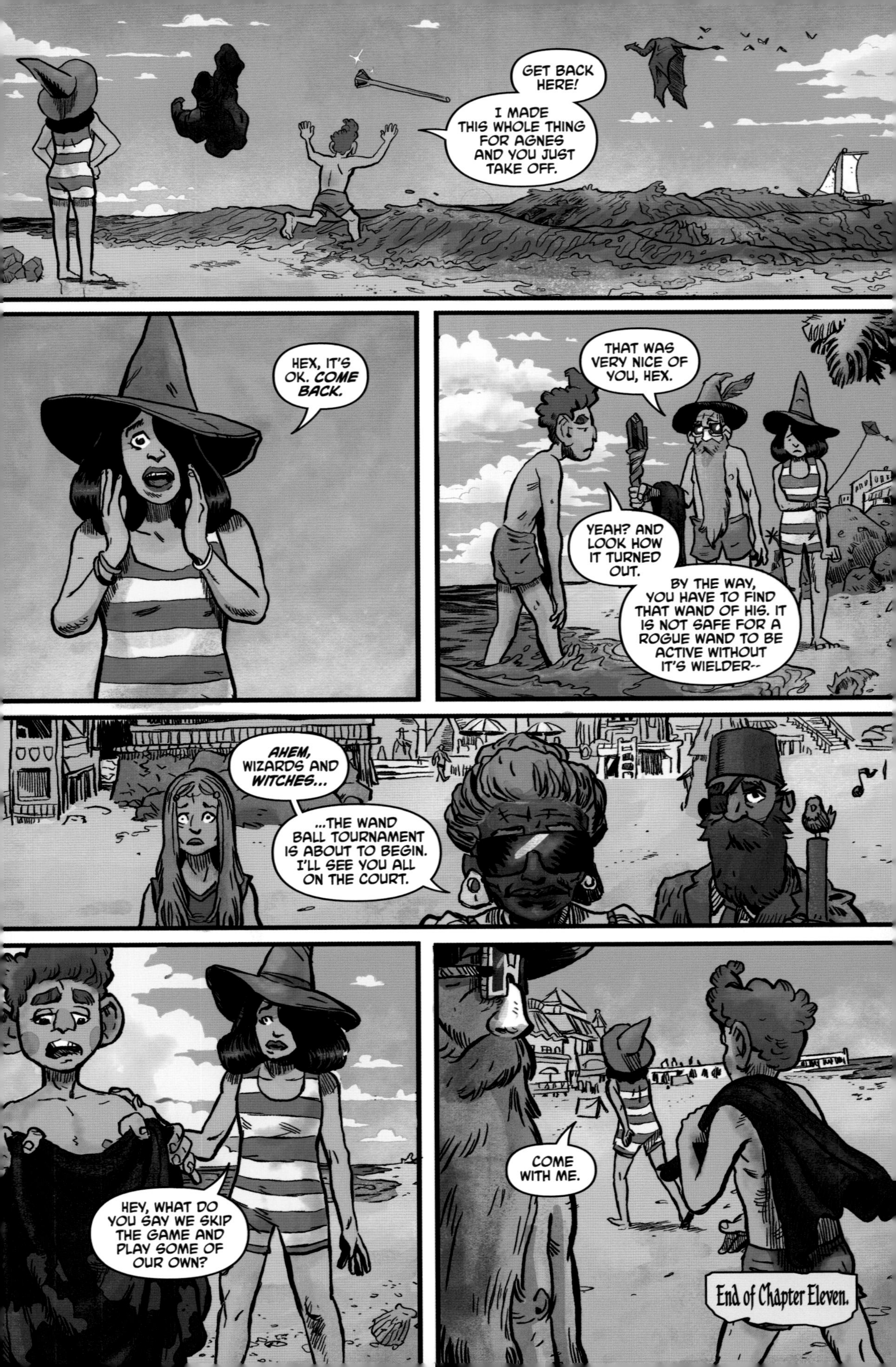
GET BACK HERE!
I MADE THIS WHOLE THING FOR AGNES AND YOU JUST TAKE OFF.
HEX, IT'S OK. COME BACK.
THAT WAS VERY NICE OF YOU, HEX.
YEAH? AND LOOK HOW IT TURNED OUT.
BY THE WAY, YOU HAVE TO FIND THAT WAND OF HIS. IT IS NOT SAFE FOR A ROGUE WAND TO BE ACTIVE WITHOUT IT'S WIELDER--
AHEM, WIZARDS AND WITCHES...
...THE WAND BALL TOURNAMENT IS ABOUT TO BEGIN. I'LL SEE YOU ALL ON THE COURT.
HEY, WHAT DO YOU SAY WE SKIP THE GAME AND PLAY SOME OF OUR OWN?
COME WITH ME.
End of Chapter Eleven.

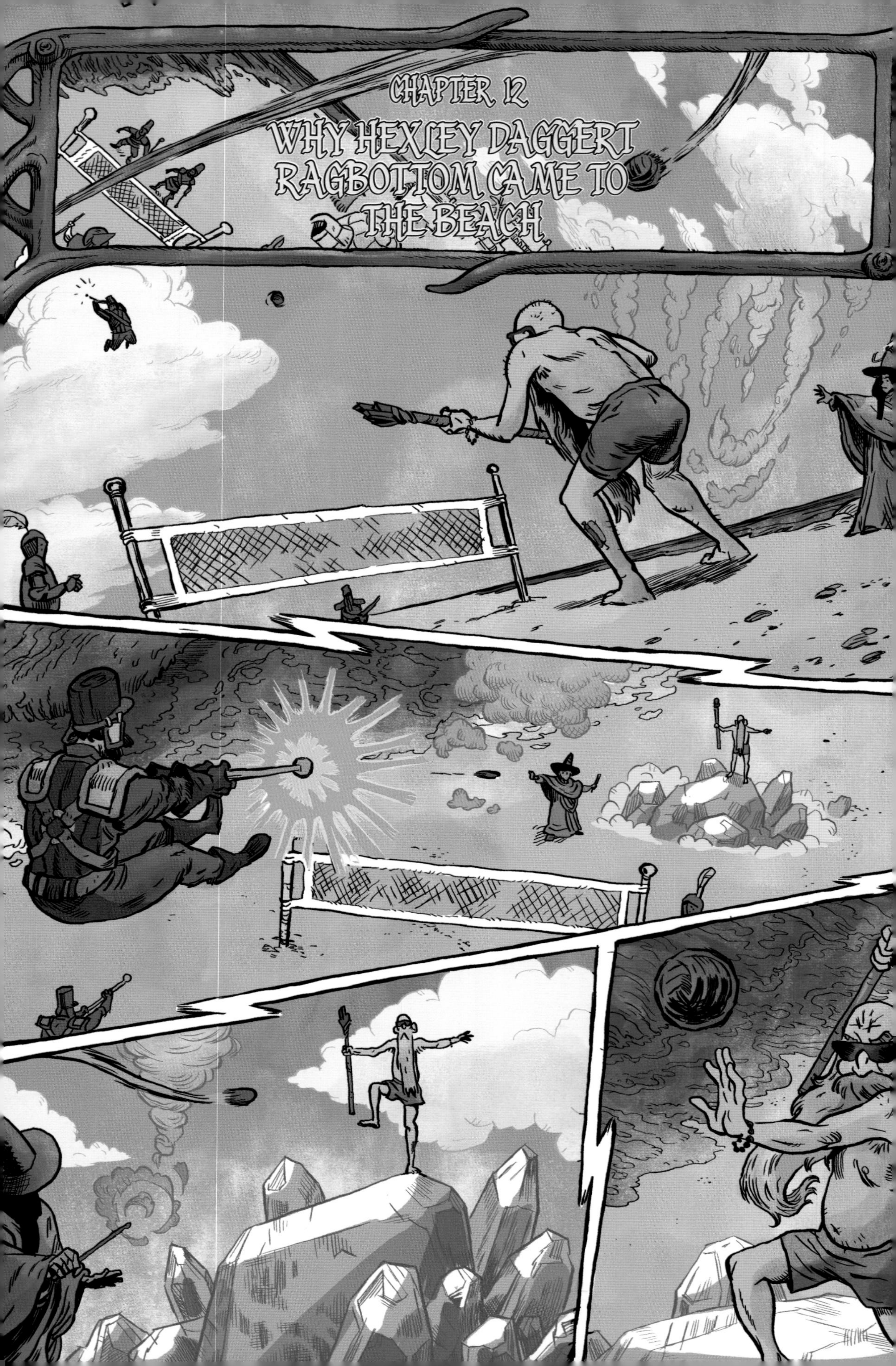
CHAPTER 12
WHY HEXLEY DAGGERT RAGBOTTOM CAME TO THE BEACH

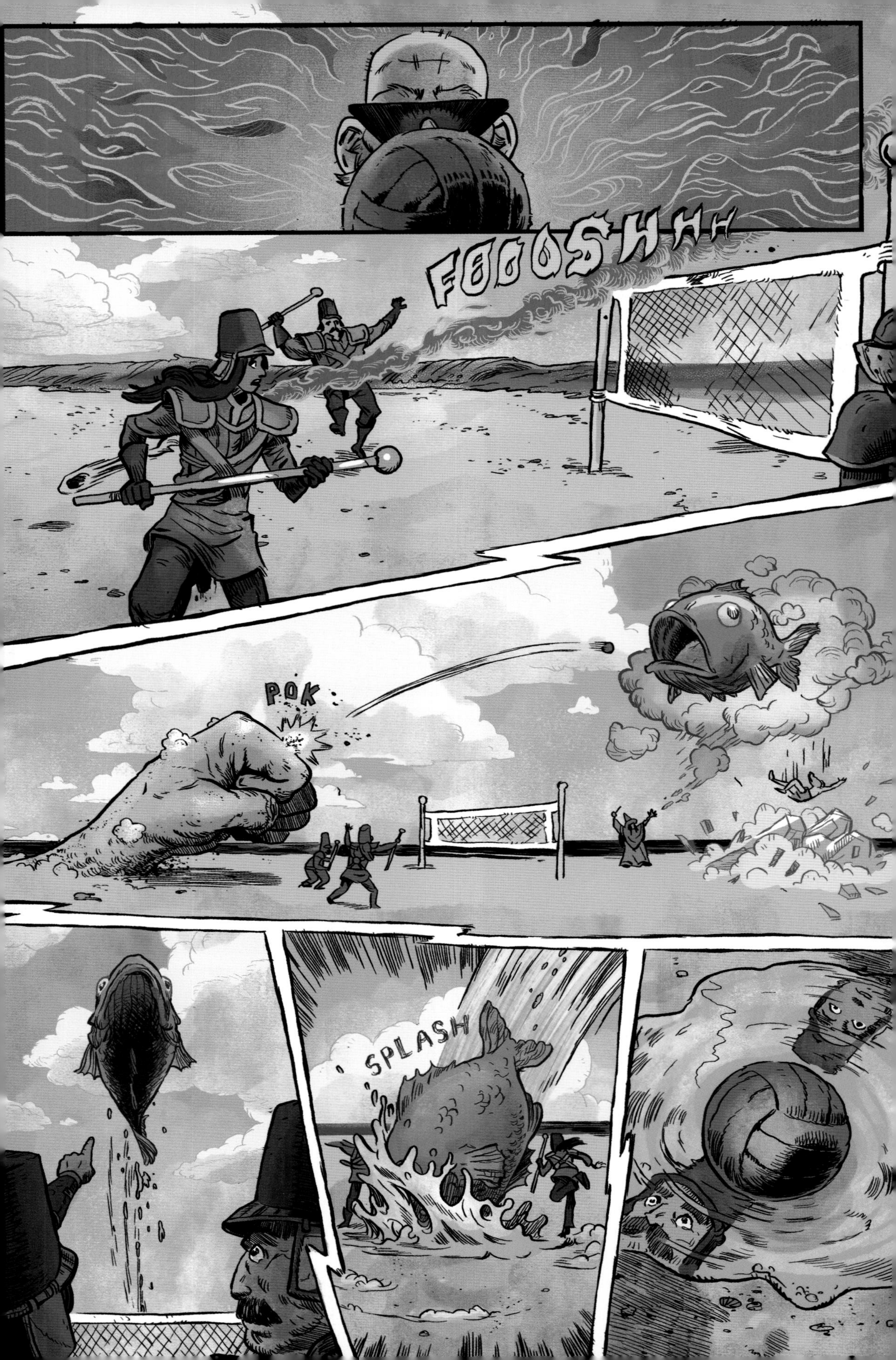
FOOOSHHH
POK
SPLASH

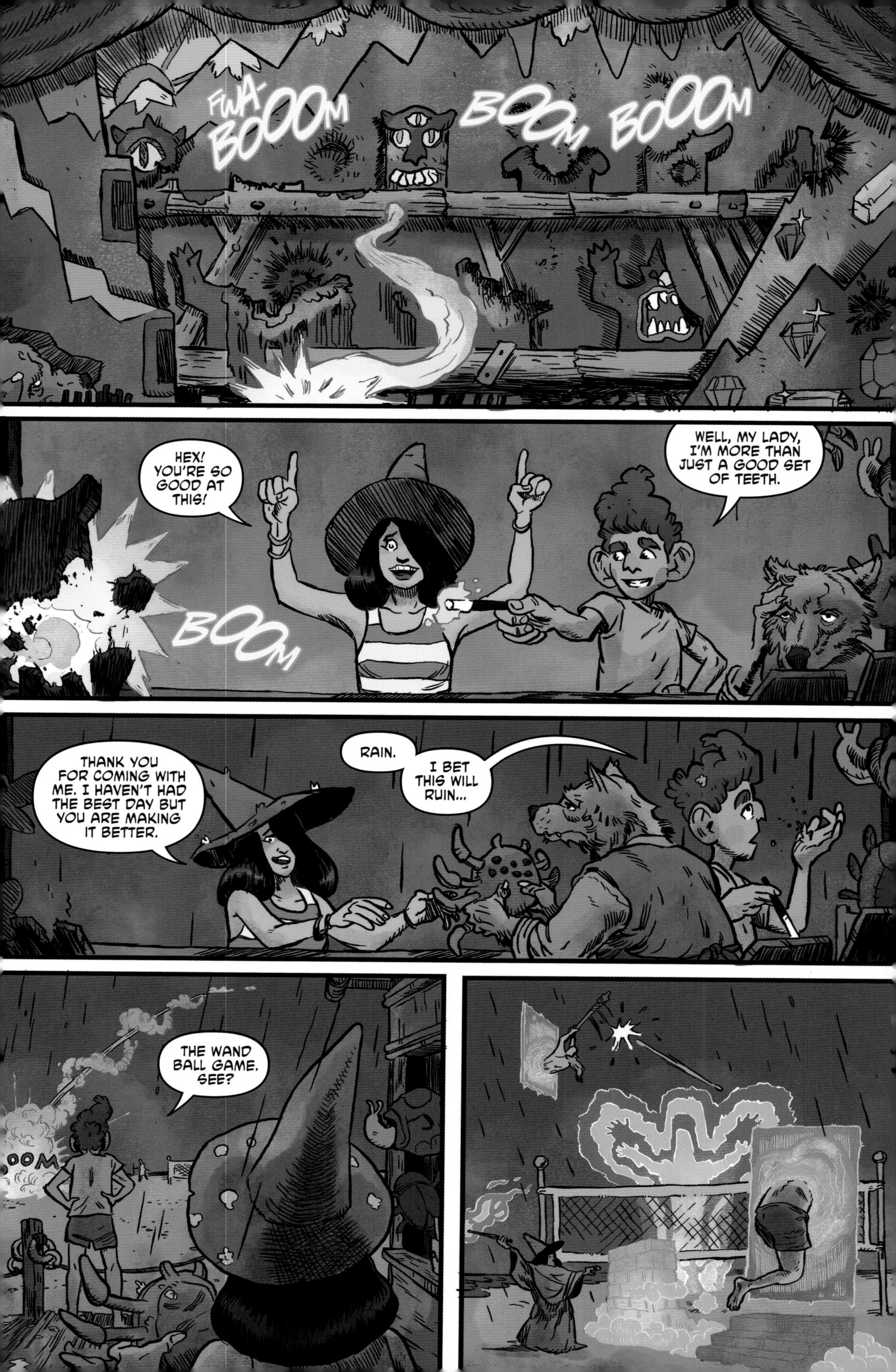
FWA-BOOOM
BOOOM
BOOOOM
HEX! YOU'RE SO GOOD AT THIS!
WELL, MY LADY, I'M MORE THAN JUST A GOOD SET OF TEETH.
BOOM
THANK YOU FOR COMING WITH ME. I HAVEN'T HAD THE BEST DAY BUT YOU ARE MAKING IT BETTER.
RAIN.
I BET THIS WILL RUIN...
THE WAND BALL GAME. SEE?

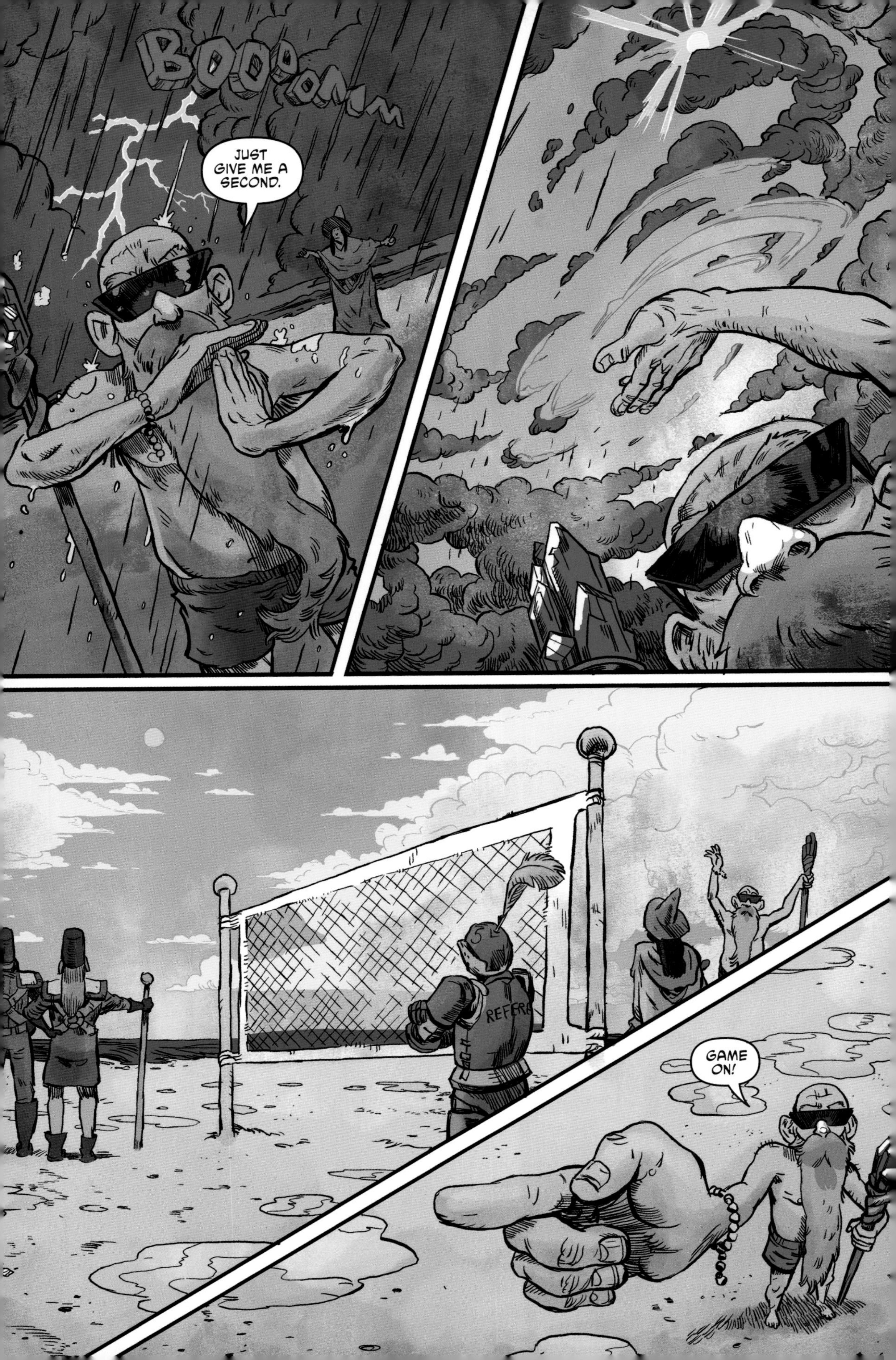
BOOOOOM
JUST GIVE ME A SECOND.
REFERA
GAME ON!

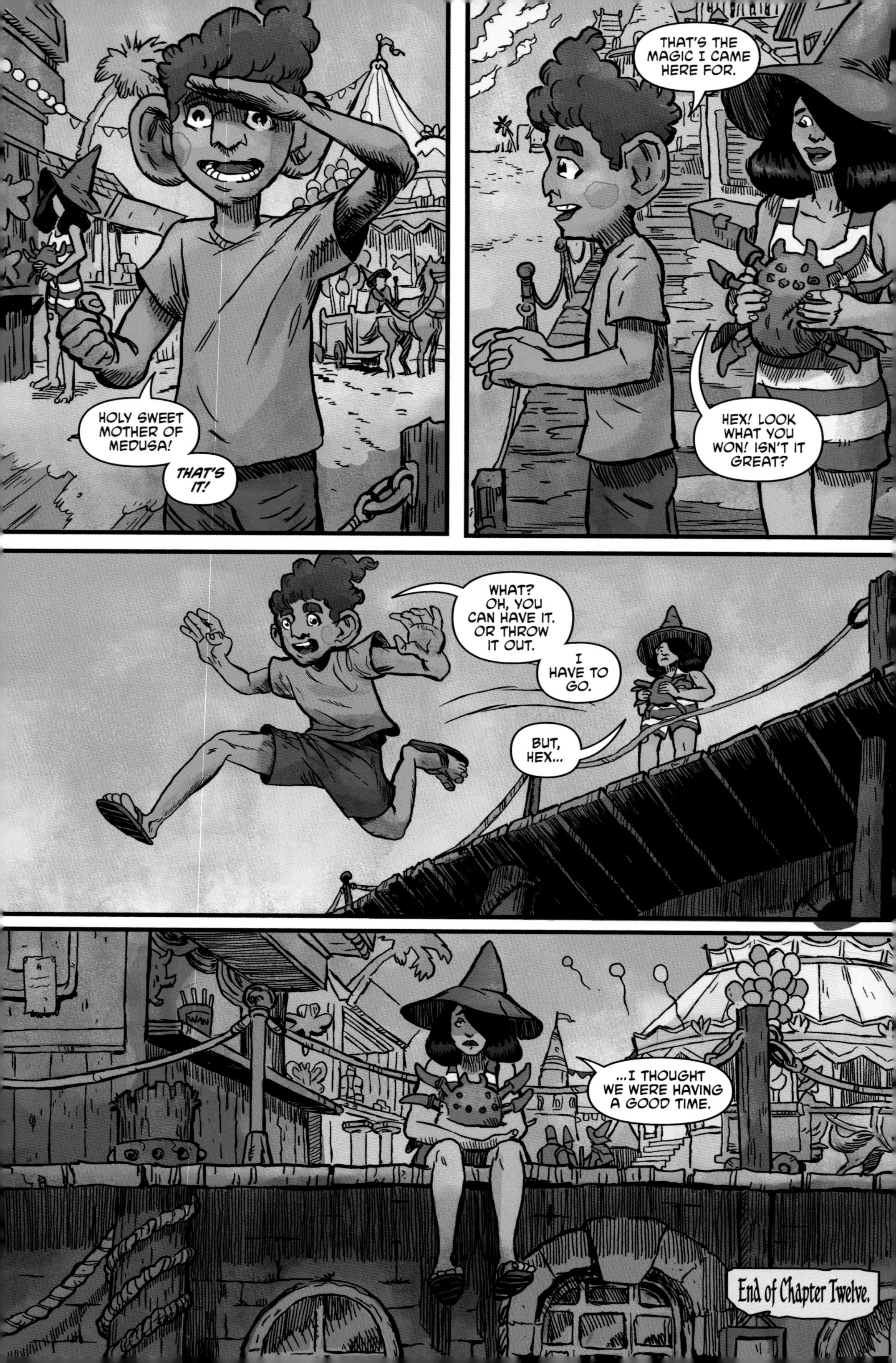
HOLY SWEET MOTHER OF MEDUSA!
THAT'S IT!
THAT'S THE MAGIC I CAME HERE FOR.
HEX! LOOK WHAT YOU WON! ISN'T IT GREAT?
WHAT? OH, YOU CAN HAVE IT. OR THROW IT OUT.
I HAVE TO GO.
BUT, HEX...
...I THOUGHT WE WERE HAVING A GOOD TIME.
End of Chapter Twelve.

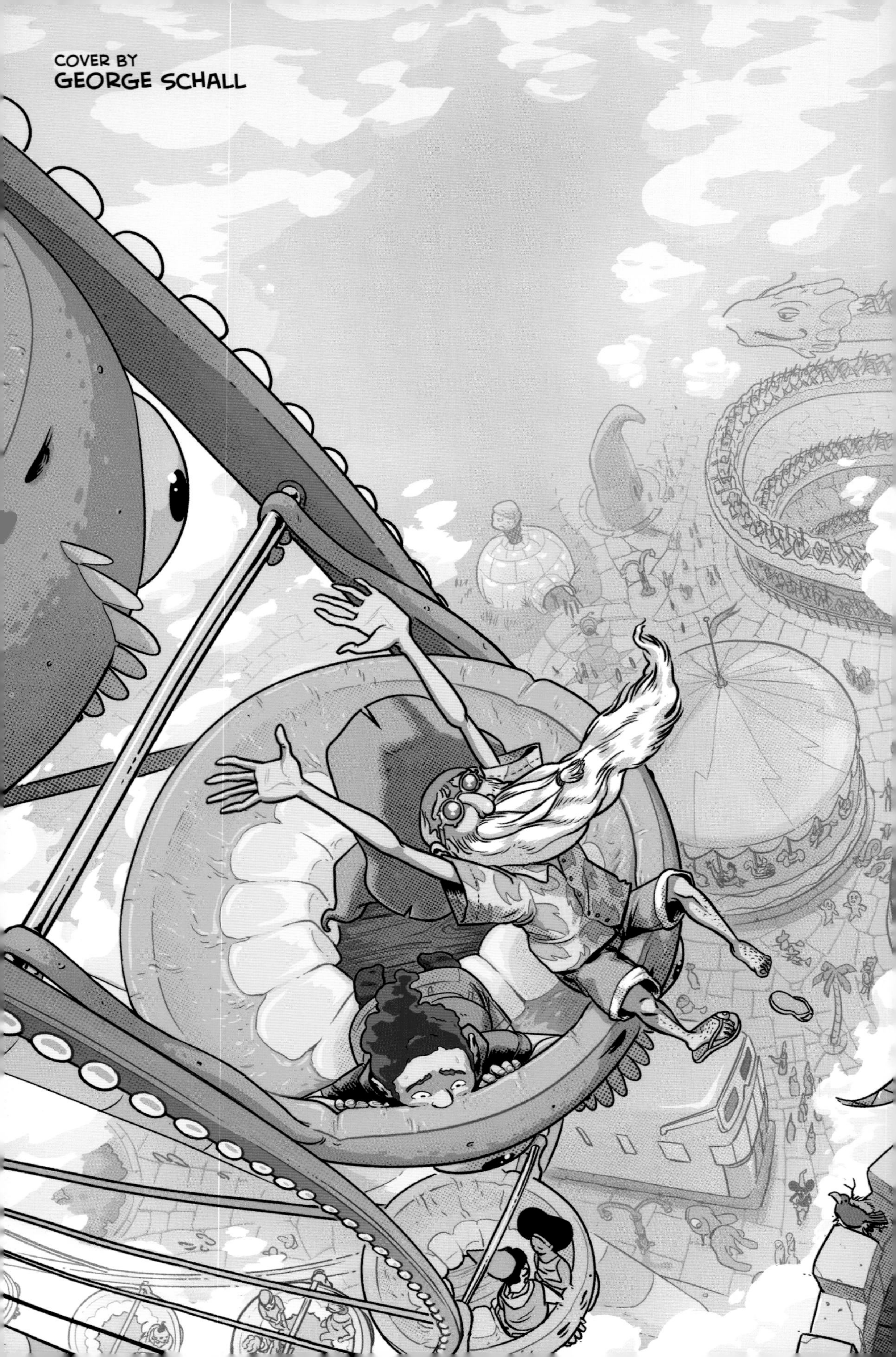

COVER BY
GEORGE SCHALL

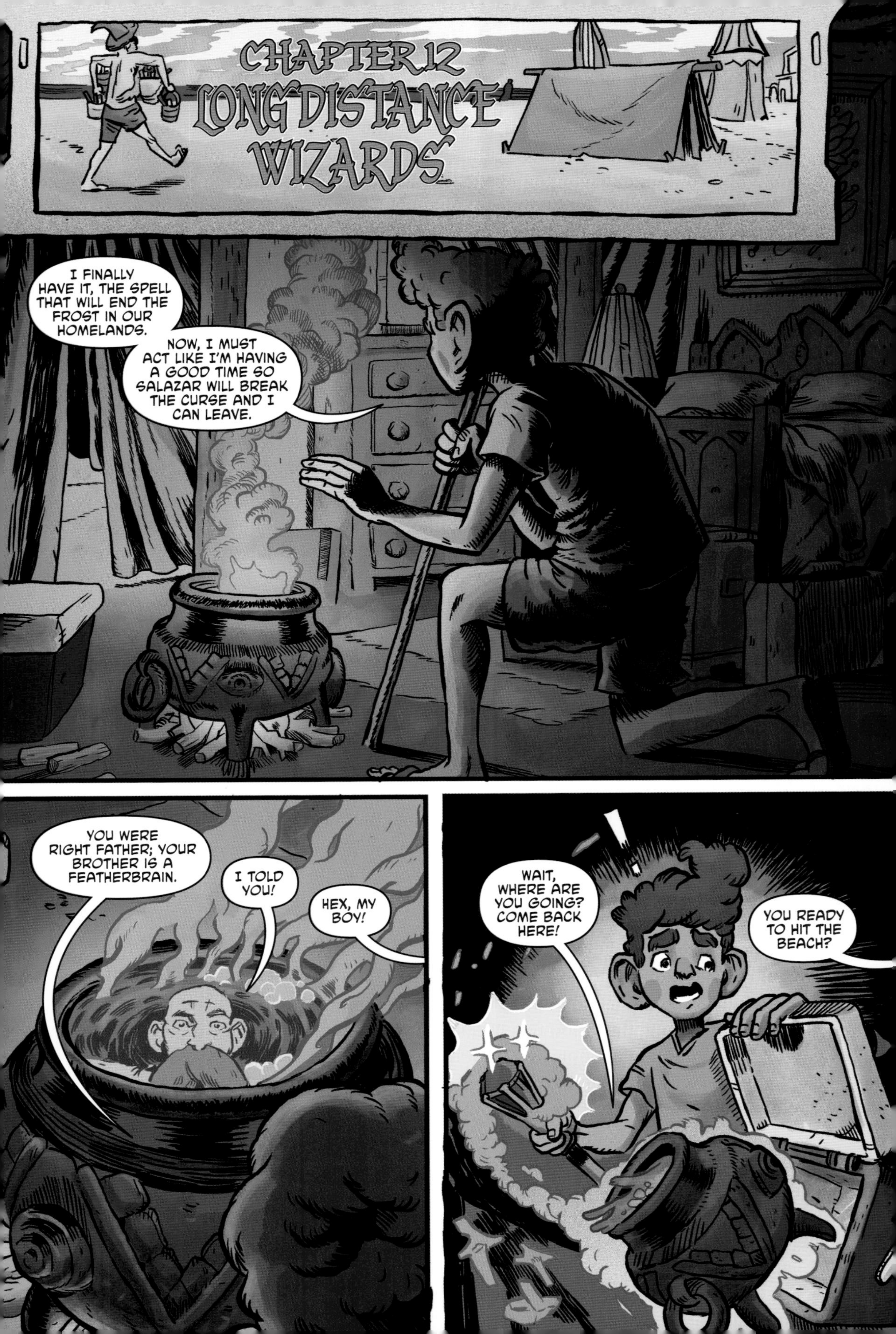
CHAPTER 12
LONG DISTANCE WIZARDS
I FINALLY HAVE IT, THE SPELL THAT WILL END THE FROST IN OUR HOMELANDS.
NOW, I MUST ACT LIKE I'M HAVING A GOOD TIME SO SALAZAR WILL BREAK THE CURSE AND I CAN LEAVE.
YOU WERE RIGHT FATHER; YOUR BROTHER IS A FEATHERBRAIN.
I TOLD YOU!
HEX, MY BOY!
!
WAIT, WHERE ARE YOU GOING? COME BACK HERE!
YOU READY TO HIT THE BEACH?

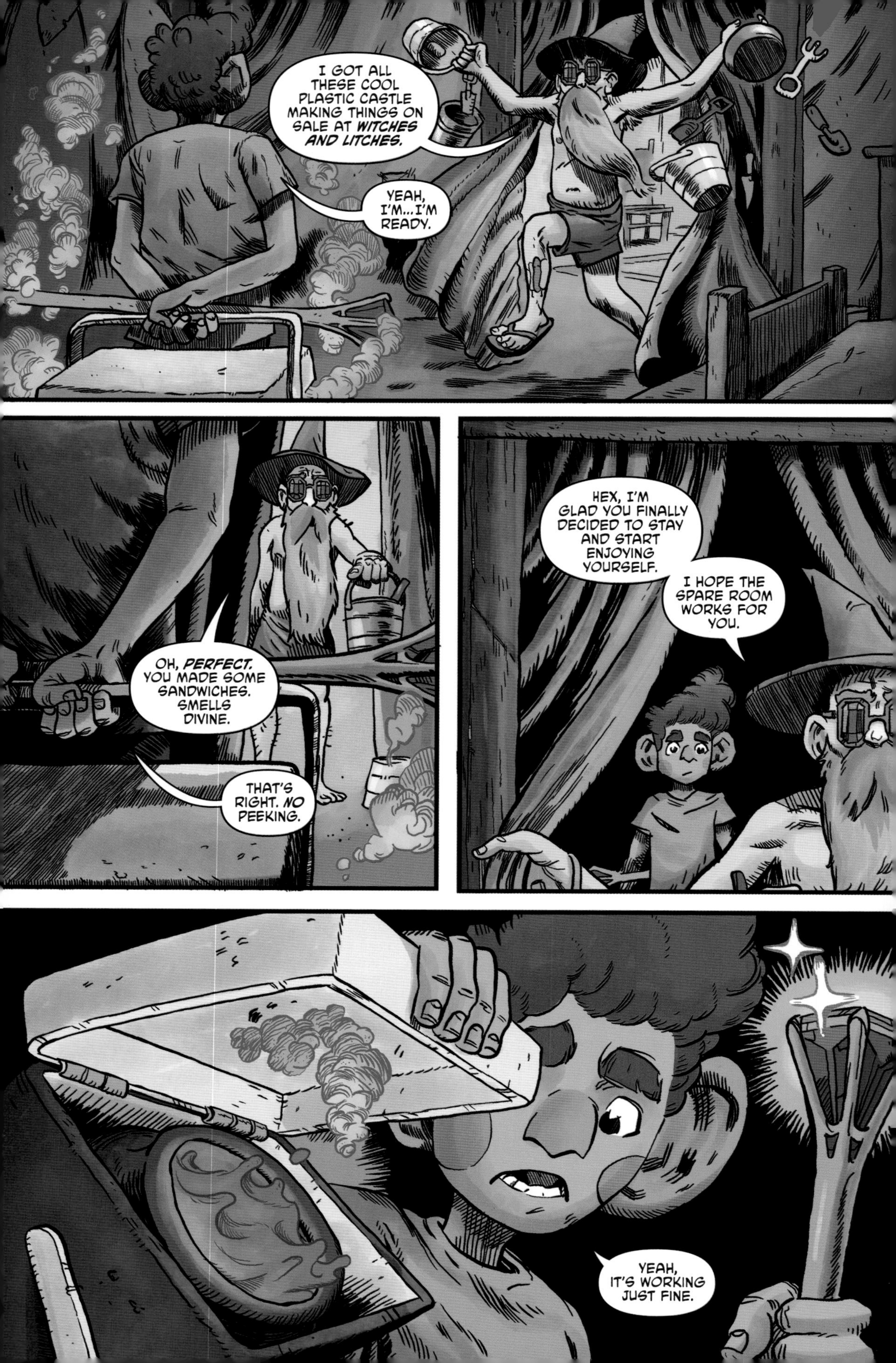
I GOT ALL THESE COOL PLASTIC CASTLE MAKING THINGS ON SALE AT *WITCHES AND LITCHES.*
YEAH, I'M...I'M READY.
OH, *PERFECT.* YOU MADE SOME SANDWICHES. SMELLS DIVINE.
THAT'S RIGHT. *NO* PEEKING.
HEX, I'M GLAD YOU FINALLY DECIDED TO STAY AND START ENJOYING YOURSELF.
I HOPE THE SPARE ROOM WORKS FOR YOU.
YEAH, IT'S WORKING JUST FINE.

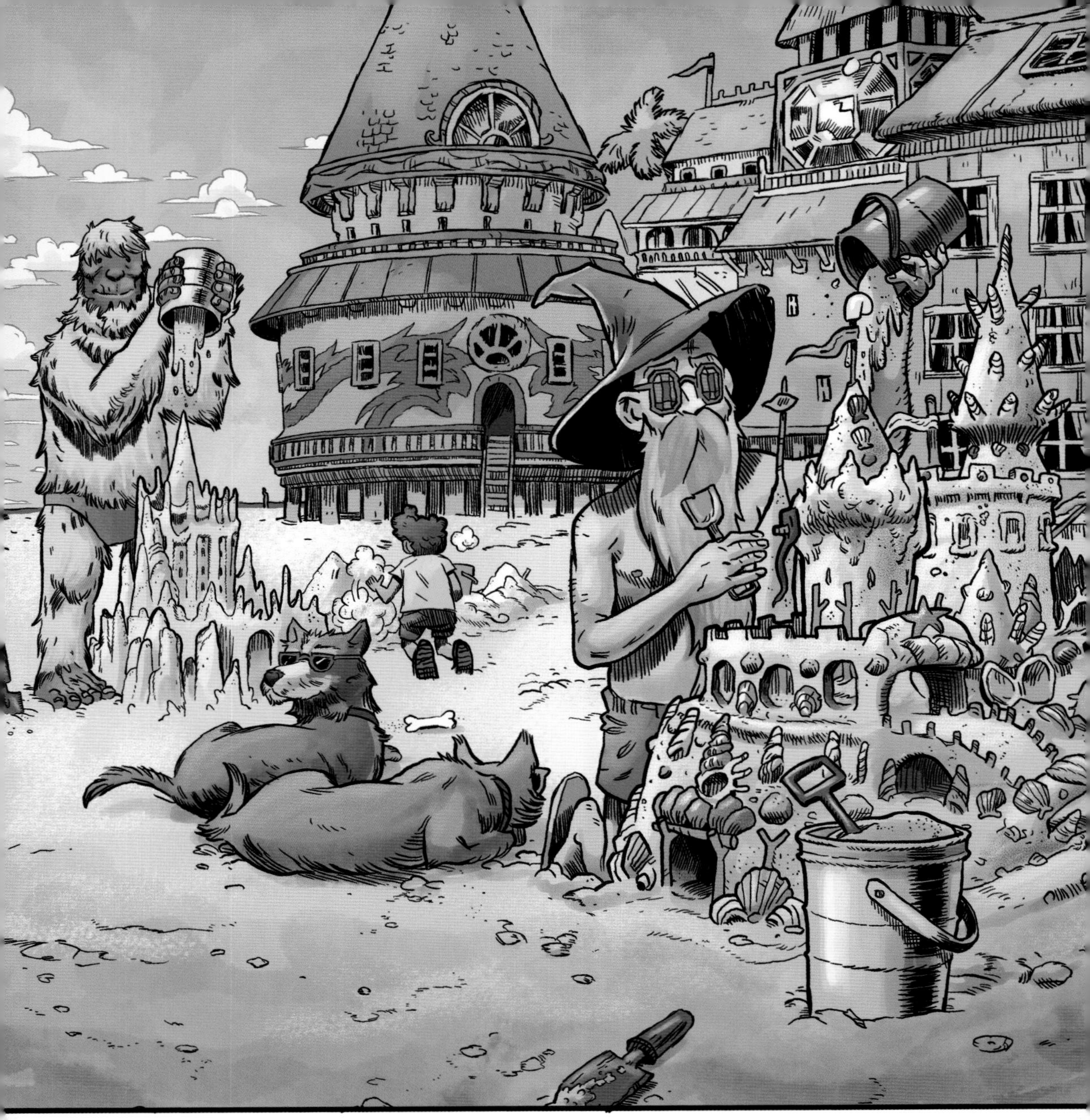
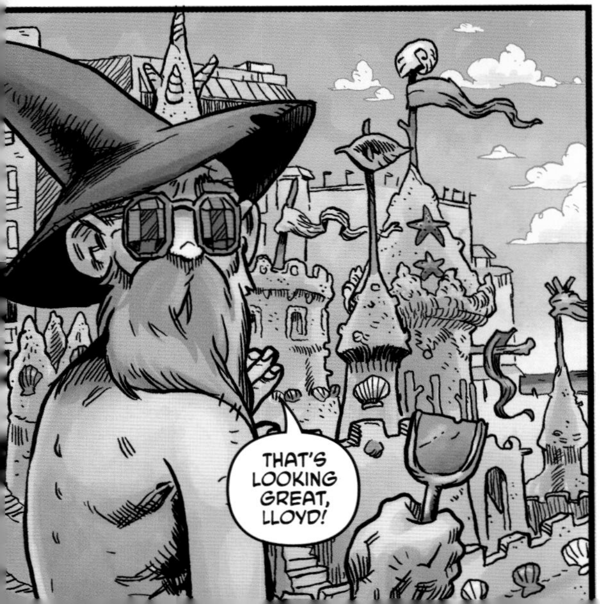
THAT'S LOOKING GREAT, LLOYD!
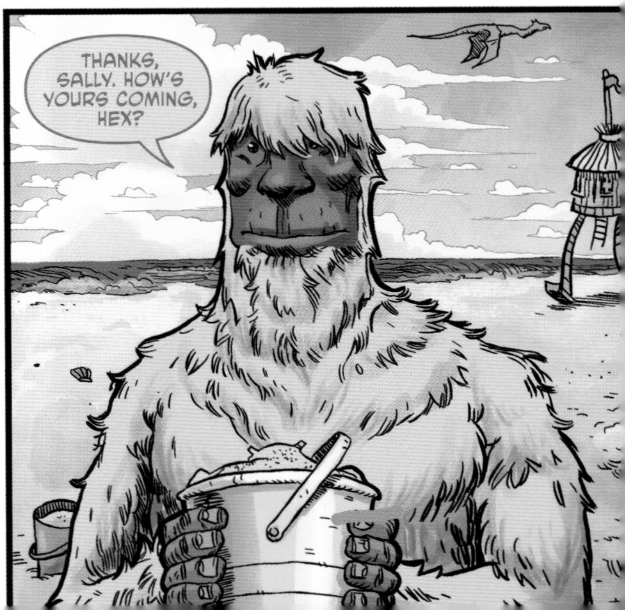
THANKS, SALLY. HOW'S YOURS COMING, HEX?

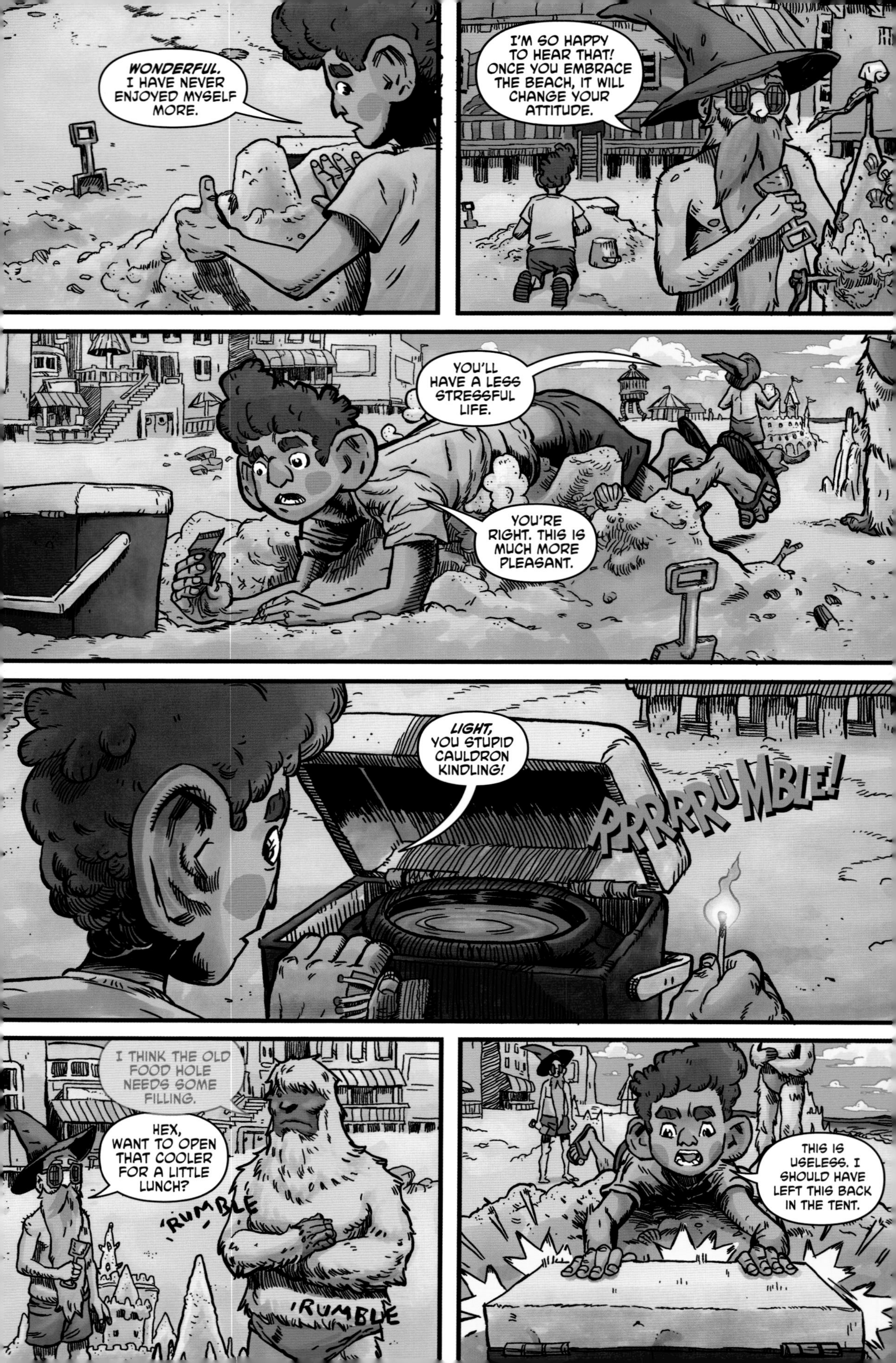
WONDERFUL. I HAVE NEVER ENJOYED MYSELF MORE.
I'M SO HAPPY TO HEAR THAT! ONCE YOU EMBRACE THE BEACH, IT WILL CHANGE YOUR ATTITUDE.
YOU'LL HAVE A LESS STRESSFUL LIFE.
YOU'RE RIGHT. THIS IS MUCH MORE PLEASANT.
LIGHT, YOU STUPID CAULDRON KINDLING!
PRRRRUMBLE!
I THINK THE OLD FOOD HOLE NEEDS SOME FILLING.
HEX, WANT TO OPEN THAT COOLER FOR A LITTLE LUNCH?
RUMBLE
RUMBLE
THIS IS USELESS. I SHOULD HAVE LEFT THIS BACK IN THE TENT.

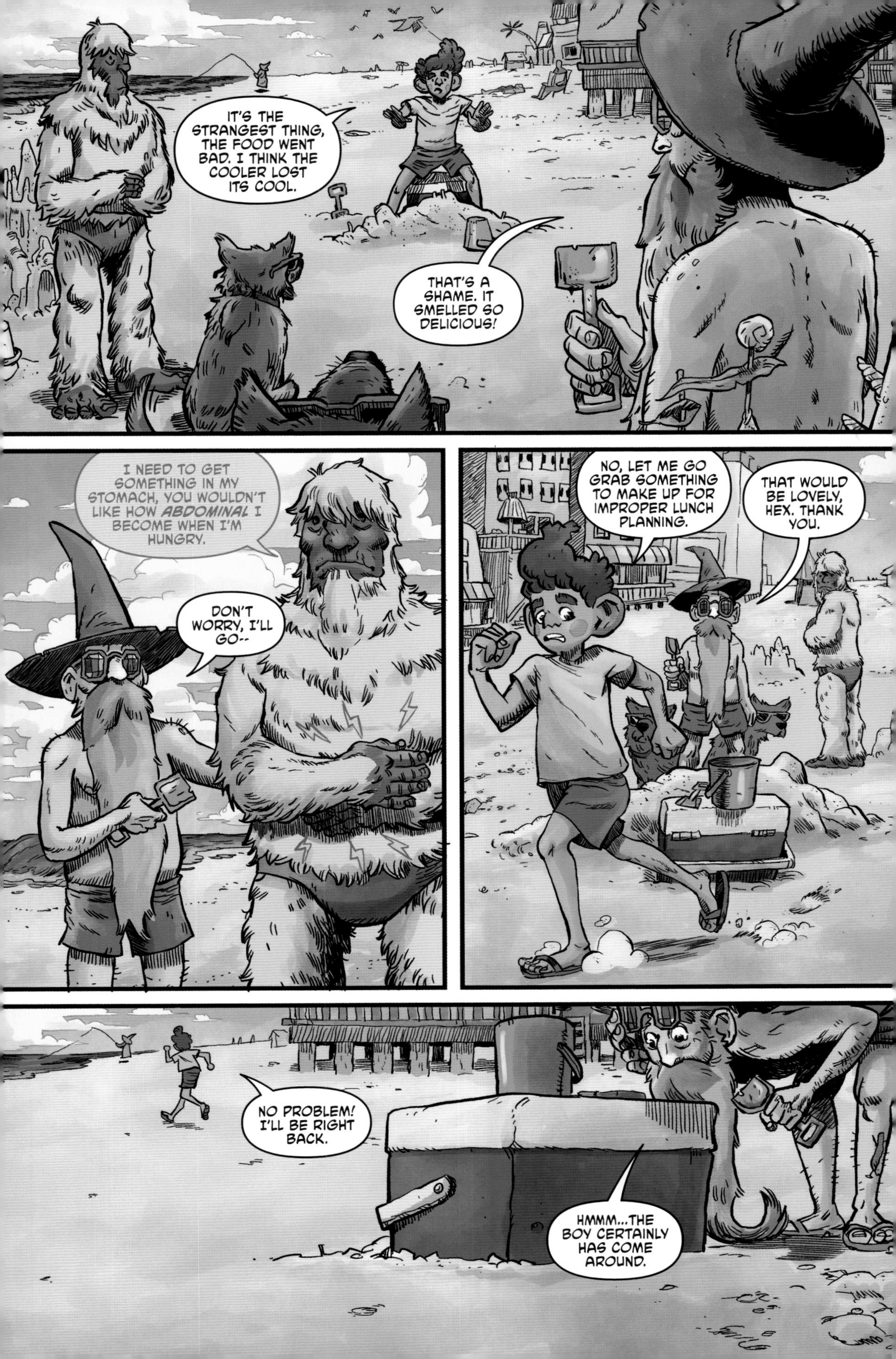
IT'S THE STRANGEST THING, THE FOOD WENT BAD. I THINK THE COOLER LOST ITS COOL.
THAT'S A SHAME. IT SMELLED SO DELICIOUS!
I NEED TO GET SOMETHING IN MY STOMACH, YOU WOULDN'T LIKE HOW *ABDOMINAL* I BECOME WHEN I'M HUNGRY.
DON'T WORRY, I'LL GO--
NO, LET ME GO GRAB SOMETHING TO MAKE UP FOR IMPROPER LUNCH PLANNING.
THAT WOULD BE LOVELY, HEX. THANK YOU.
NO PROBLEM! I'LL BE RIGHT BACK.
HMMM...THE BOY CERTAINLY HAS COME AROUND.

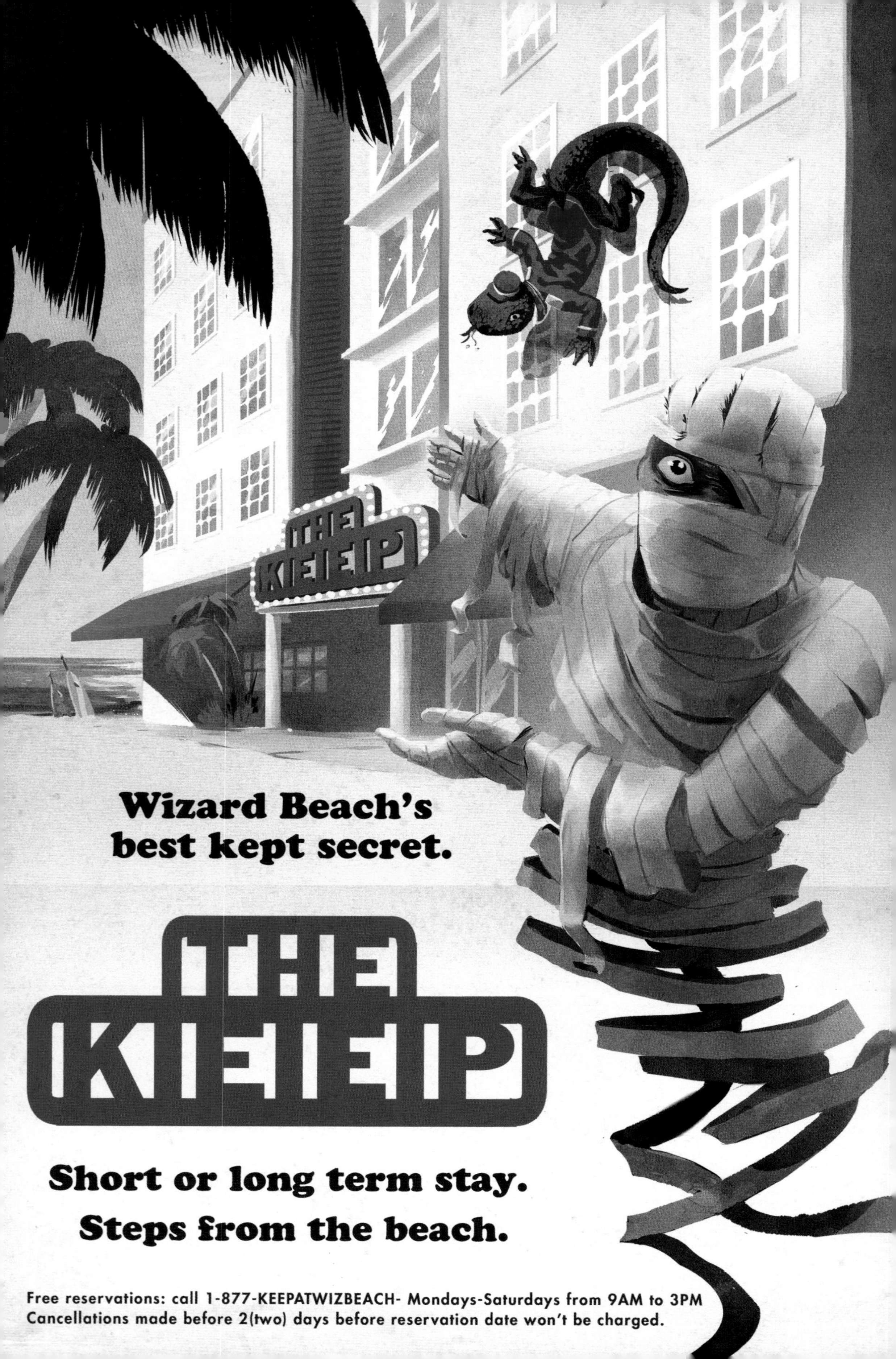
THE KEEP
Wizard Beach's
best kept secret.
THE KEEP
Short or long term stay.
Steps from the beach.
Free reservations: call 1-877-KEEPATWIZBEACH- Mondays-Saturdays from 9AM to 3PM
Cancellations made before 2(two) days before reservation date won't be charged.

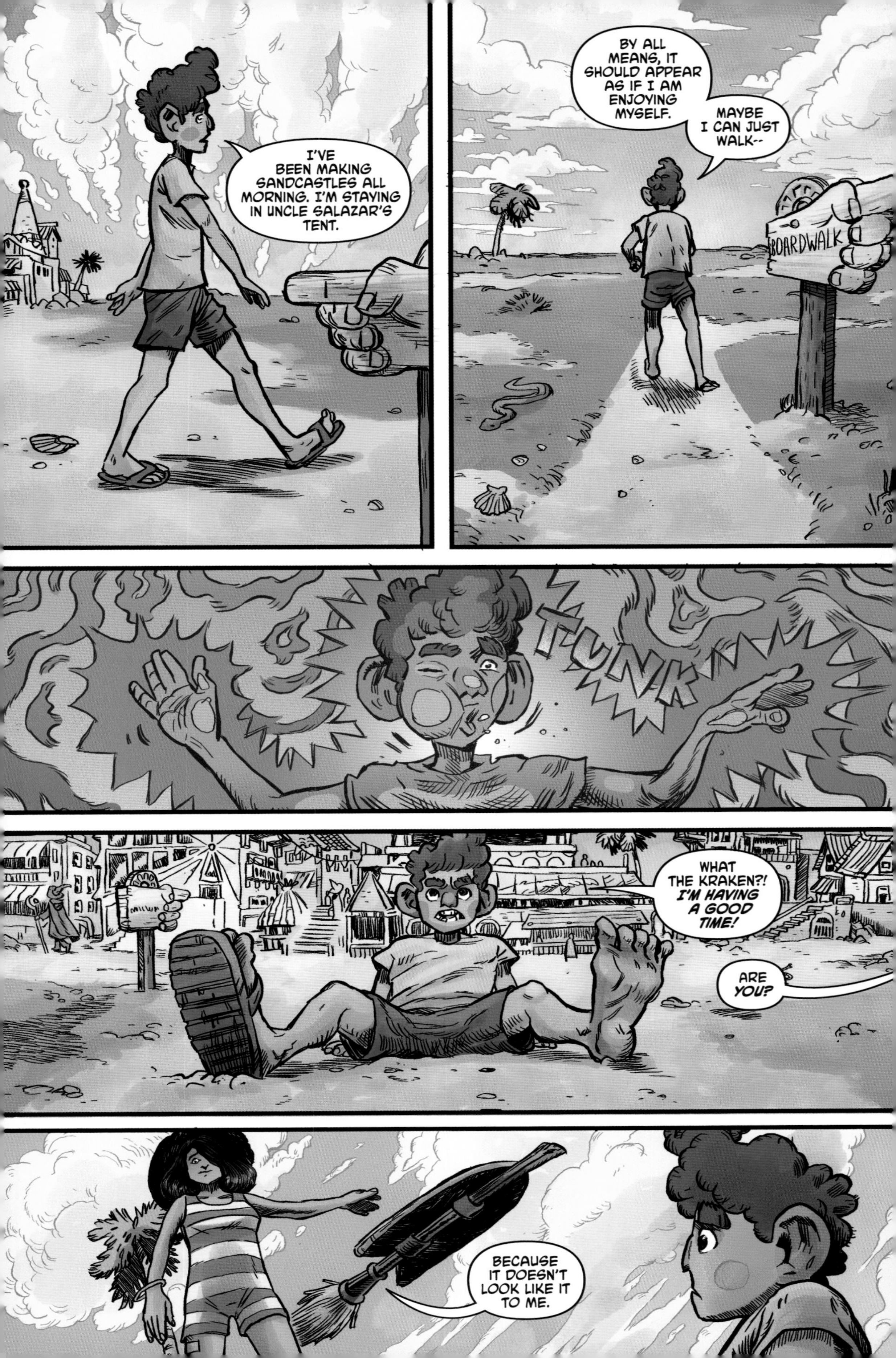
I'VE BEEN MAKING SANDCASTLES ALL MORNING. I'M STAYING IN UNCLE SALAZAR'S TENT.
BY ALL MEANS, IT SHOULD APPEAR AS IF I AM ENJOYING MYSELF.
MAYBE I CAN JUST WALK--
BOARDWALK
TUNK
WHAT THE KRAKEN?! *I'M HAVING A GOOD TIME!*
ARE *YOU?*
BECAUSE IT DOESN'T LOOK LIKE IT TO ME.

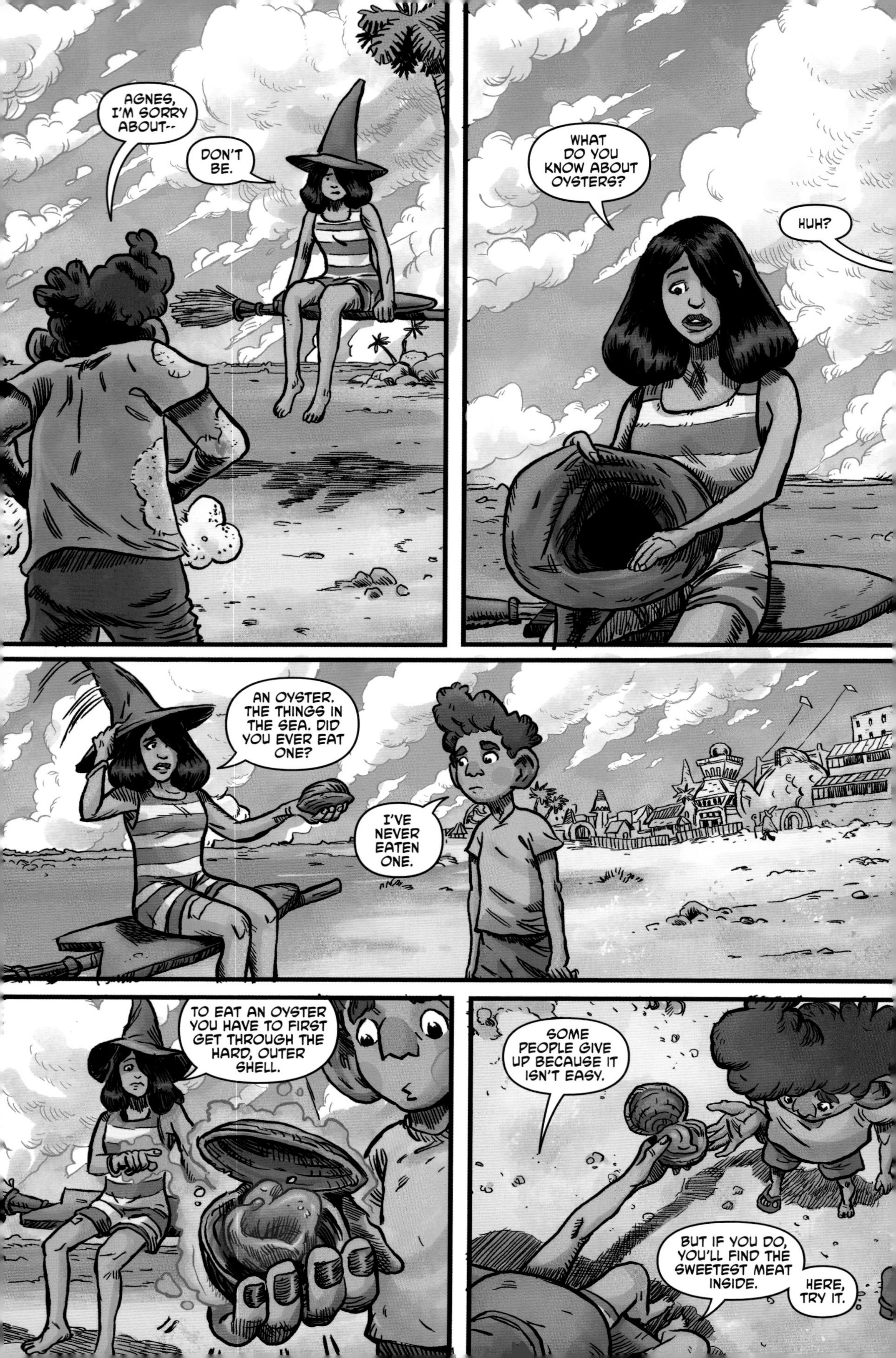
AGNES, I'M SORRY ABOUT--
DON'T BE.
WHAT DO YOU KNOW ABOUT OYSTERS?
HUH?
AN OYSTER. THE THINGS IN THE SEA. DID YOU EVER EAT ONE?
I'VE NEVER EATEN ONE.
TO EAT AN OYSTER YOU HAVE TO FIRST GET THROUGH THE HARD, OUTER SHELL.
SOME PEOPLE GIVE UP BECAUSE IT ISN'T EASY.
BUT IF YOU DO, YOU'LL FIND THE SWEETEST MEAT INSIDE.
HERE, TRY IT.

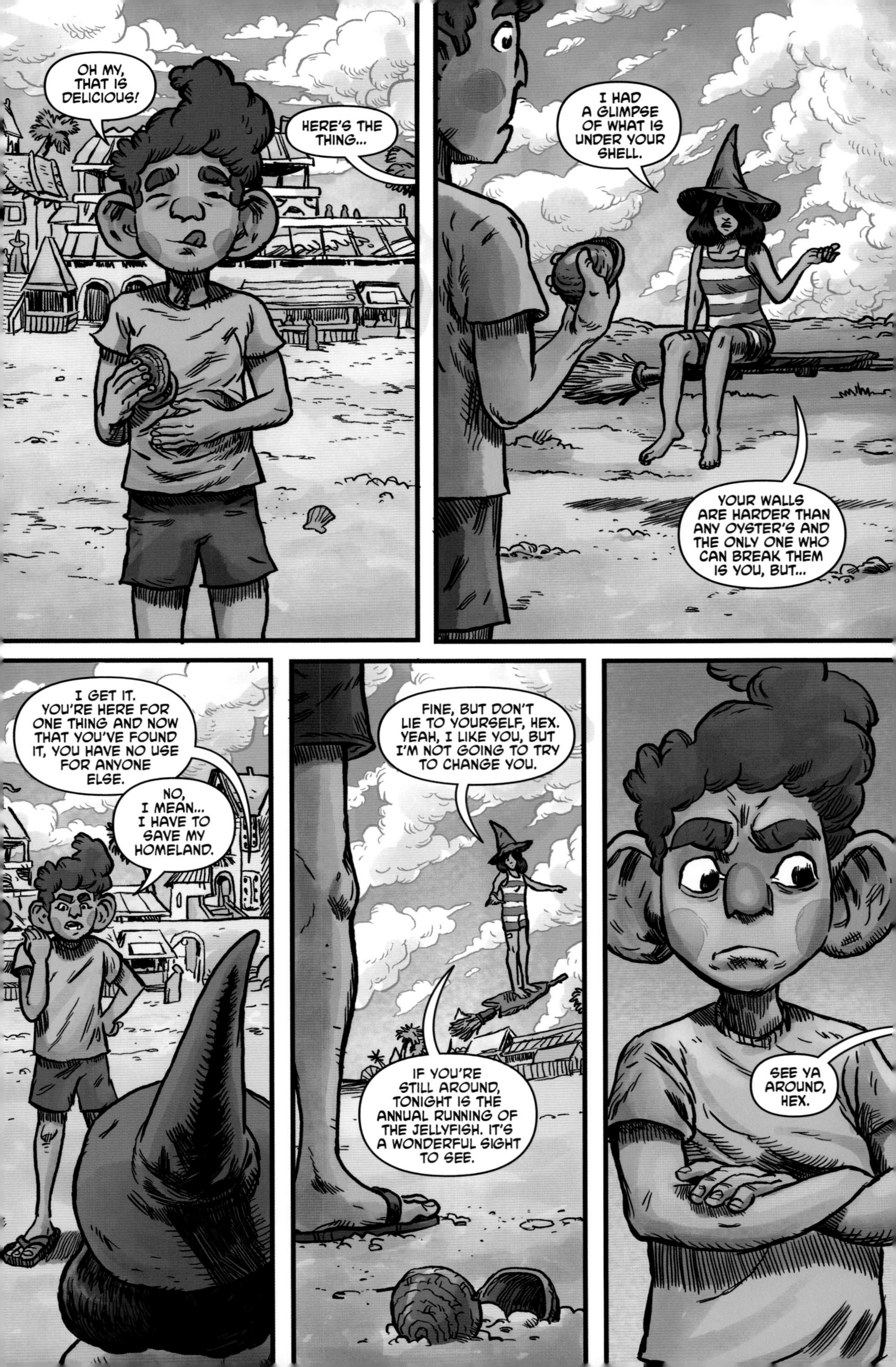
OH MY, THAT IS DELICIOUS!
HERE'S THE THING...
I HAD A GLIMPSE OF WHAT IS UNDER YOUR SHELL.
YOUR WALLS ARE HARDER THAN ANY OYSTER'S AND THE ONLY ONE WHO CAN BREAK THEM IS YOU, BUT...
I GET IT. YOU'RE HERE FOR ONE THING AND NOW THAT YOU'VE FOUND IT, YOU HAVE NO USE FOR ANYONE ELSE.
NO, I MEAN... I HAVE TO SAVE MY HOMELAND.
FINE, BUT DON'T LIE TO YOURSELF, HEX. YEAH, I LIKE YOU, BUT I'M NOT GOING TO TRY TO CHANGE YOU.
IF YOU'RE STILL AROUND, TONIGHT IS THE ANNUAL RUNNING OF THE JELLYFISH. IT'S A WONDERFUL SIGHT TO SEE.
SEE YA AROUND, HEX.

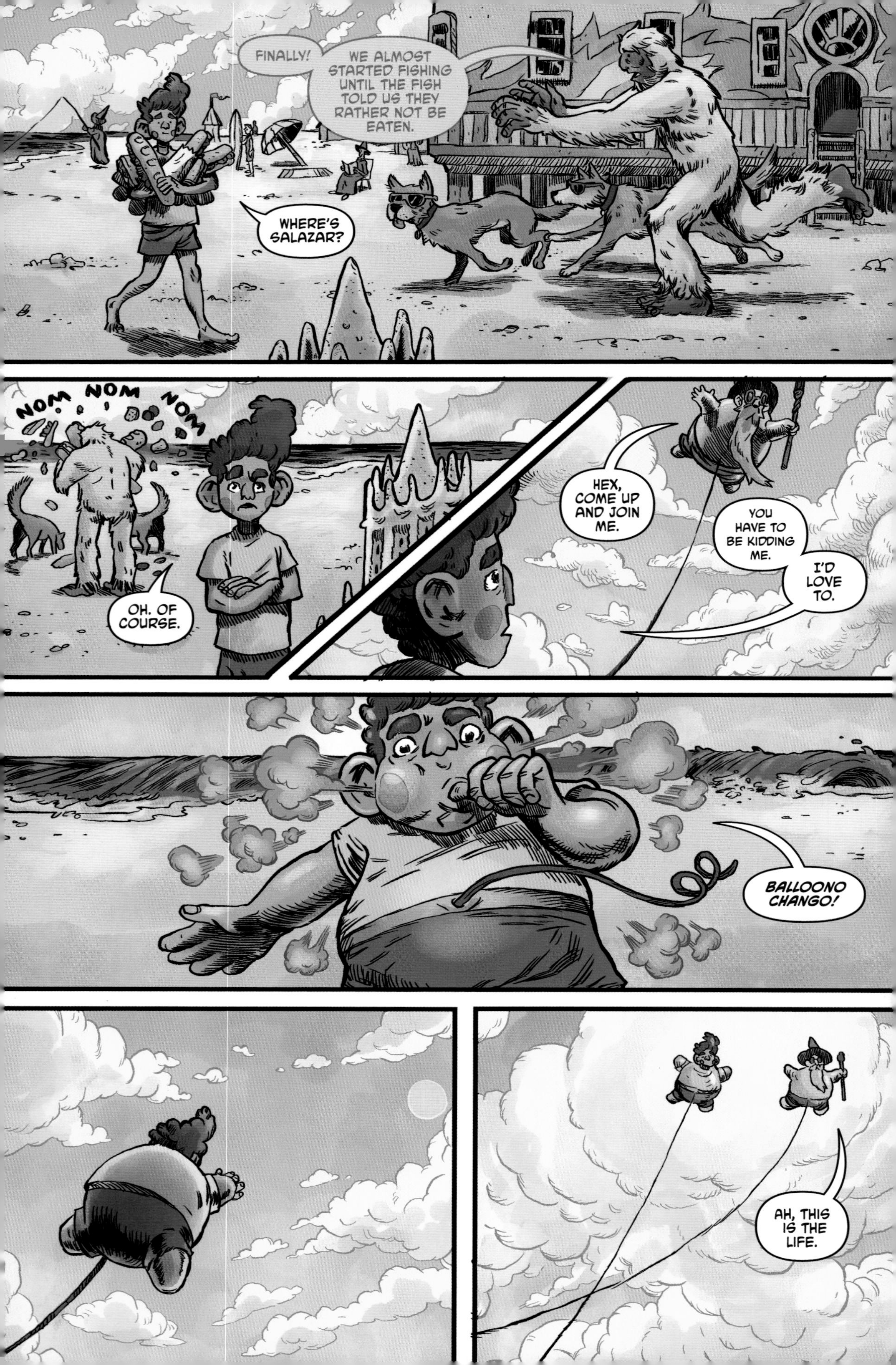
FINALLY!
WE ALMOST STARTED FISHING UNTIL THE FISH TOLD US THEY RATHER NOT BE EATEN.
WHERE'S SALAZAR?
NOM NOM NOM
OH. OF COURSE.
HEX, COME UP AND JOIN ME.
YOU HAVE TO BE KIDDING ME.
I'D LOVE TO.
BALLOONO CHANGO!
AH, THIS IS THE LIFE.

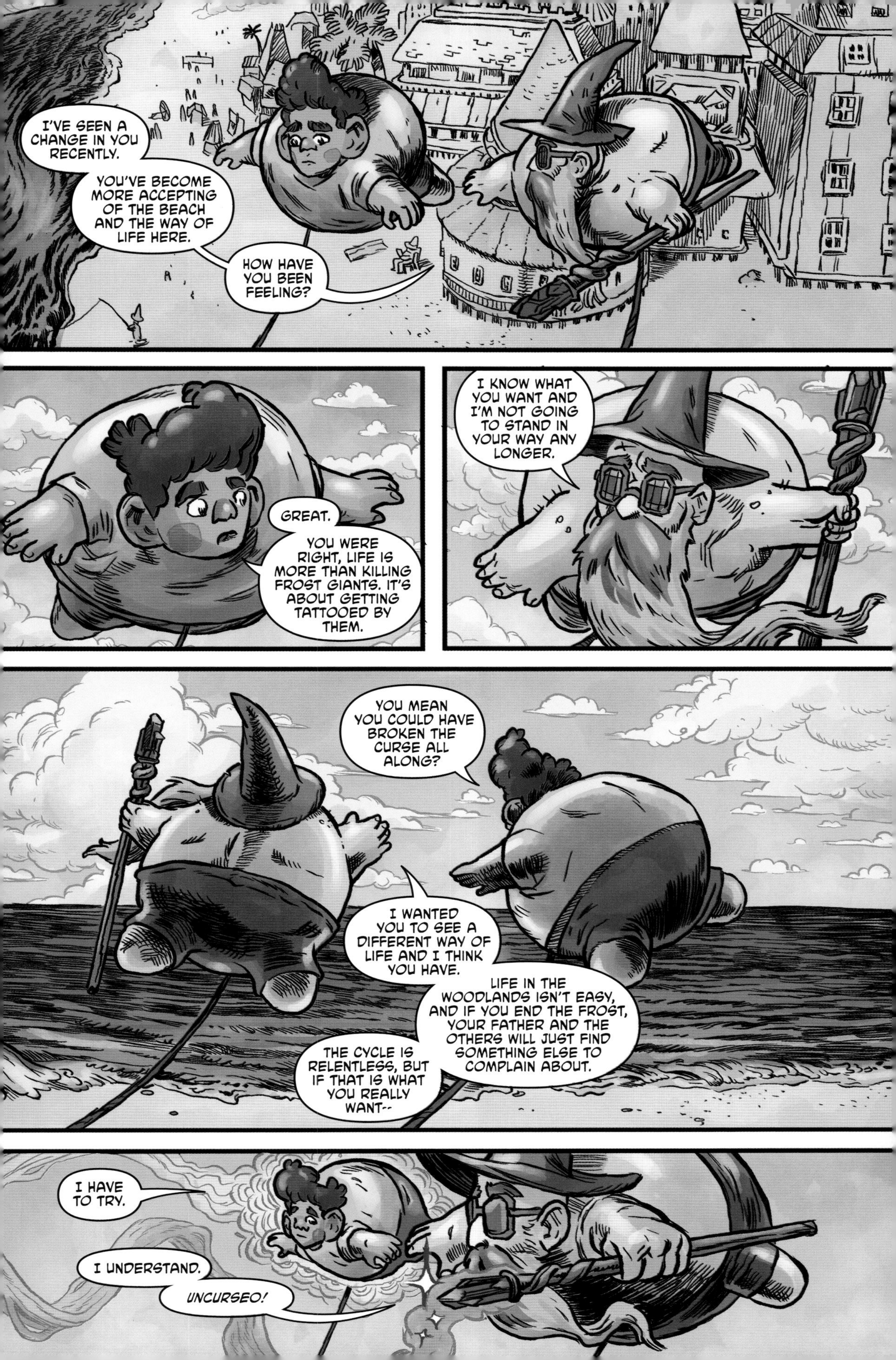
I'VE SEEN A CHANGE IN YOU RECENTLY.
YOU'VE BECOME MORE ACCEPTING OF THE BEACH AND THE WAY OF LIFE HERE.
HOW HAVE YOU BEEN FEELING?
GREAT.
YOU WERE RIGHT, LIFE IS MORE THAN KILLING FROST GIANTS. IT'S ABOUT GETTING TATTOOED BY THEM.
I KNOW WHAT YOU WANT AND I'M NOT GOING TO STAND IN YOUR WAY ANY LONGER.
YOU MEAN YOU COULD HAVE BROKEN THE CURSE ALL ALONG?
I WANTED YOU TO SEE A DIFFERENT WAY OF LIFE AND I THINK YOU HAVE.
LIFE IN THE WOODLANDS ISN'T EASY, AND IF YOU END THE FROST, YOUR FATHER AND THE OTHERS WILL JUST FIND SOMETHING ELSE TO COMPLAIN ABOUT.
THE CYCLE IS RELENTLESS, BUT IF THAT IS WHAT YOU REALLY WANT--
I HAVE TO TRY.
I UNDERSTAND.
UNCURSEO!

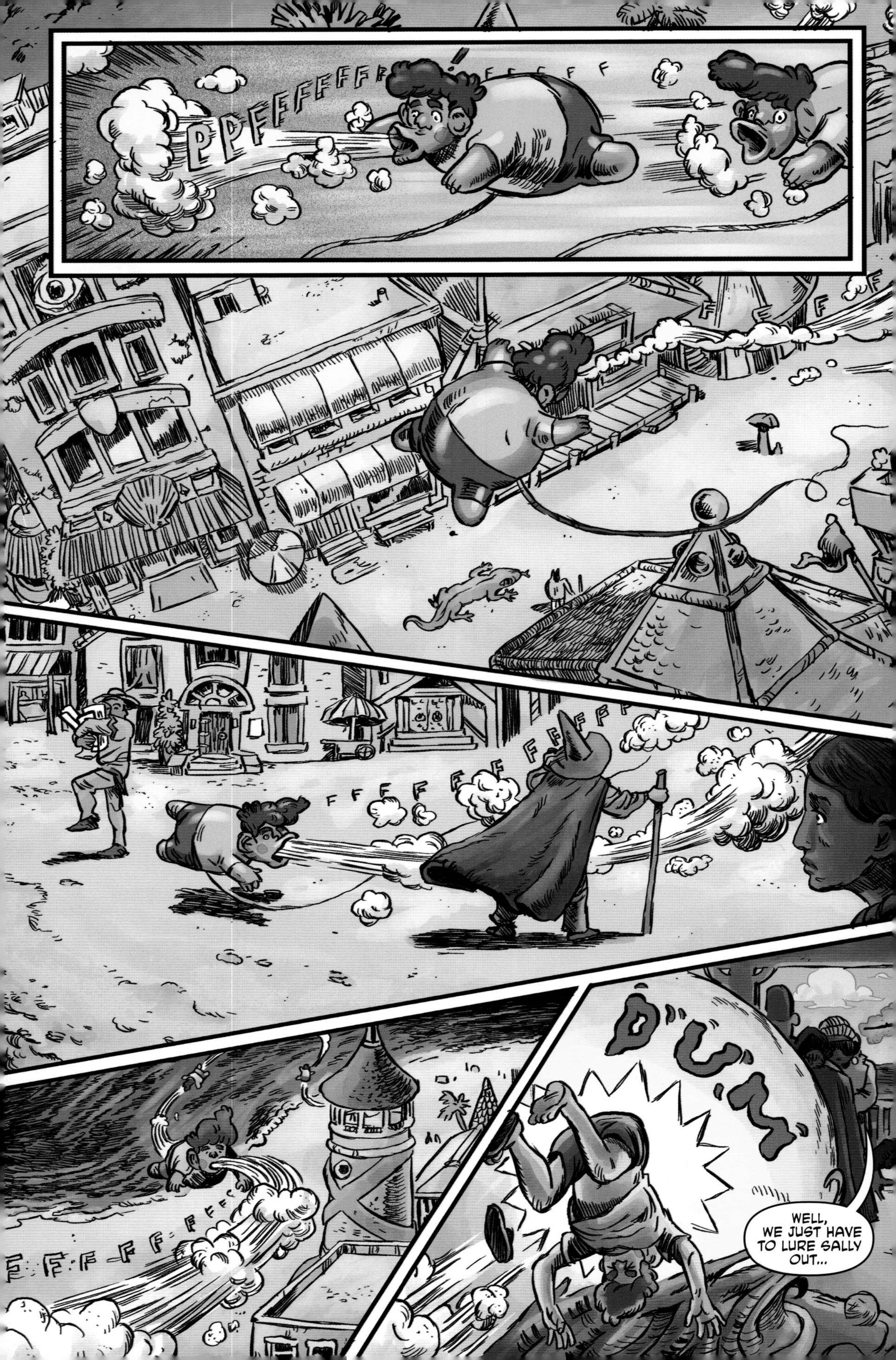
DUM
WELL, WE JUST HAVE TO LURE SALLY OUT...

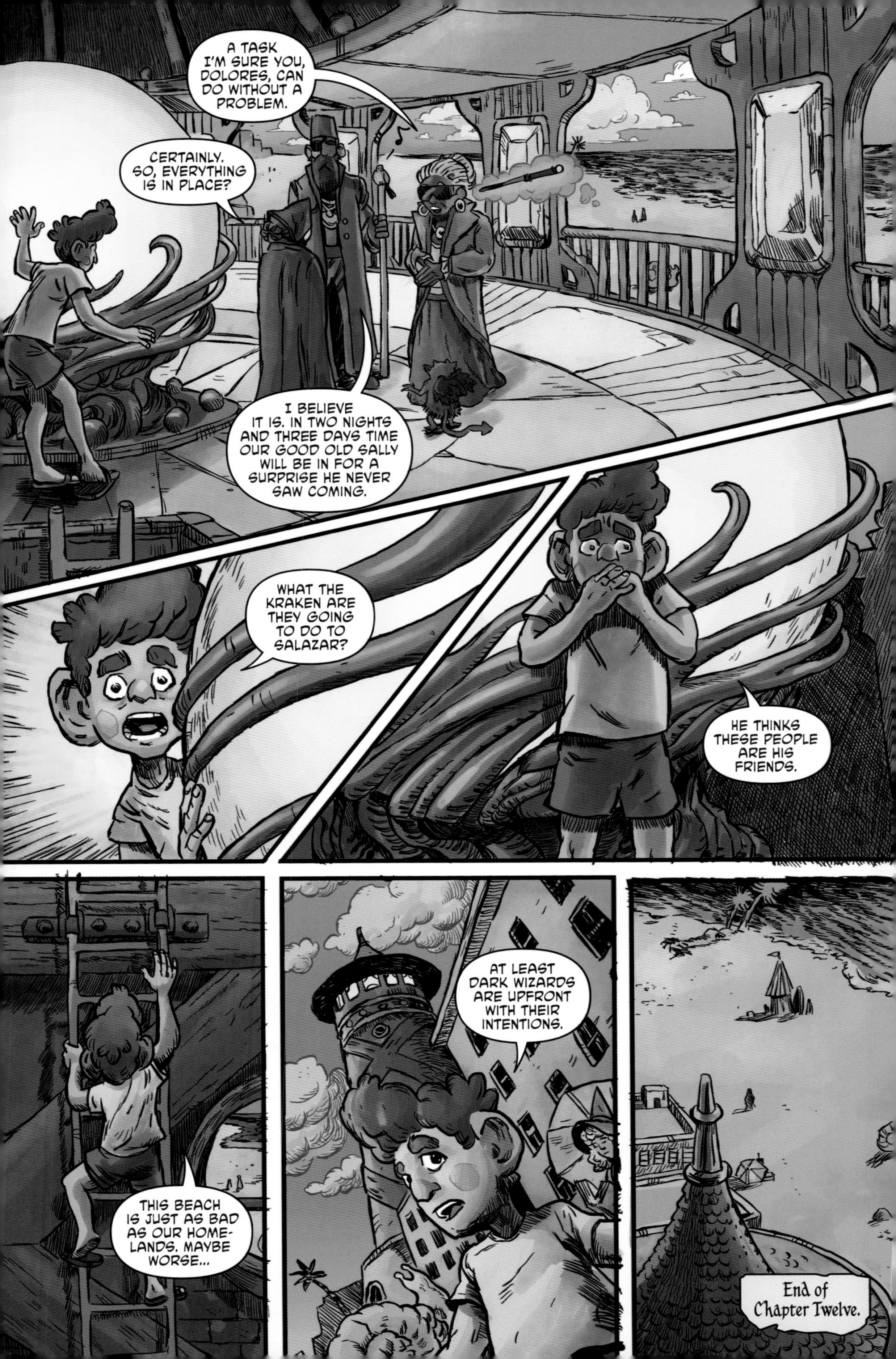
A TASK I'M SURE YOU, DOLORES, CAN DO WITHOUT A PROBLEM.
CERTAINLY. SO, EVERYTHING IS IN PLACE?
I BELIEVE IT IS. IN TWO NIGHTS AND THREE DAYS TIME OUR GOOD OLD SALLY WILL BE IN FOR A SURPRISE HE NEVER SAW COMING.
WHAT THE KRAKEN ARE THEY GOING TO DO TO SALAZAR?
HE THINKS THESE PEOPLE ARE HIS FRIENDS.
THIS BEACH IS JUST AS BAD AS OUR HOME-LANDS. MAYBE WORSE...
AT LEAST DARK WIZARDS ARE UPFRONT WITH THEIR INTENTIONS.
End of Chapter Twelve.

Wizard Beach
GARBAGE DAY

Mondays	**ORGANICS**
Tuesdays	**RECYCLED**
Wednesdays	**WASTE**
Thursdays	**POISON**
Fridays	**ENCHANTED**

As stated by the **Beach Council** and **Wizard Beach Department of Public Works**, all citizens and visitors of Wizard Beach - **no exceptions** - must deposit their trash in the appropriate spots for incineration according to the categories and dates determined in the schedule displayed above. Those failing to comply might be subject to penalties ruling from small fine to permanent expulsion from the Beach premises on the occasion of multiple reincident infractions. Don't say we didn't warn ya

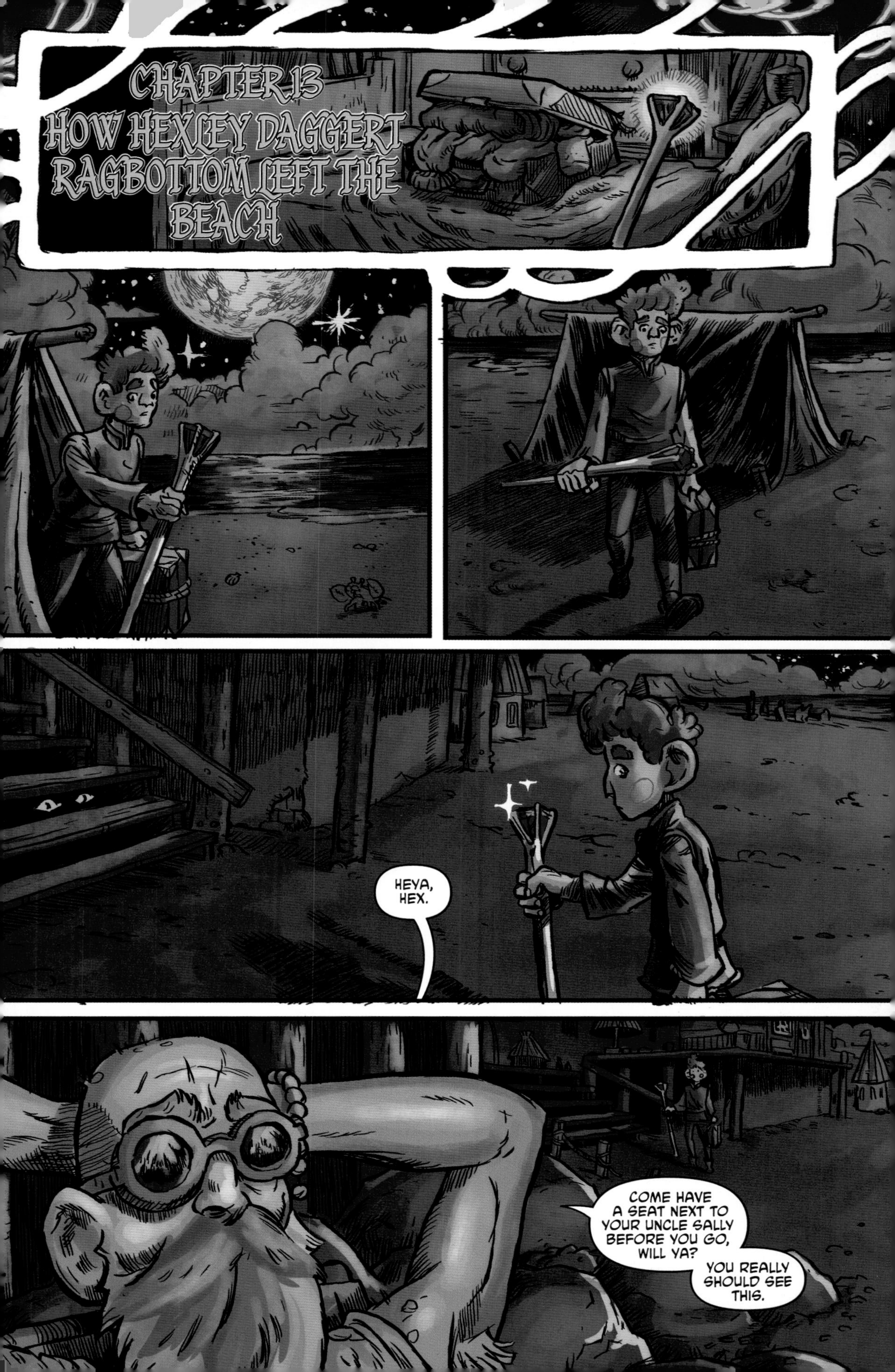
CHAPTER 13
HOW HEXLEY DAGGERT RAGBOTTOM LEFT THE BEACH
HEYA, HEX.
COME HAVE A SEAT NEXT TO YOUR UNCLE SALLY BEFORE YOU GO, WILL YA?
YOU REALLY SHOULD SEE THIS.

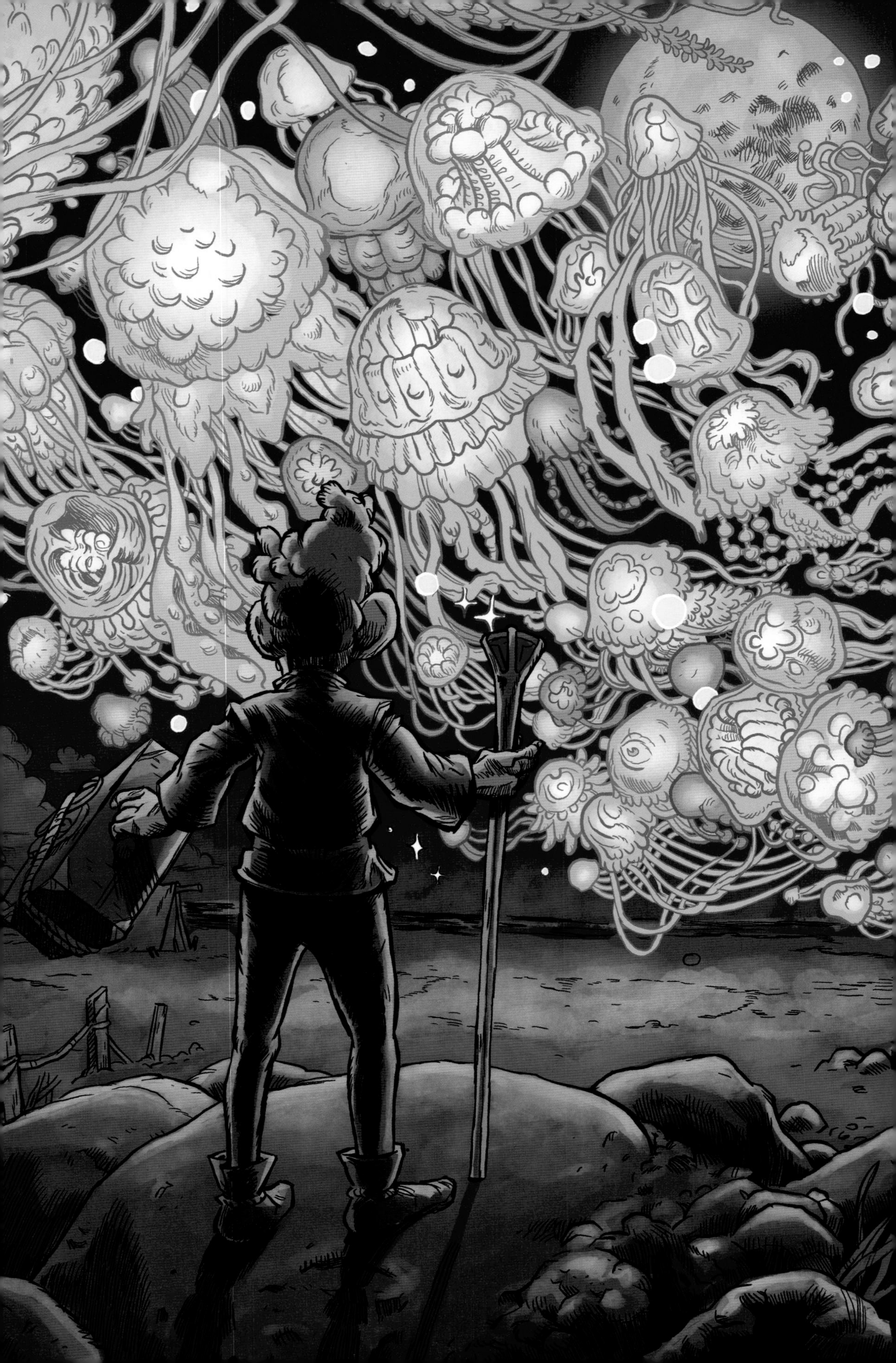

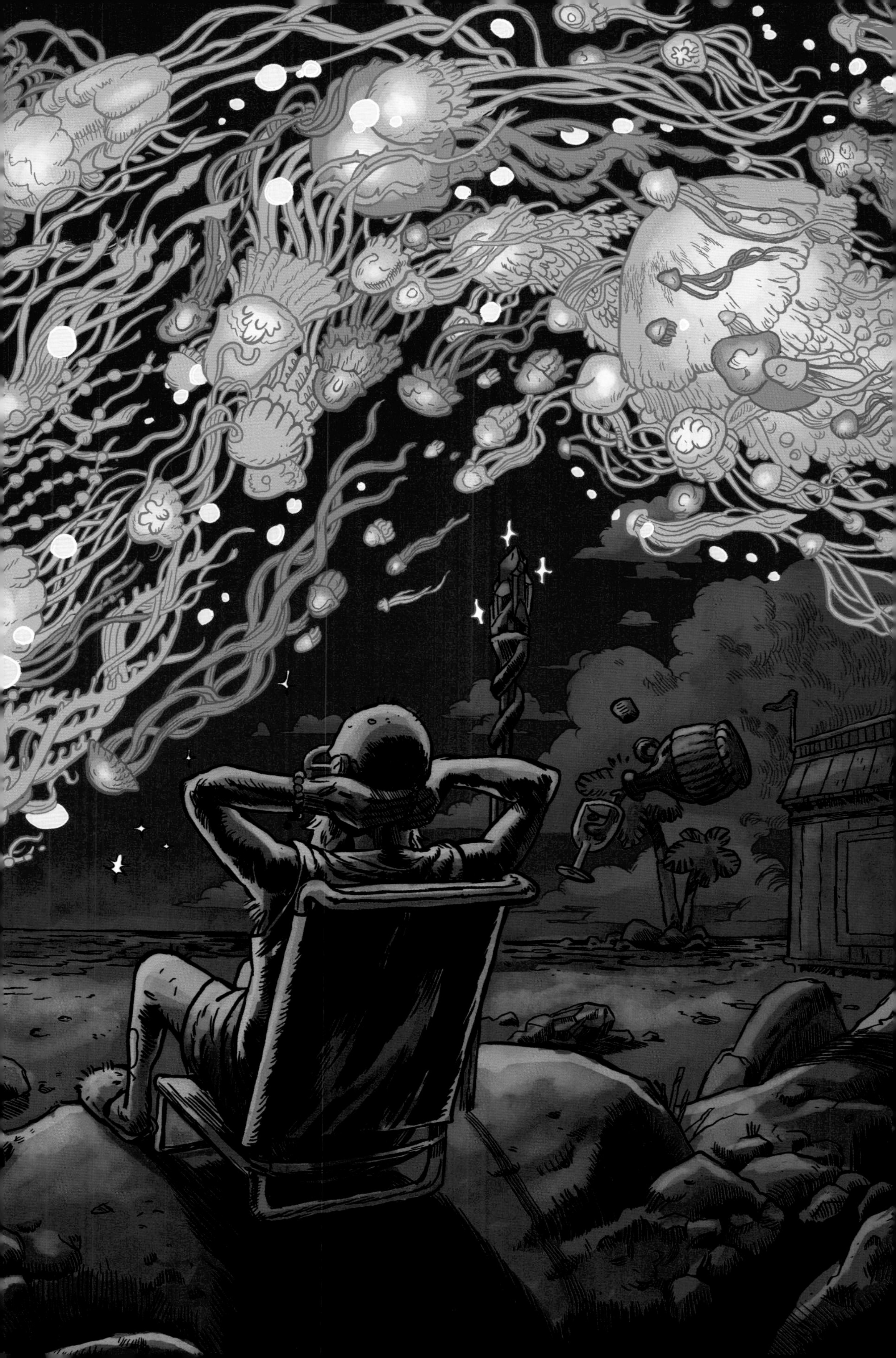

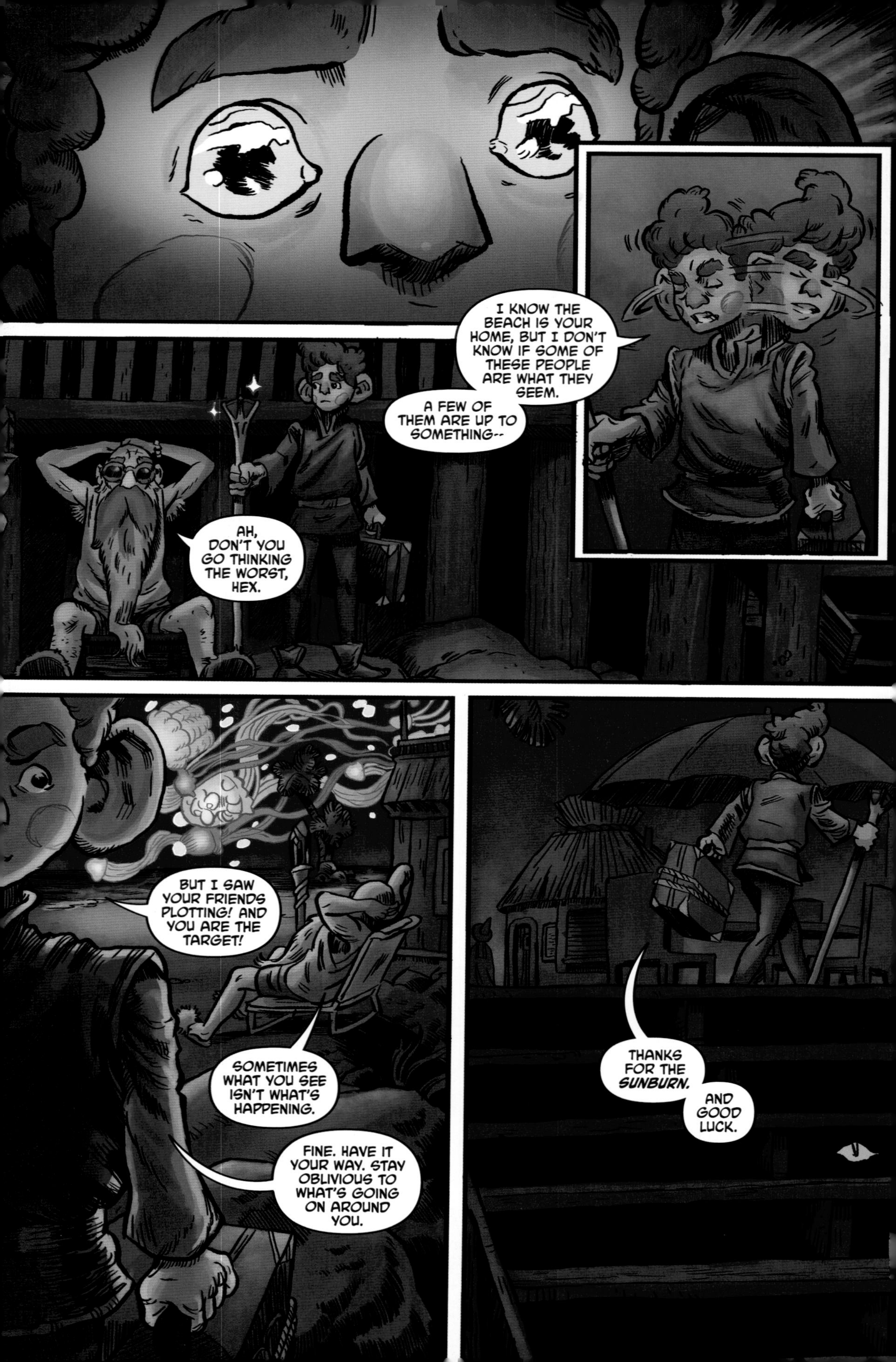
I KNOW THE BEACH IS YOUR HOME, BUT I DON'T KNOW IF SOME OF THESE PEOPLE ARE WHAT THEY SEEM.
A FEW OF THEM ARE UP TO SOMETHING--
AH, DON'T YOU GO THINKING THE WORST, HEX.
BUT I SAW YOUR FRIENDS PLOTTING! AND YOU ARE THE TARGET!
SOMETIMES WHAT YOU SEE ISN'T WHAT'S HAPPENING.
FINE. HAVE IT YOUR WAY. STAY OBLIVIOUS TO WHAT'S GOING ON AROUND YOU.
THANKS FOR THE *SUNBURN.*
AND GOOD LUCK.

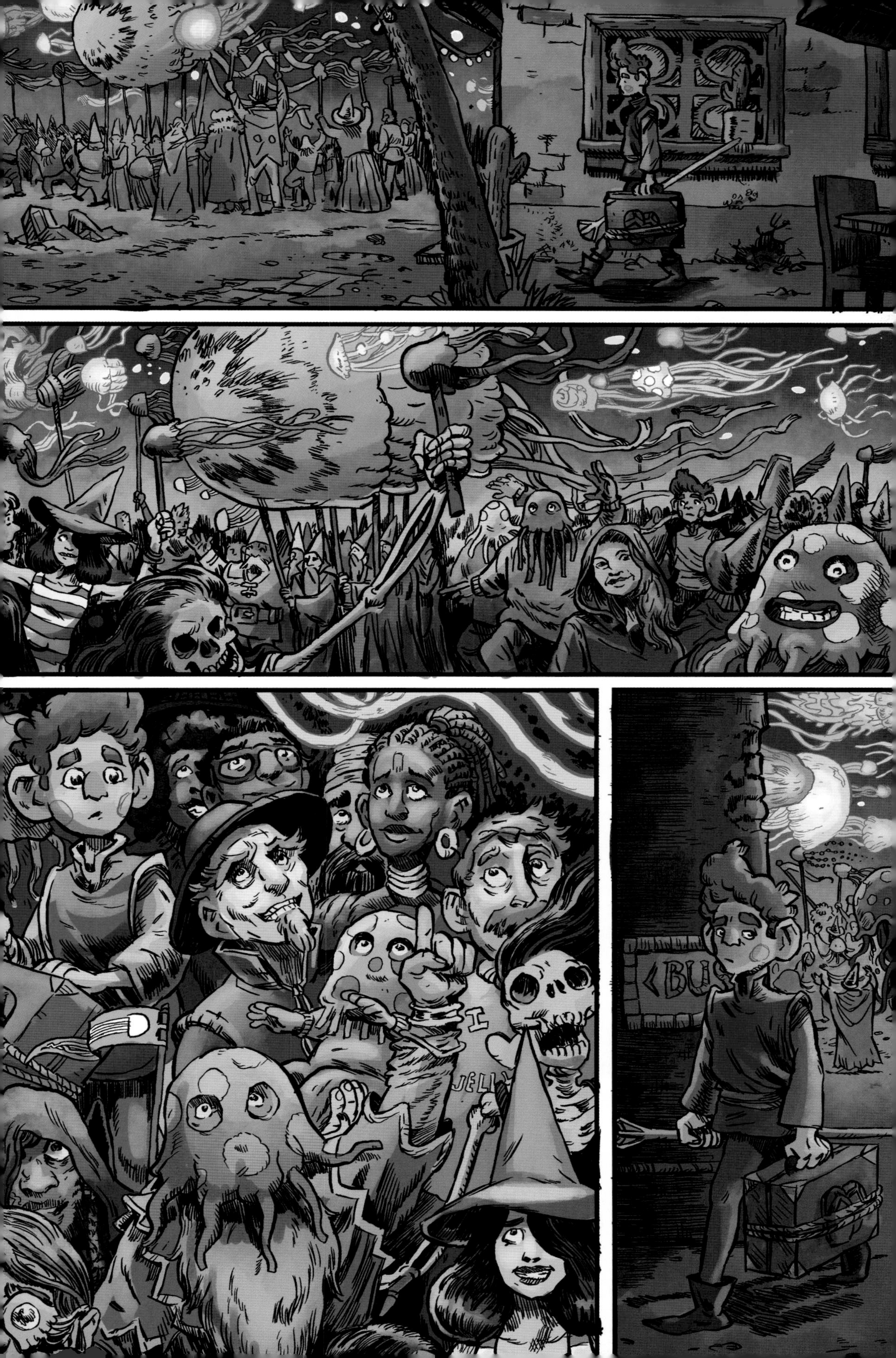
BU

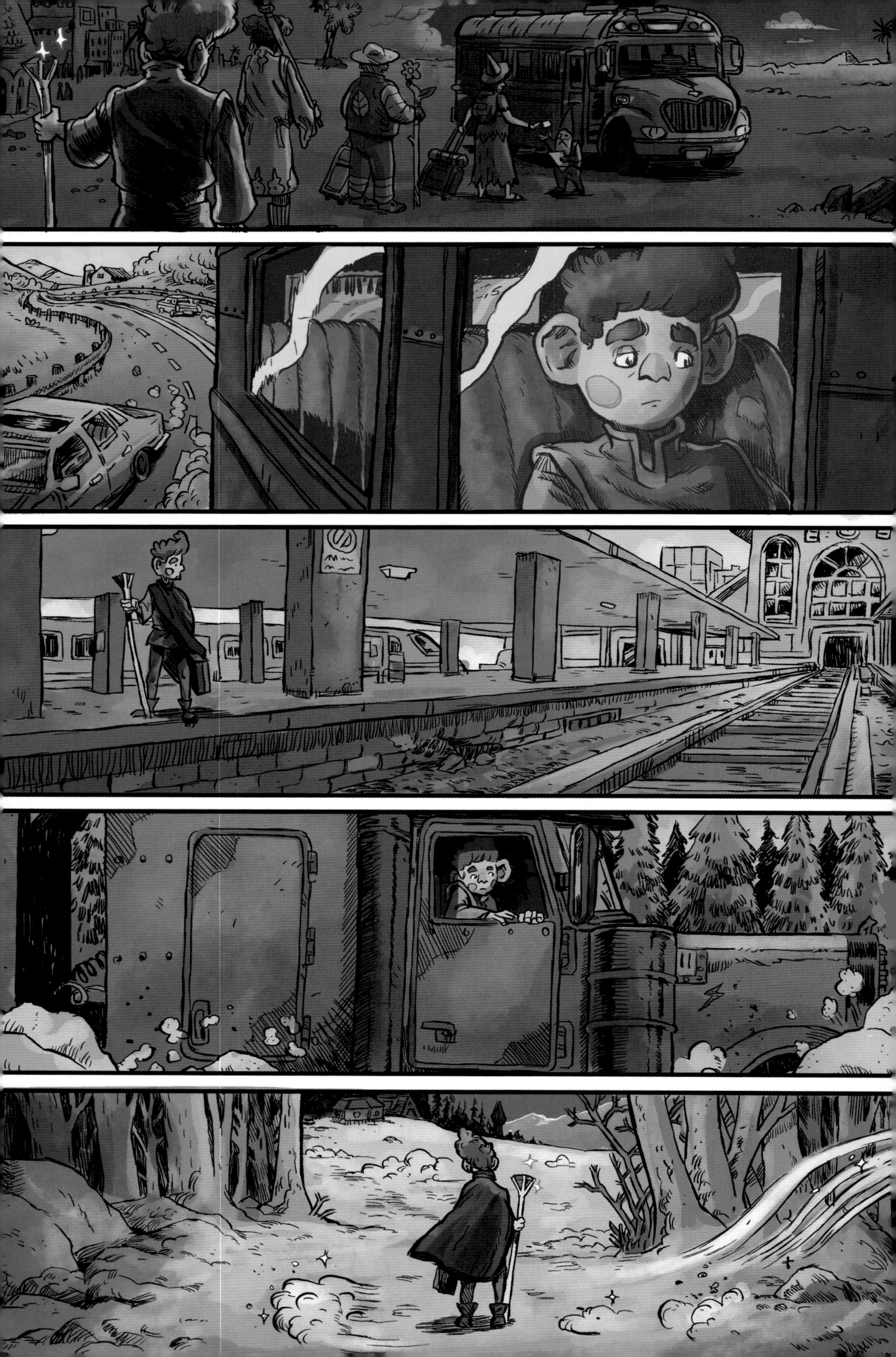

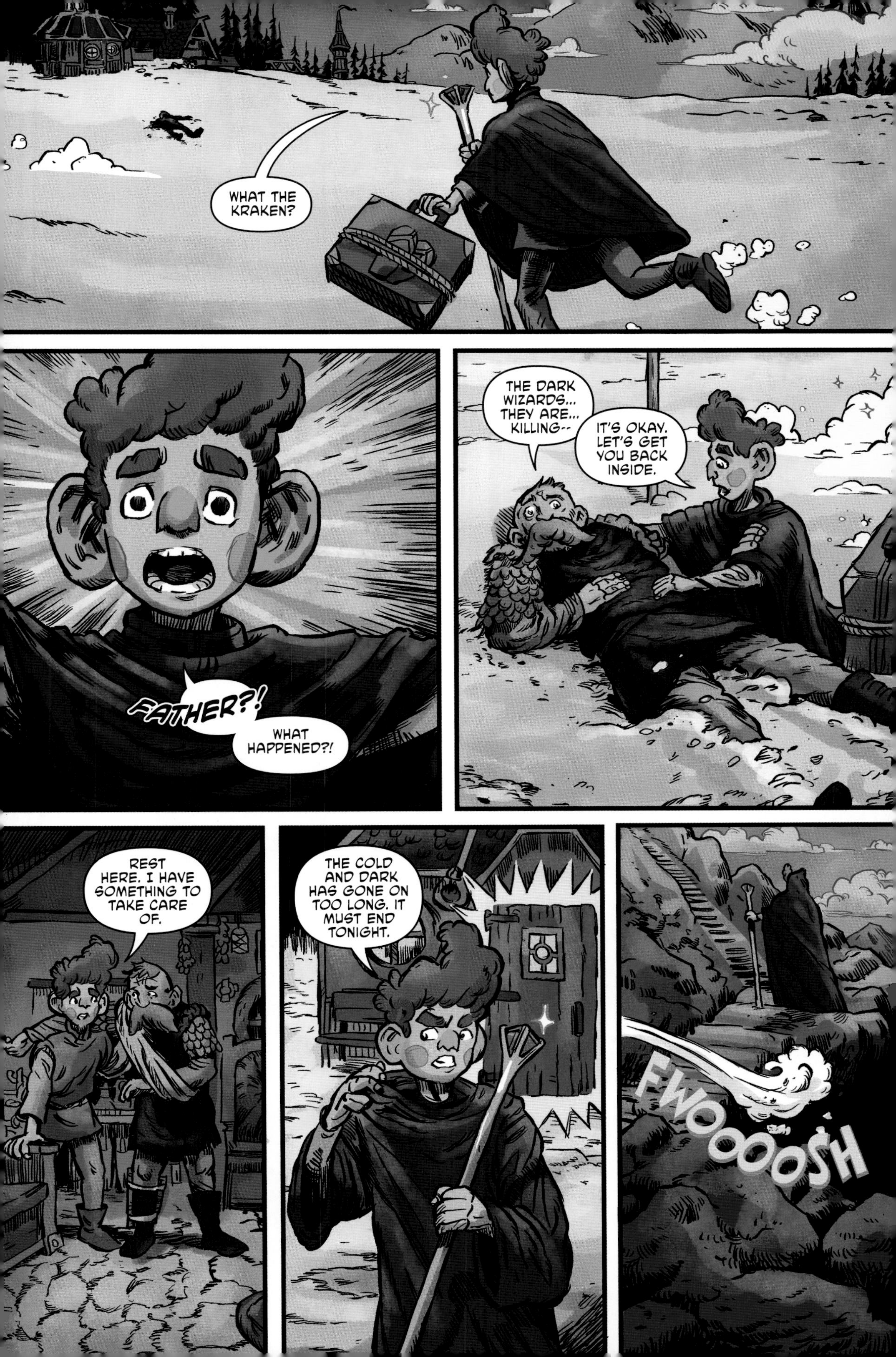
WHAT THE KRAKEN?
FATHER?!
WHAT HAPPENED?!
THE DARK WIZARDS... THEY ARE... KILLING--
IT'S OKAY. LET'S GET YOU BACK INSIDE.
REST HERE. I HAVE SOMETHING TO TAKE CARE OF.
THE COLD AND DARK HAS GONE ON TOO LONG. IT MUST END TONIGHT.
FWOOOOSH

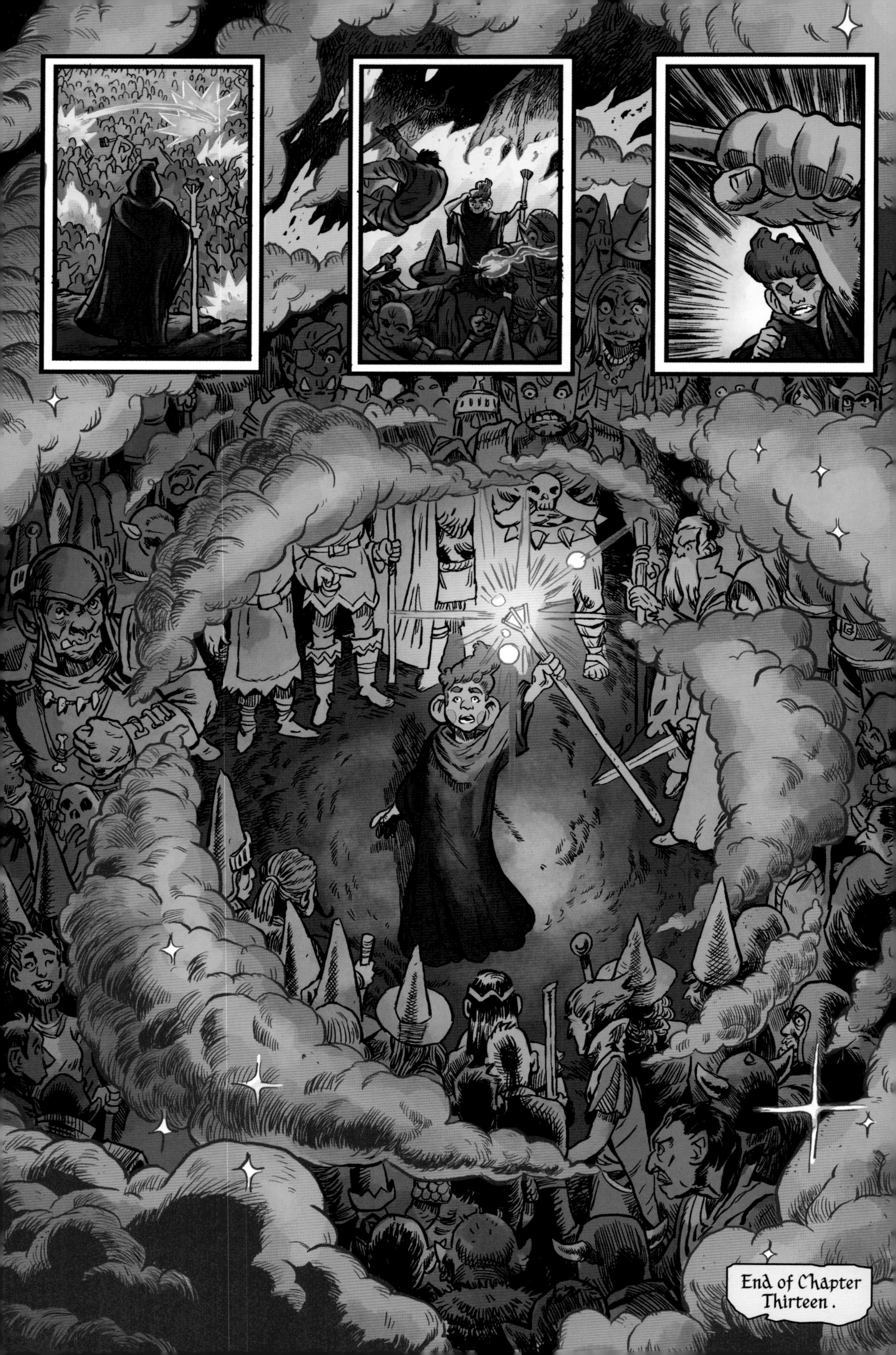
End of Chapter
Thirteen.

COVER BY
CONOR NOLAN

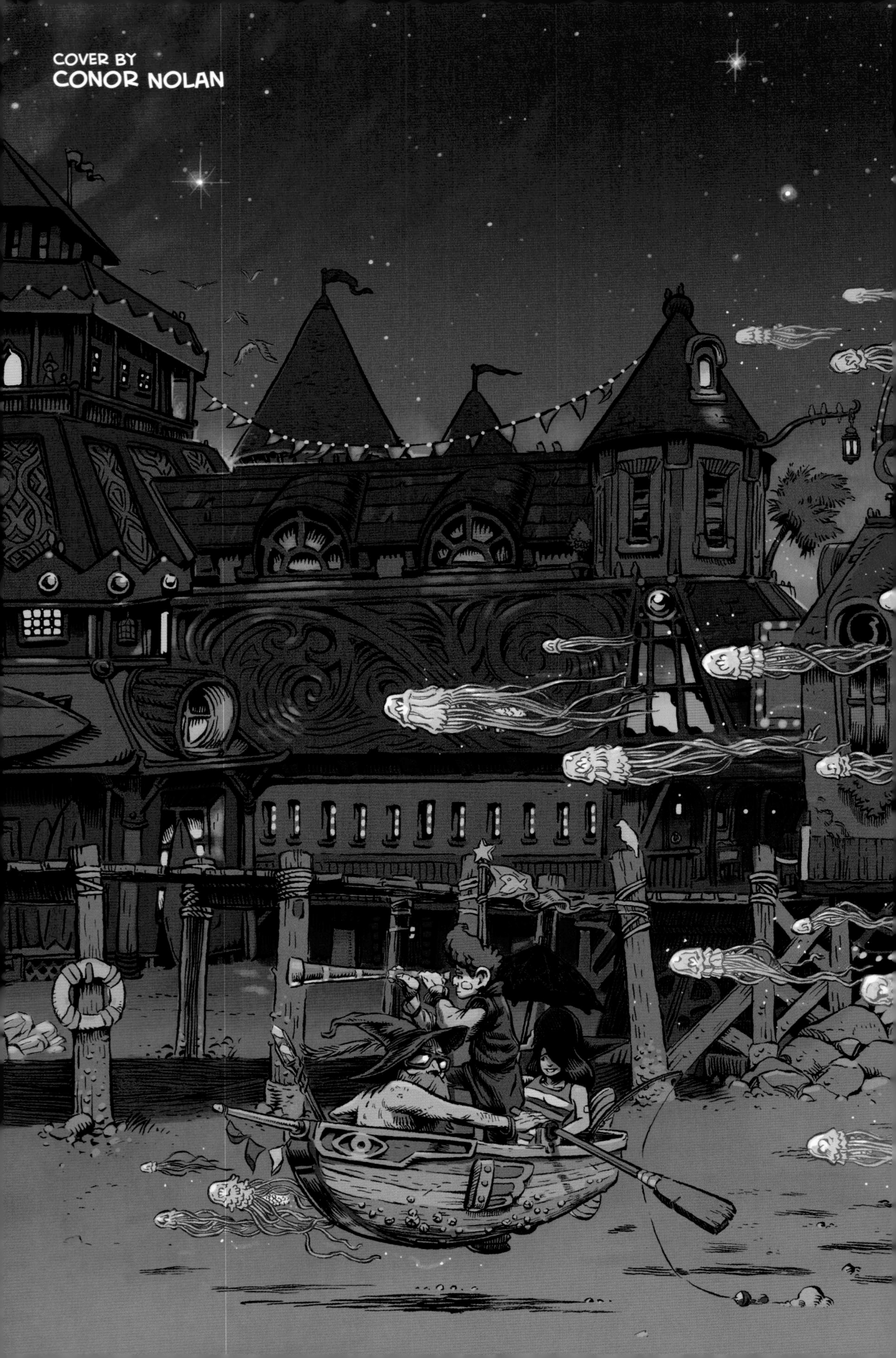

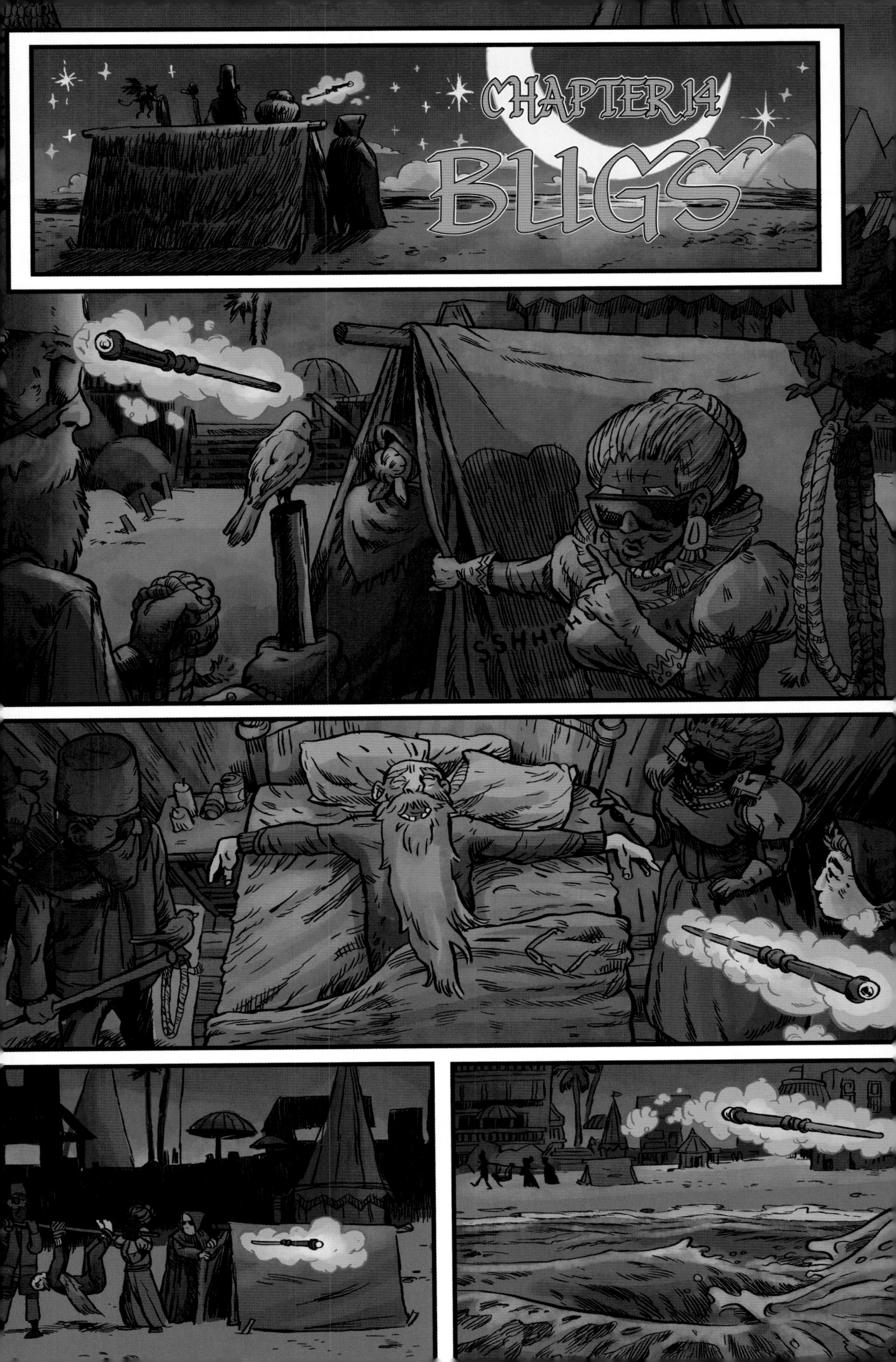
CHAPTER 14
BUGS
SSHHHHH

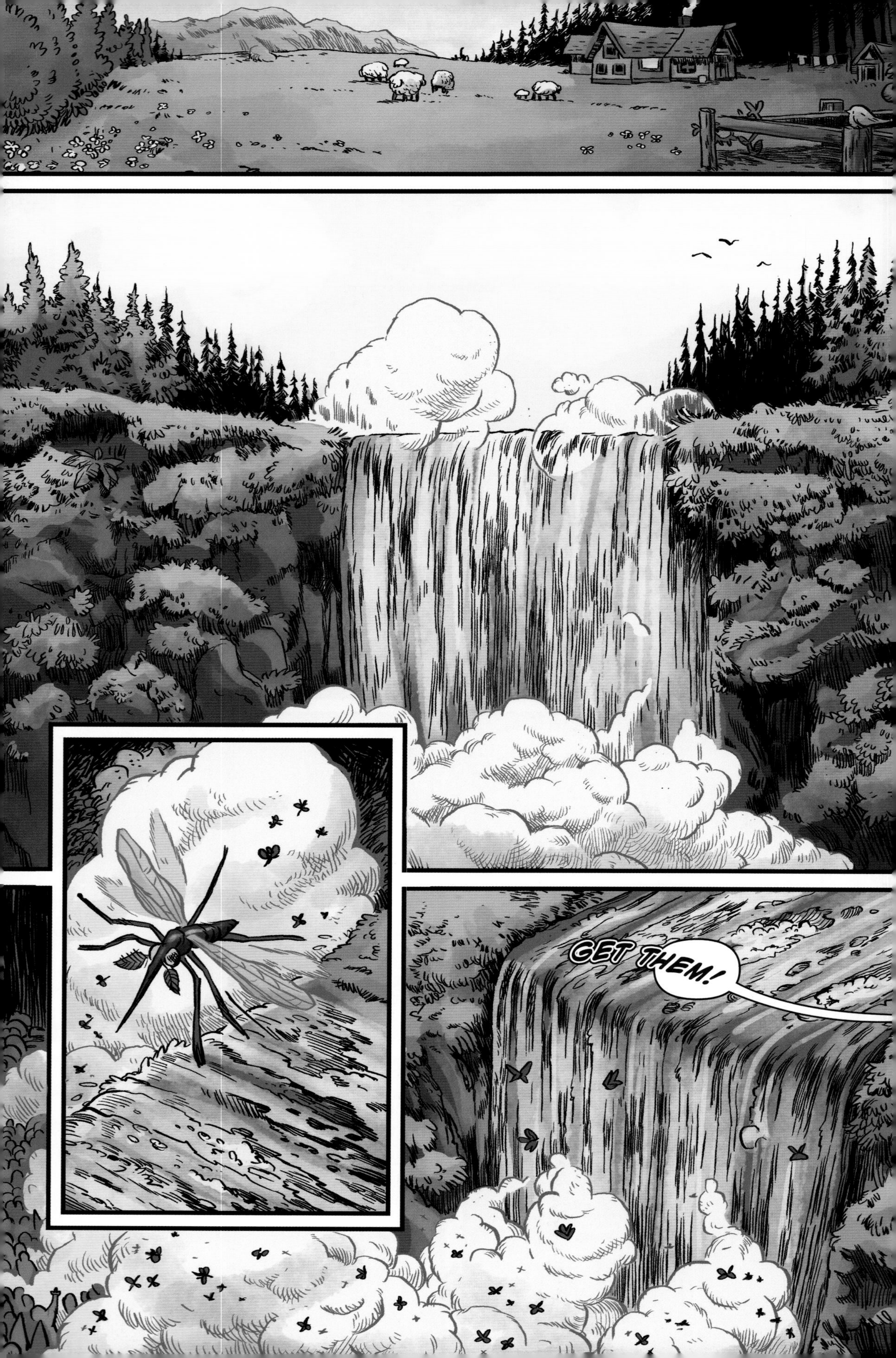
GET THEM!

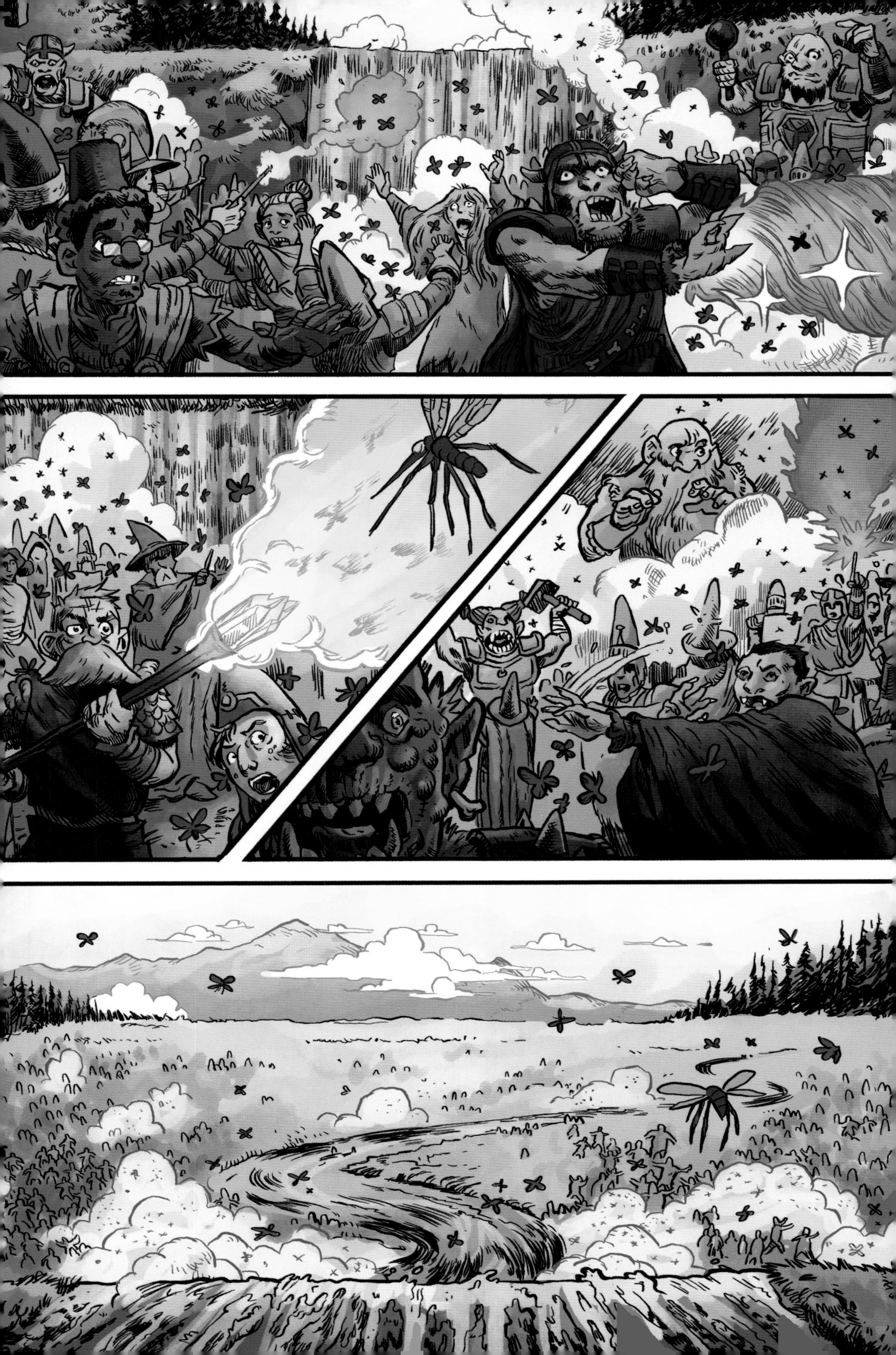

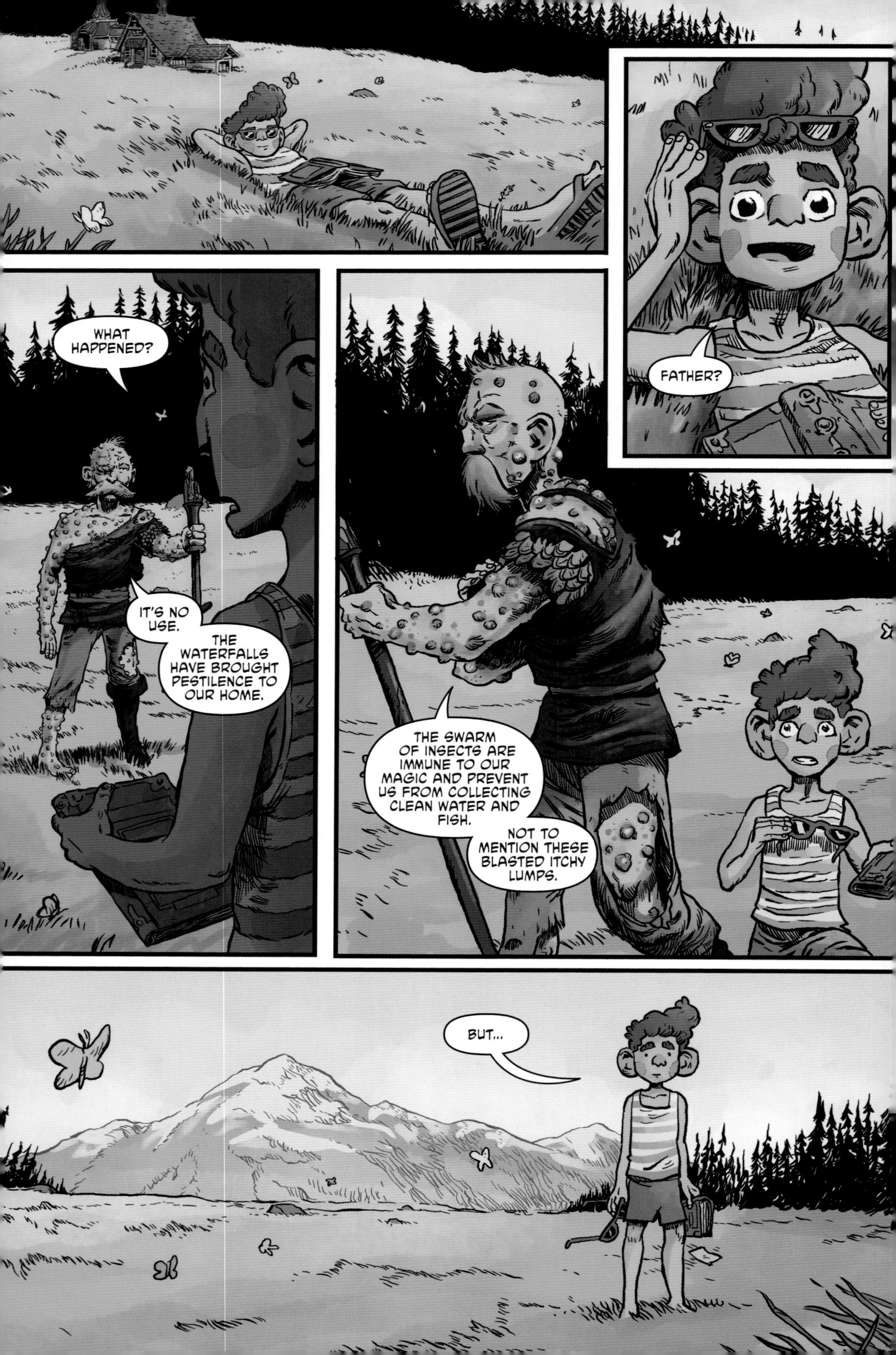
FATHER?
WHAT HAPPENED?
IT'S NO USE.
THE WATERFALLS HAVE BROUGHT PESTILENCE TO OUR HOME.
THE SWARM OF INSECTS ARE IMMUNE TO OUR MAGIC AND PREVENT US FROM COLLECTING CLEAN WATER AND FISH.
NOT TO MENTION THESE BLASTED ITCHY LUMPS.
BUT...

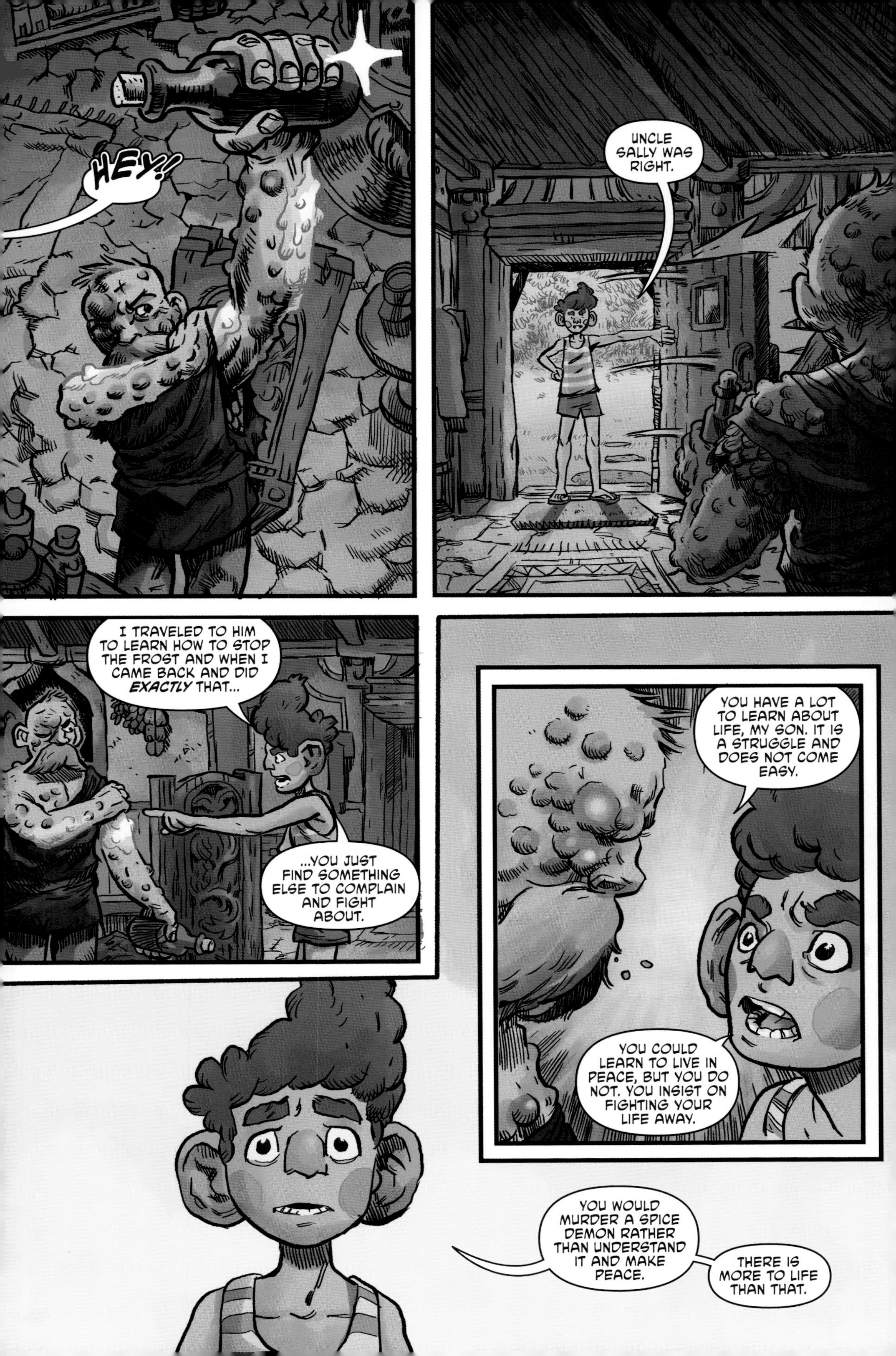
HEY!!
UNCLE SALLY WAS RIGHT.
I TRAVELED TO HIM TO LEARN HOW TO STOP THE FROST AND WHEN I CAME BACK AND DID *EXACTLY* THAT...
...YOU JUST FIND SOMETHING ELSE TO COMPLAIN AND FIGHT ABOUT.
YOU HAVE A LOT TO LEARN ABOUT LIFE, MY SON. IT IS A STRUGGLE AND DOES NOT COME EASY.
YOU COULD LEARN TO LIVE IN PEACE, BUT YOU DO NOT. YOU INSIST ON FIGHTING YOUR LIFE AWAY.
YOU WOULD MURDER A SPICE DEMON RATHER THAN UNDERSTAND IT AND MAKE PEACE.
THERE IS MORE TO LIFE THAN THAT.

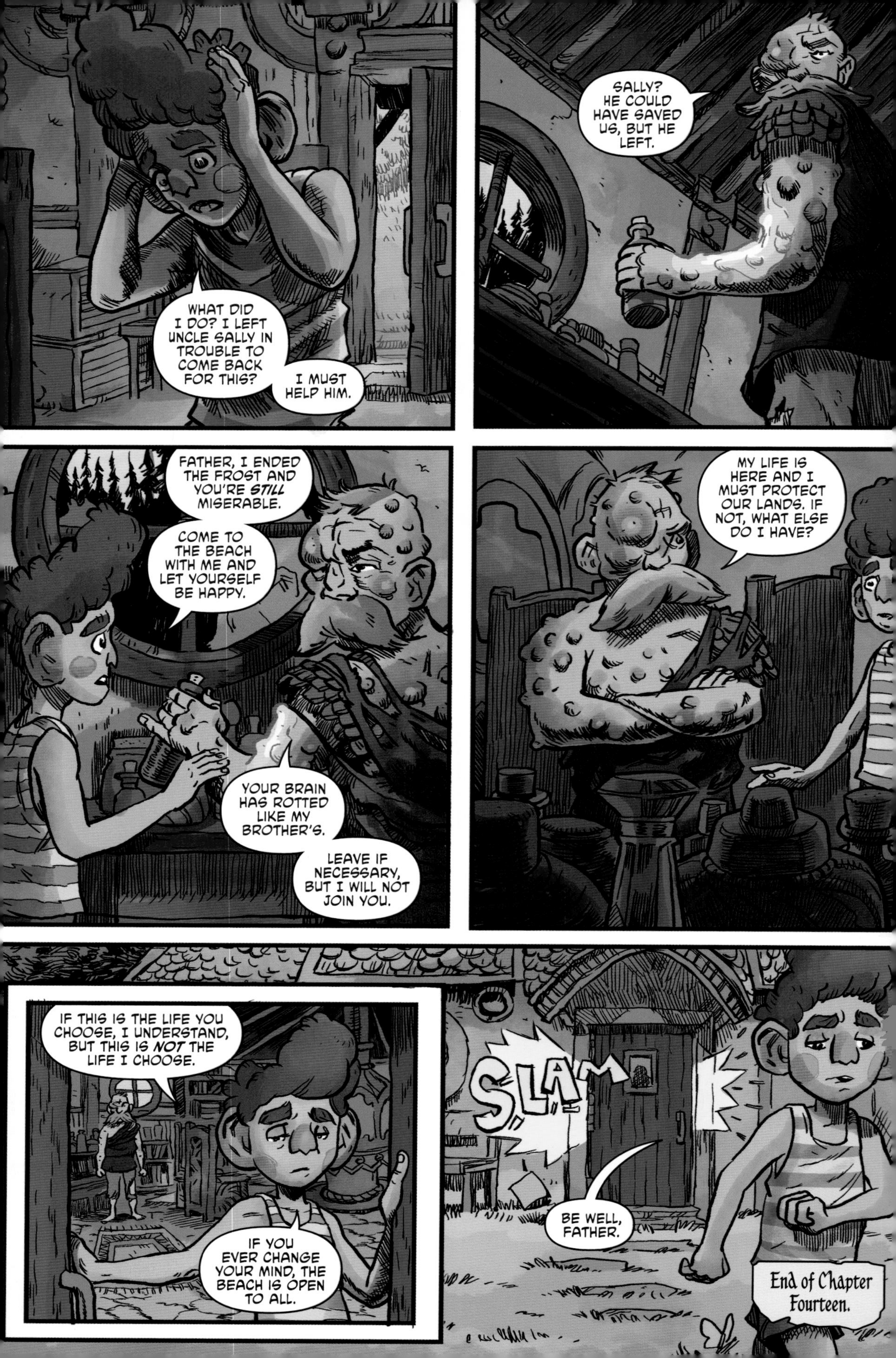
WHAT DID I DO? I LEFT UNCLE SALLY IN TROUBLE TO COME BACK FOR THIS?
I MUST HELP HIM.
SALLY? HE COULD HAVE SAVED US, BUT HE LEFT.
FATHER, I ENDED THE FROST AND YOU'RE STILL MISERABLE.
COME TO THE BEACH WITH ME AND LET YOURSELF BE HAPPY.
YOUR BRAIN HAS ROTTED LIKE MY BROTHER'S.
LEAVE IF NECESSARY, BUT I WILL NOT JOIN YOU.
MY LIFE IS HERE AND I MUST PROTECT OUR LANDS. IF NOT, WHAT ELSE DO I HAVE?
IF THIS IS THE LIFE YOU CHOOSE, I UNDERSTAND, BUT THIS IS NOT THE LIFE I CHOOSE.
IF YOU EVER CHANGE YOUR MIND, THE BEACH IS OPEN TO ALL.
SLAM
BE WELL, FATHER.
End of Chapter Fourteen.

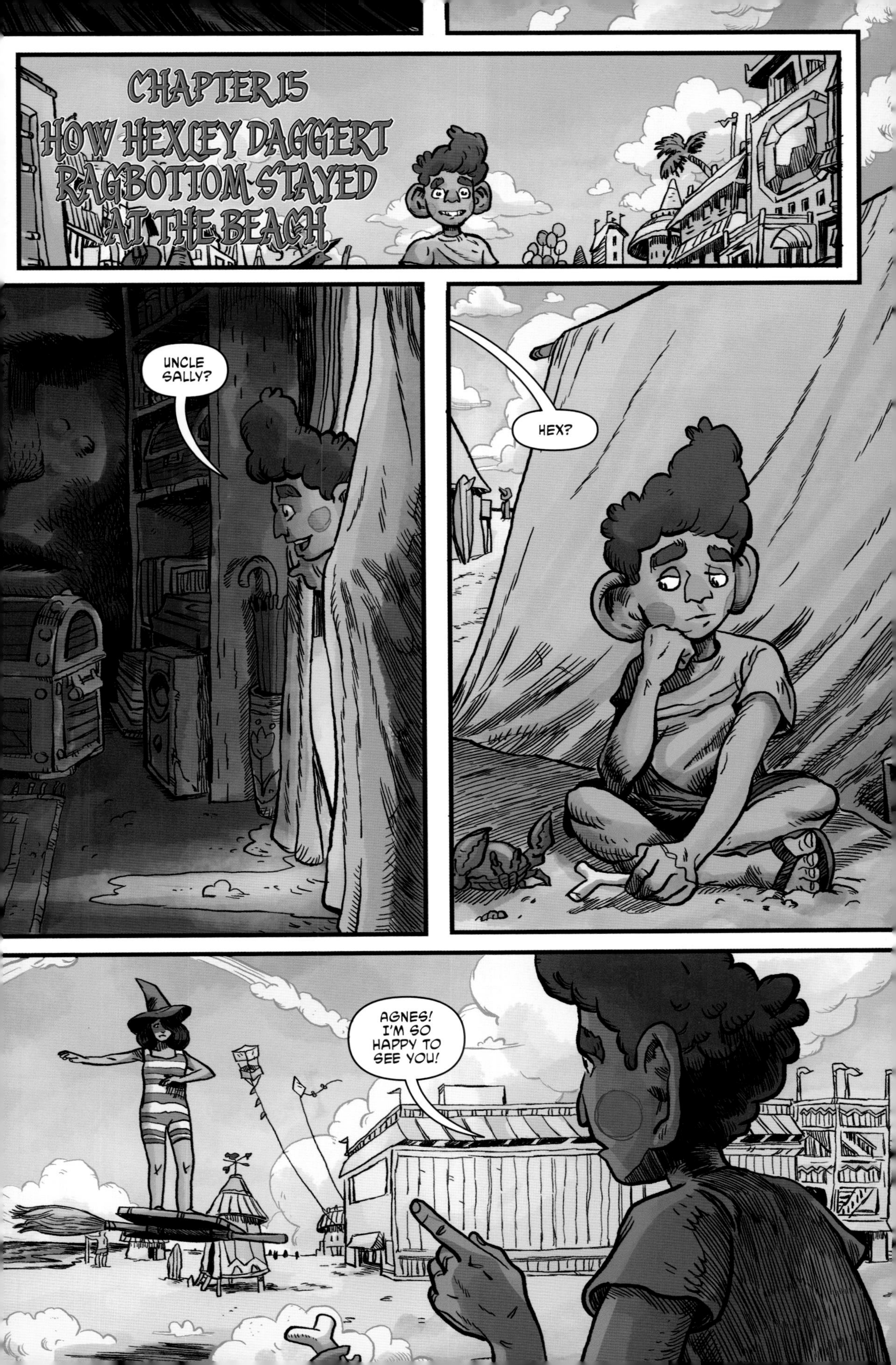
CHAPTER 15
HOW HEXLEY DAGGERT RAGBOTTOM STAYED AT THE BEACH
UNCLE SALLY?
HEX?
AGNES! I'M SO HAPPY TO SEE YOU!

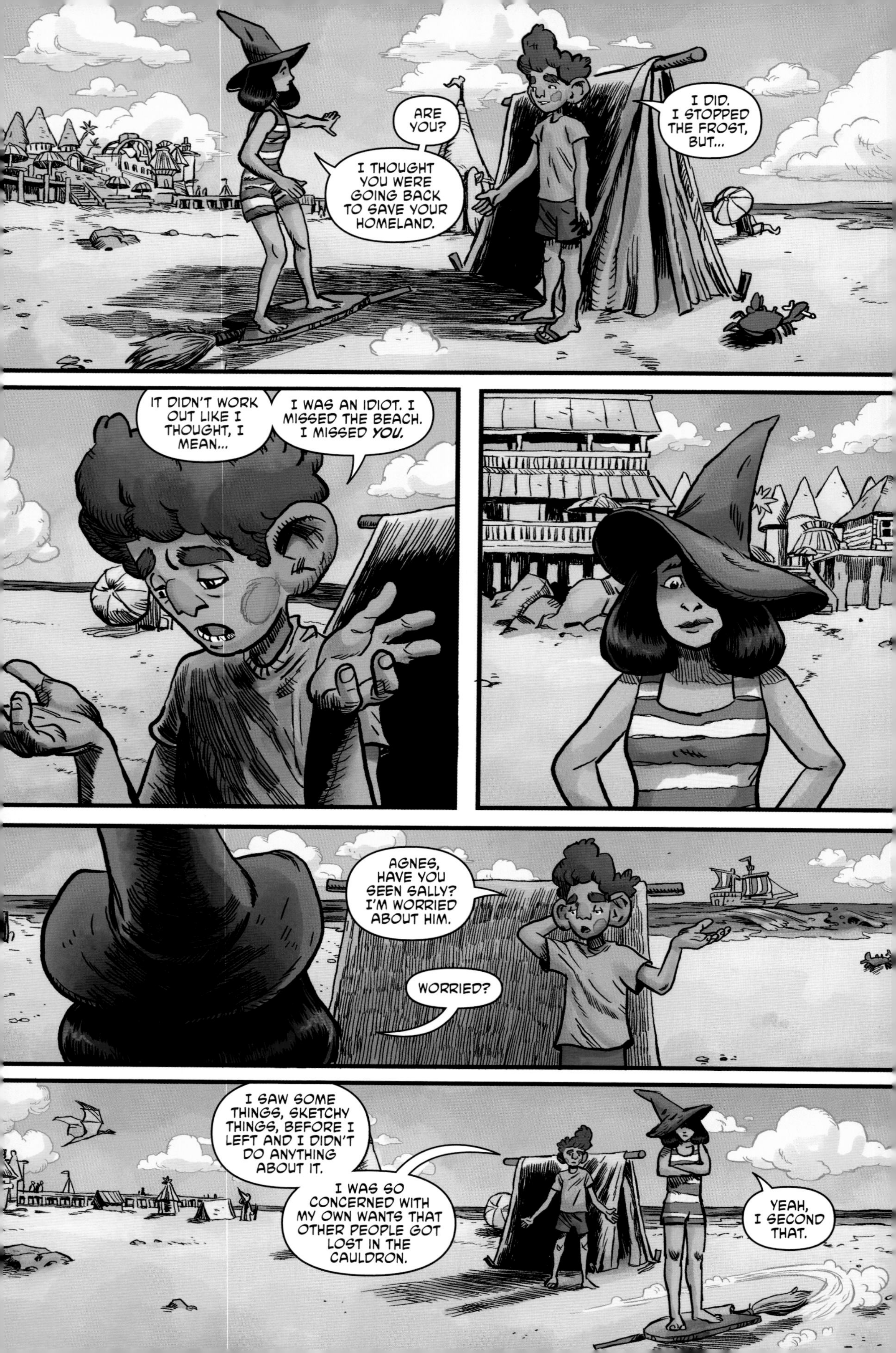
ARE YOU?
I THOUGHT YOU WERE GOING BACK TO SAVE YOUR HOMELAND.
I DID. I STOPPED THE FROST, BUT...
IT DIDN'T WORK OUT LIKE I THOUGHT, I MEAN...
I WAS AN IDIOT. I MISSED THE BEACH. I MISSED *YOU.*
AGNES, HAVE YOU SEEN SALLY? I'M WORRIED ABOUT HIM.
WORRIED?
I SAW SOME THINGS, SKETCHY THINGS, BEFORE I LEFT AND I DIDN'T DO ANYTHING ABOUT IT.
I WAS SO CONCERNED WITH MY OWN WANTS THAT OTHER PEOPLE GOT LOST IN THE CAULDRON.
YEAH, I SECOND THAT.

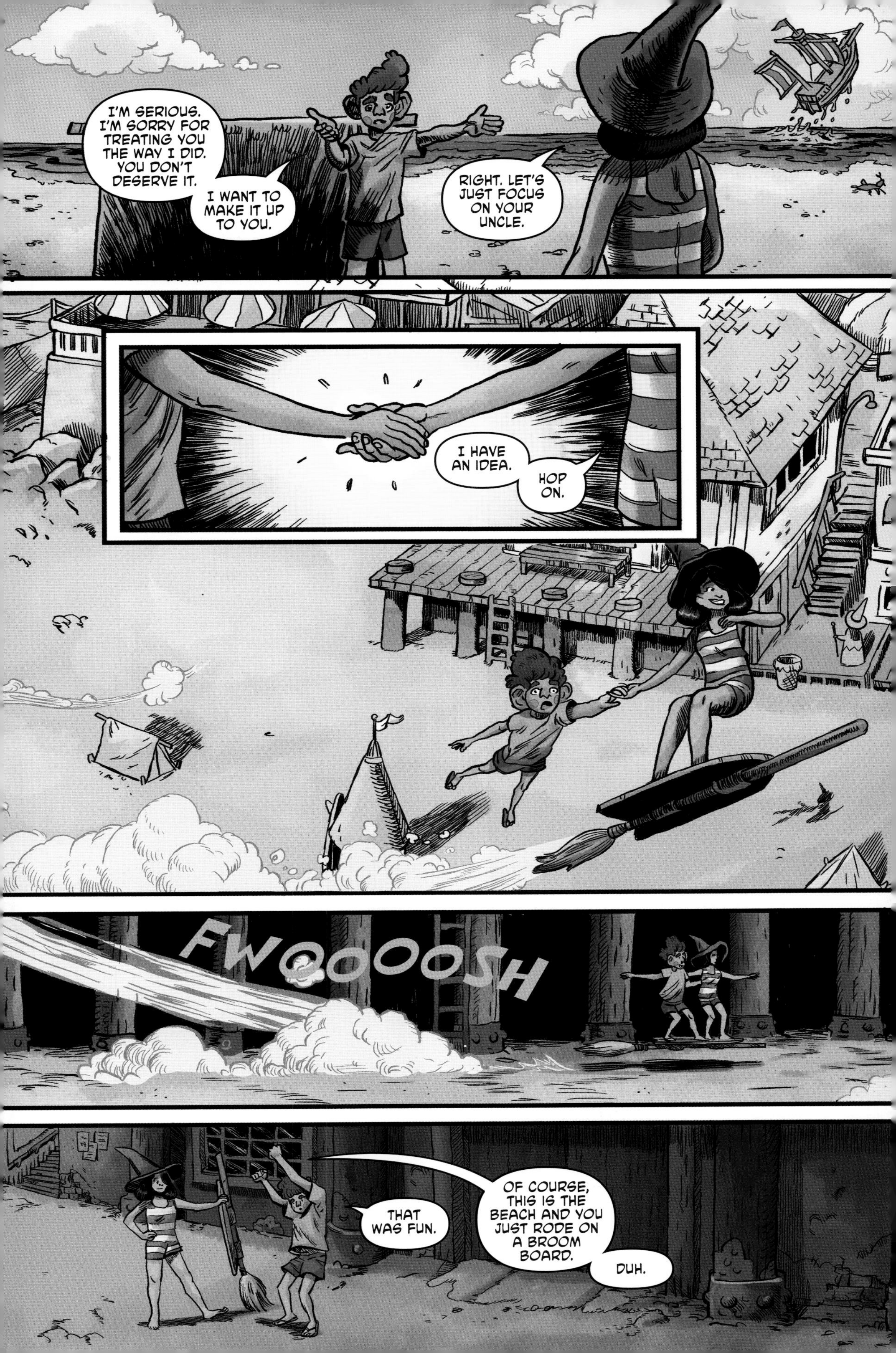
I'M SERIOUS. I'M SORRY FOR TREATING YOU THE WAY I DID. YOU DON'T DESERVE IT.
I WANT TO MAKE IT UP TO YOU.
RIGHT. LET'S JUST FOCUS ON YOUR UNCLE.
I HAVE AN IDEA.
HOP ON.
FWOOOOSH
THAT WAS FUN.
OF COURSE, THIS IS THE BEACH AND YOU JUST RODE ON A BROOM BOARD.
DUH.

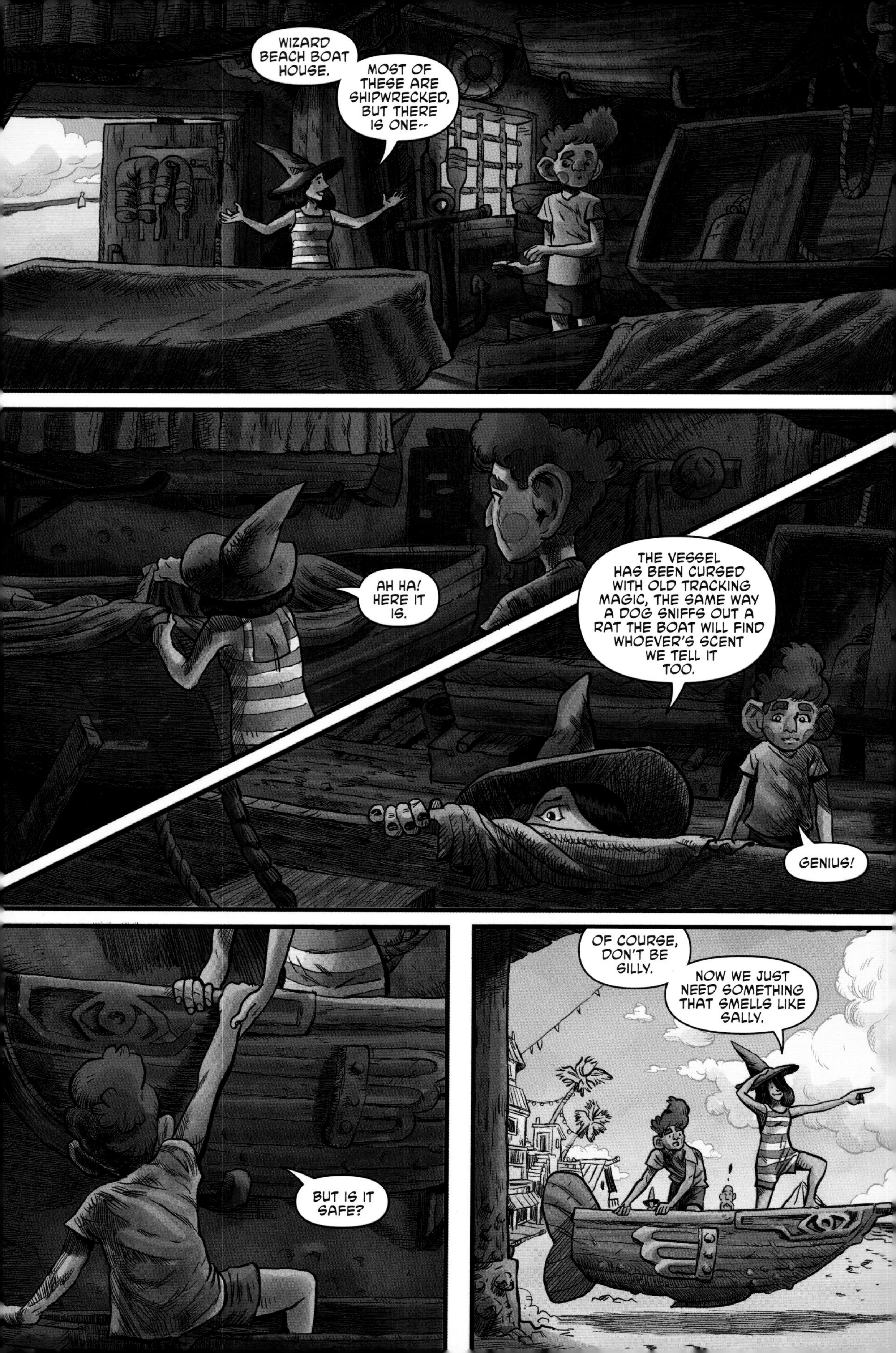
WIZARD BEACH BOAT HOUSE.
MOST OF THESE ARE SHIPWRECKED, BUT THERE IS ONE--
AH HA! HERE IT IS.
THE VESSEL HAS BEEN CURSED WITH OLD TRACKING MAGIC, THE SAME WAY A DOG SNIFFS OUT A RAT THE BOAT WILL FIND WHOEVER'S SCENT WE TELL IT TOO.
GENIUS!
BUT IS IT SAFE?
OF COURSE, DON'T BE SILLY.
NOW WE JUST NEED SOMETHING THAT SMELLS LIKE SALLY.

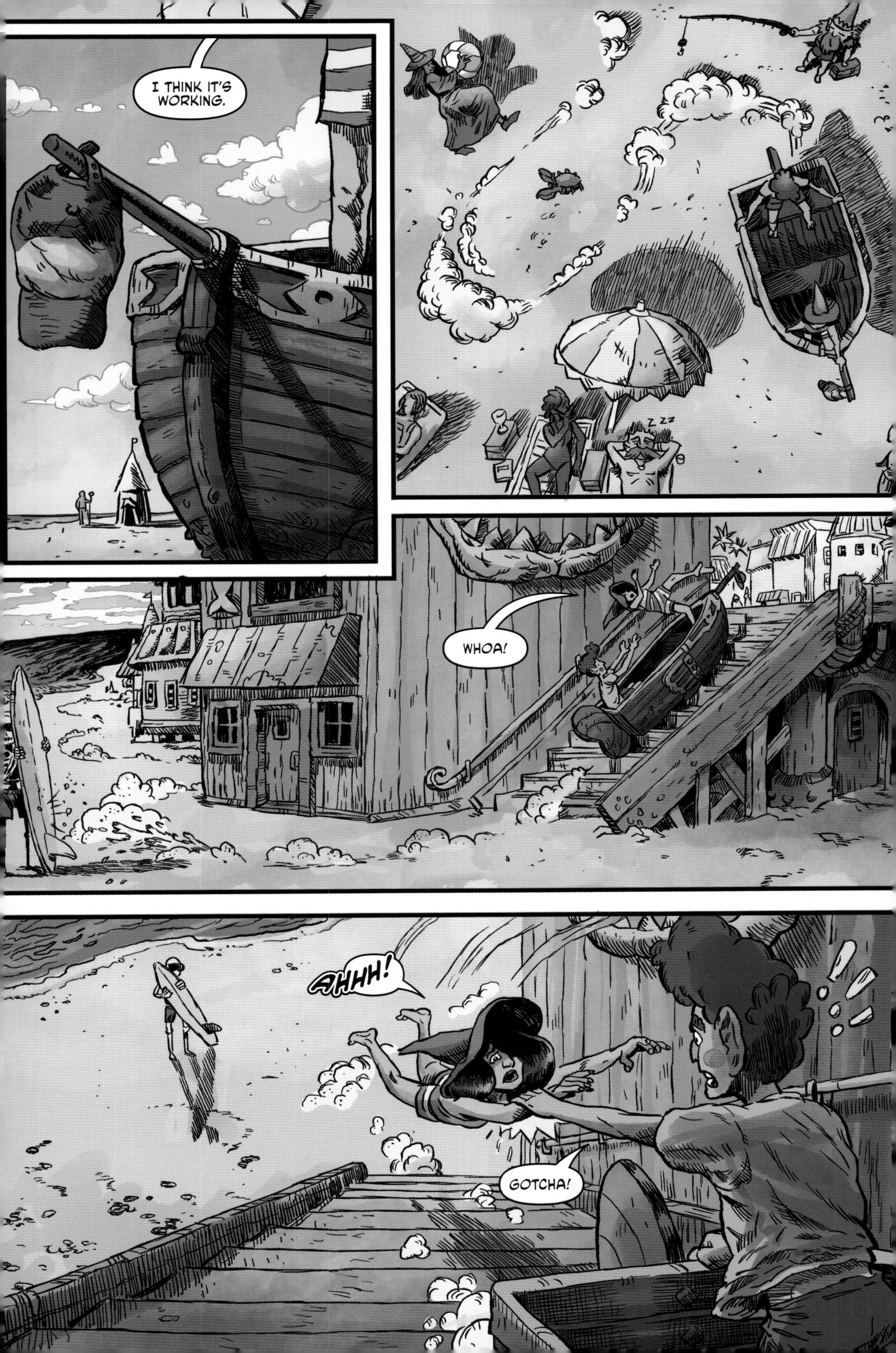
I THINK IT'S WORKING.
WHOA!
AHHH!
GOTCHA!

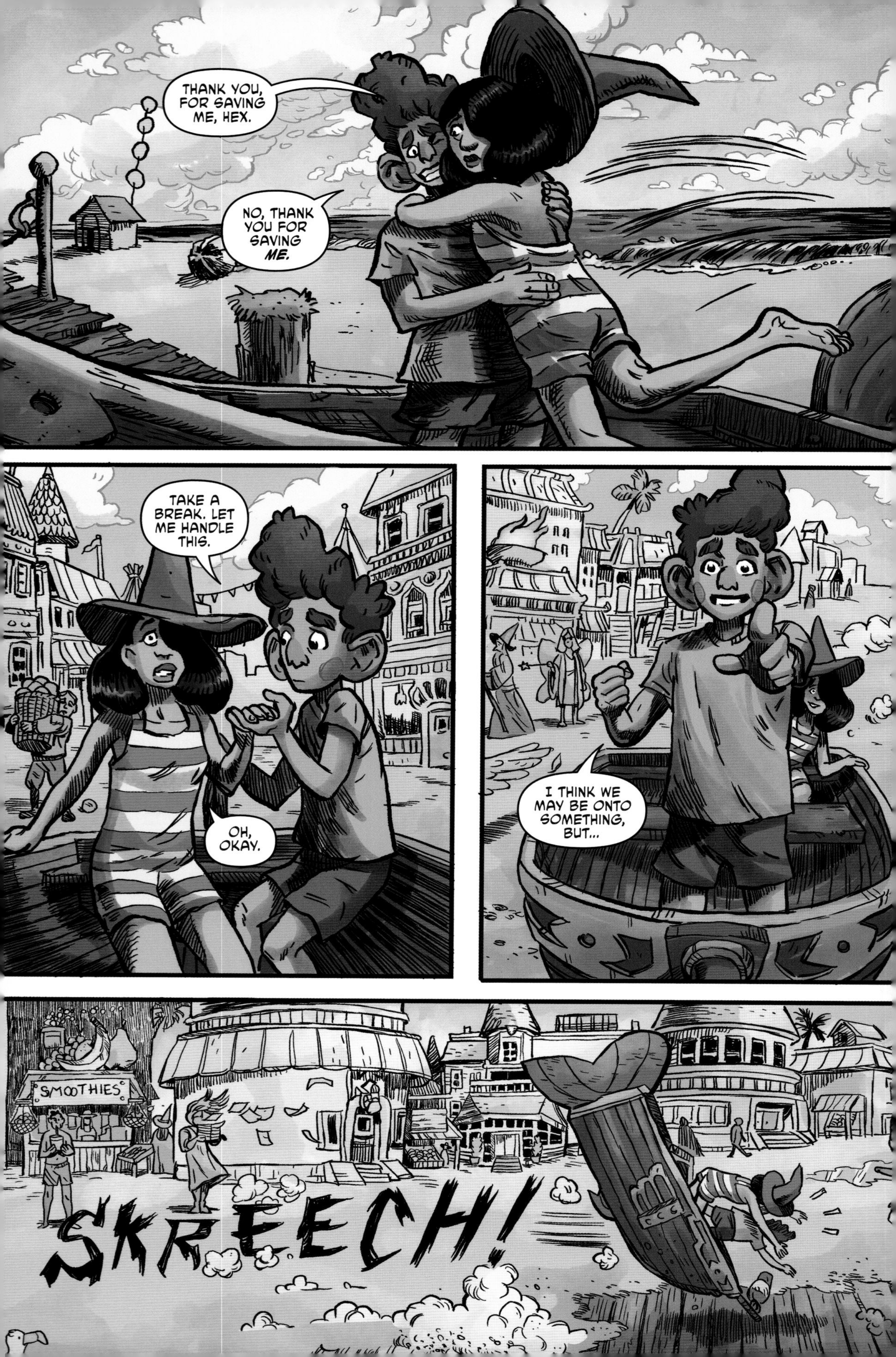
THANK YOU, FOR SAVING ME, HEX.
NO, THANK YOU FOR SAVING *ME.*
TAKE A BREAK. LET ME HANDLE THIS.
OH, OKAY.
I THINK WE MAY BE ONTO SOMETHING, BUT...
SMOOTHIES
SKREECH!

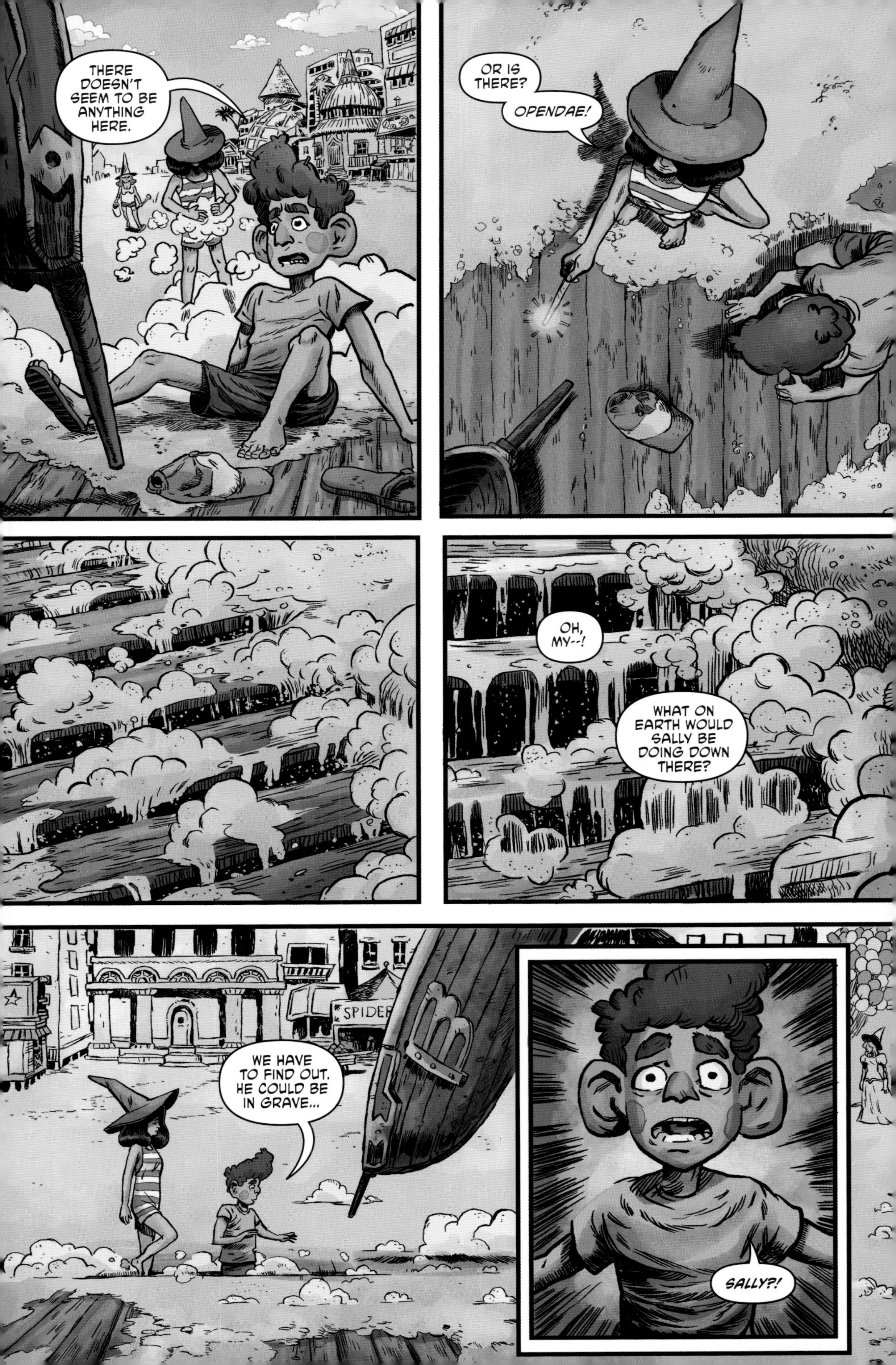
THERE DOESN'T SEEM TO BE ANYTHING HERE.
OR IS THERE?
OPENDAE!
OH, MY--!
WHAT ON EARTH WOULD SALLY BE DOING DOWN THERE?
SPIDER
WE HAVE TO FIND OUT. HE COULD BE IN GRAVE...
SALLY?!

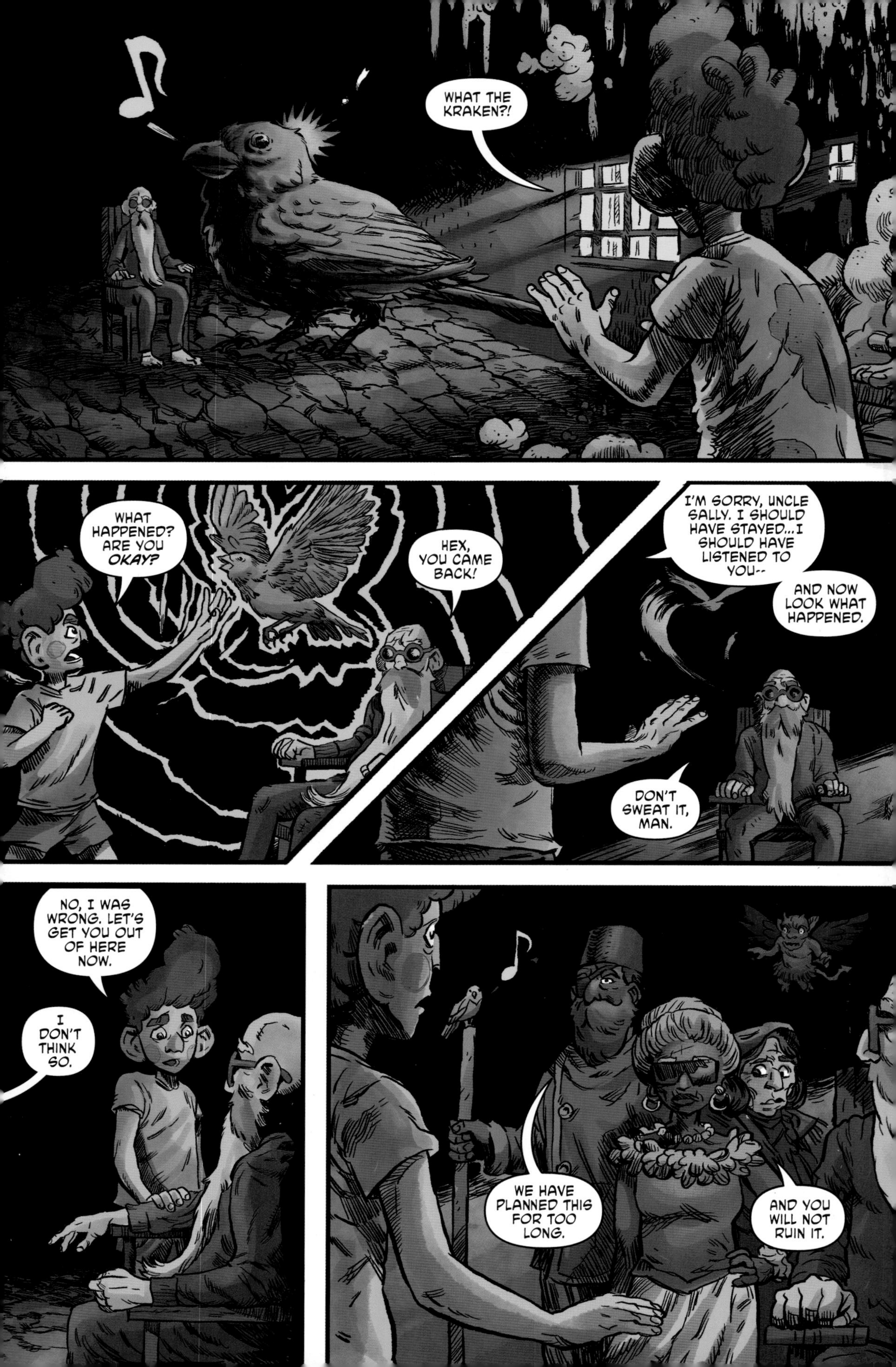
WHAT THE KRAKEN?!
WHAT HAPPENED? ARE YOU *OKAY?*
HEX, YOU CAME BACK!
I'M SORRY, UNCLE SALLY. I SHOULD HAVE STAYED...I SHOULD HAVE LISTENED TO YOU--
AND NOW LOOK WHAT HAPPENED.
DON'T SWEAT IT, MAN.
NO, I WAS WRONG. LET'S GET YOU OUT OF HERE NOW.
I DON'T THINK SO.
WE HAVE PLANNED THIS FOR TOO LONG.
AND YOU WILL NOT RUIN IT.

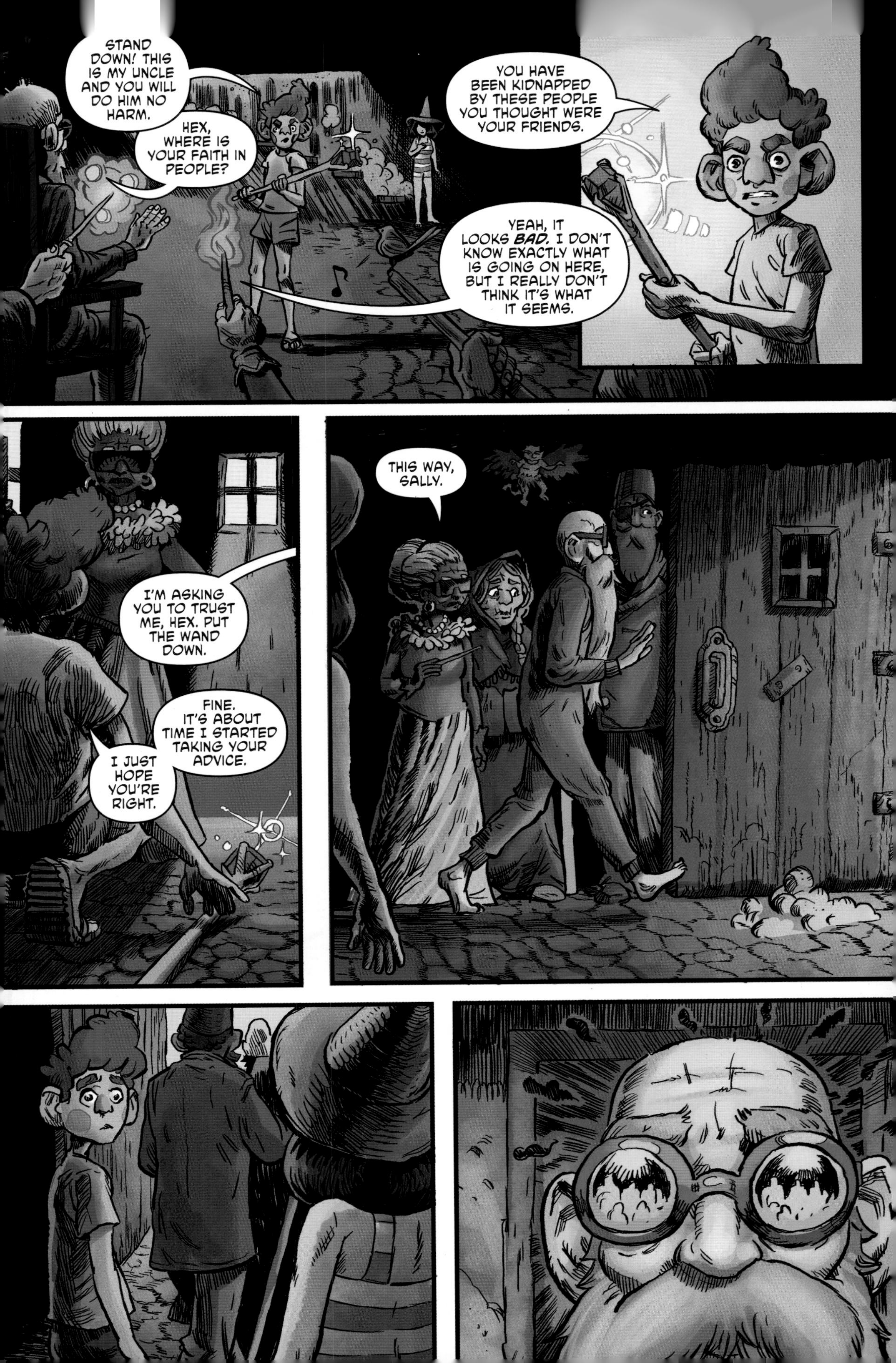
STAND DOWN! THIS IS MY UNCLE AND YOU WILL DO HIM NO HARM.
HEX, WHERE IS YOUR FAITH IN PEOPLE?
YOU HAVE BEEN KIDNAPPED BY THESE PEOPLE YOU THOUGHT WERE YOUR FRIENDS.
YEAH, IT LOOKS BAD. I DON'T KNOW EXACTLY WHAT IS GOING ON HERE, BUT I REALLY DON'T THINK IT'S WHAT IT SEEMS.
I'M ASKING YOU TO TRUST ME, HEX. PUT THE WAND DOWN.
FINE. IT'S ABOUT TIME I STARTED TAKING YOUR ADVICE.
I JUST HOPE YOU'RE RIGHT.
THIS WAY, SALLY.

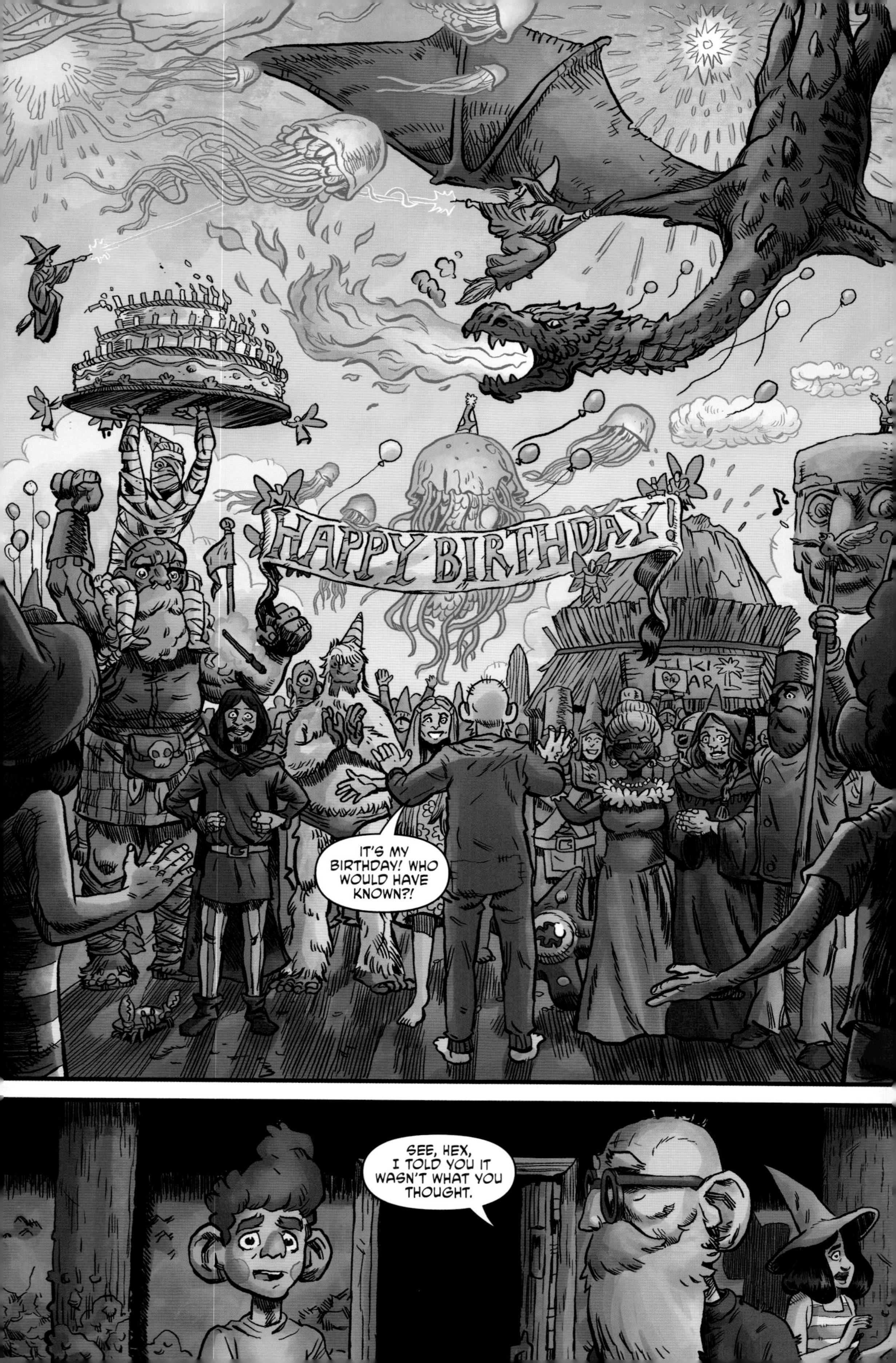
HAPPY BIRTHDAY!
IT'S MY BIRTHDAY! WHO WOULD HAVE KNOWN?!
SEE, HEX, I TOLD YOU IT WASN'T WHAT YOU THOUGHT.

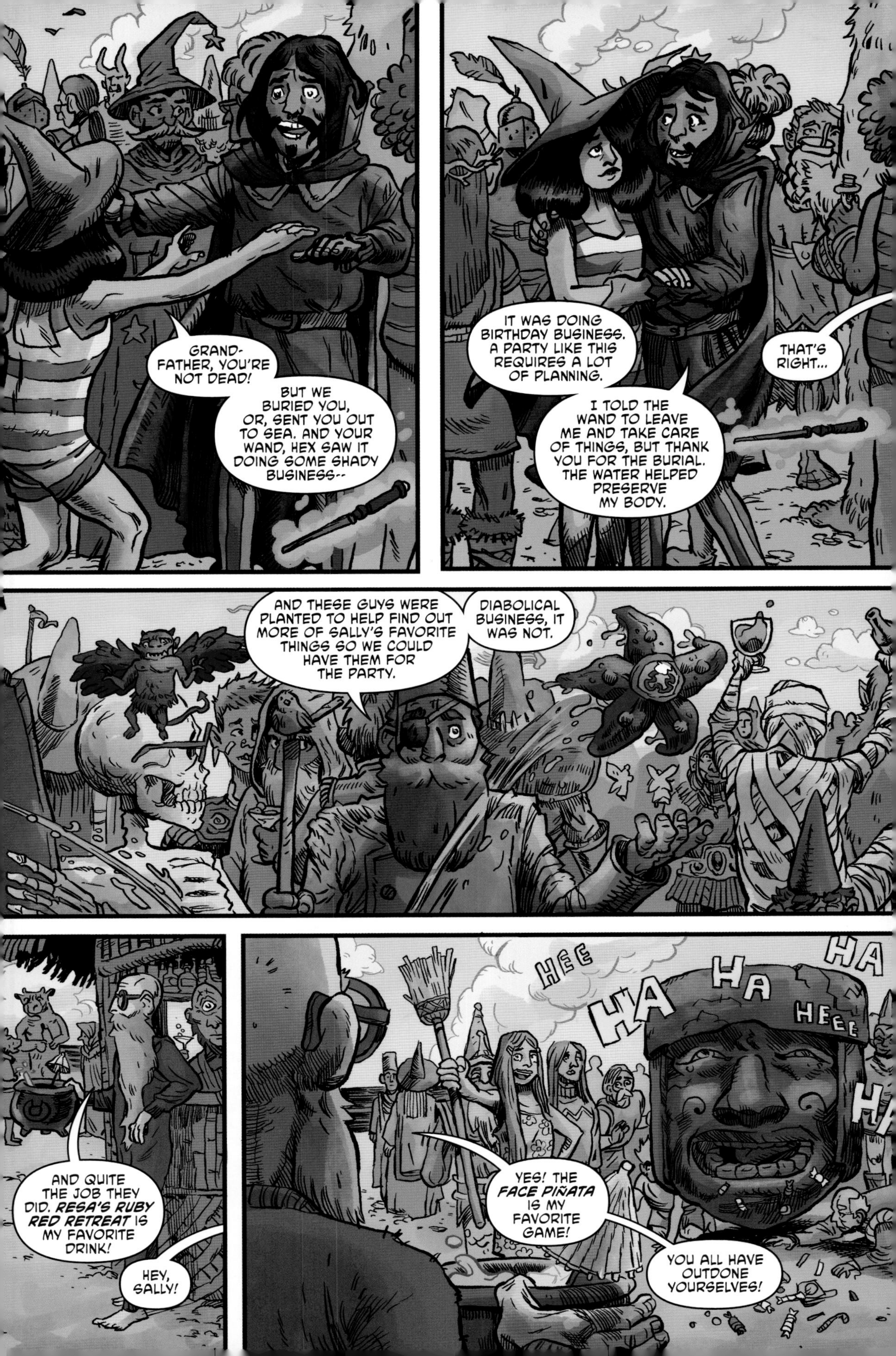
GRAND-FATHER, YOU'RE NOT DEAD!
BUT WE BURIED YOU, OR, SENT YOU OUT TO SEA. AND YOUR WAND, HEX SAW IT DOING SOME SHADY BUSINESS--
IT WAS DOING BIRTHDAY BUSINESS. A PARTY LIKE THIS REQUIRES A LOT OF PLANNING.
I TOLD THE WAND TO LEAVE ME AND TAKE CARE OF THINGS, BUT THANK YOU FOR THE BURIAL. THE WATER HELPED PRESERVE MY BODY.
THAT'S RIGHT...
AND THESE GUYS WERE PLANTED TO HELP FIND OUT MORE OF SALLY'S FAVORITE THINGS SO WE COULD HAVE THEM FOR THE PARTY.
DIABOLICAL BUSINESS, IT WAS NOT.
AND QUITE THE JOB THEY DID. *RESA'S RUBY RED RETREAT* IS MY FAVORITE DRINK!
HEY, SALLY!
HEE
HA
HA
HA
HEEE
HA
YES! THE *FACE PIÑATA* IS MY FAVORITE GAME!
YOU ALL HAVE OUTDONE YOURSELVES!

FACE PIÑATA!
A.K.A. FACATA!

INSTRUCTIONS BY FRANK IERO **(NOT FOCACCIA!)**

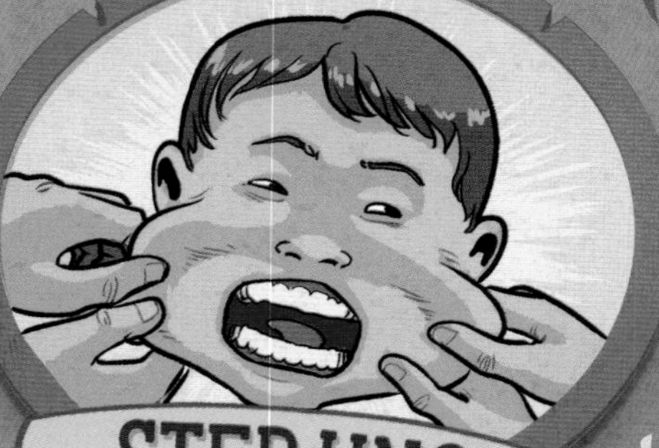

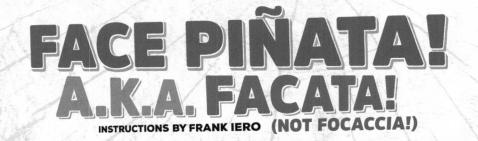

STEP UNO

Stretch open face hole for optimum packing capabilities. Use fingers, tongue, hands belonging to others, and/or feet to reach desired floppiness of mouth coverings.

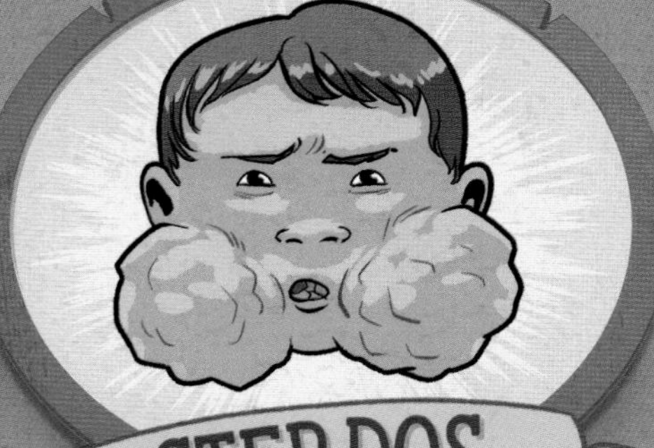

STEP DOS

Gather delicious treats and/or treasures then recklessly insert hundreds of them into your gaping cheek pouches. *Unwrapped candies or dissolvables may work to your advantage!

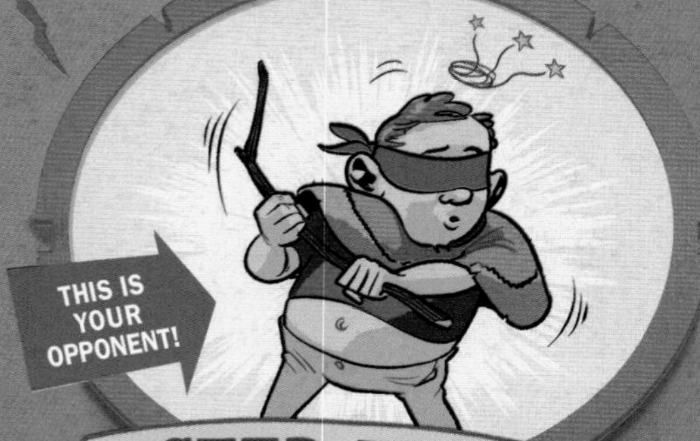
THIS IS YOUR OPPONENT!

STEP TRES

Blindfold and bewilder a small child, elderly adult, or anyone you feel confident in withstanding many blows to the head from.

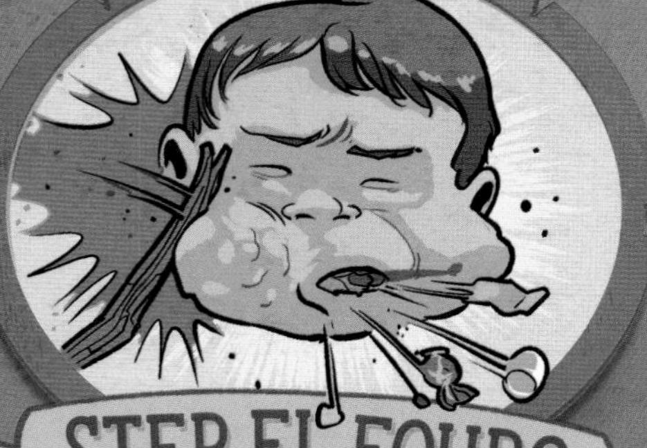

STEP EL FOURO

Do Battle!
Feel free to arm the weakened attacker with a stick or simply convince them to use their provided appendages to loosen your hold on the precious mouth jewels. Swinging and flailing, the dizzied assailant must remove as many riches as they can from your FACATA!™

If the spoils are forcibly extracted from the head holes and spill out onto the floor, they can and must be enjoyed by all in attendance!

However, if the owner of the face swallows more goodies than the armed combatant can mine, the face owner is the sole winner!

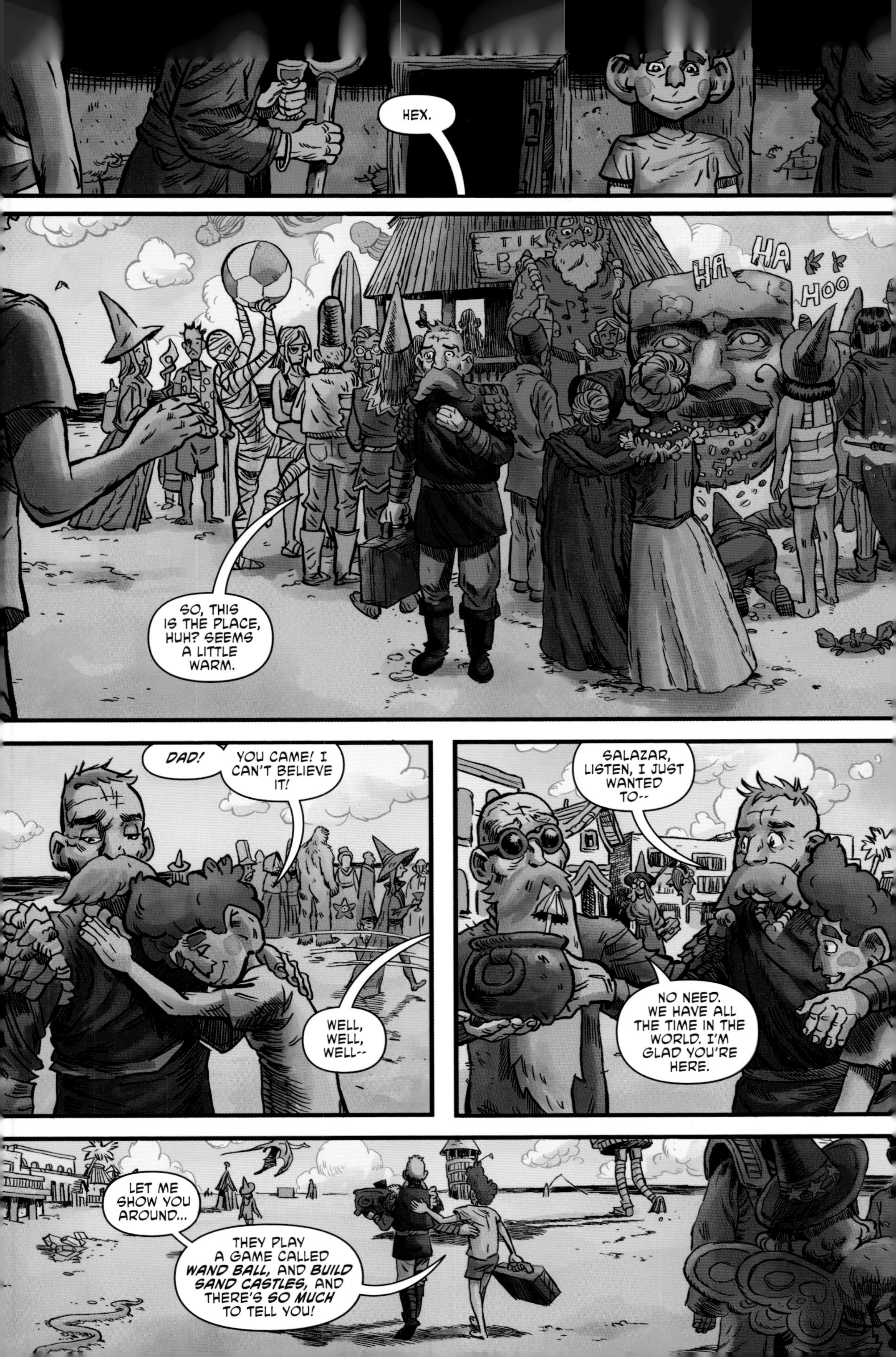

HEX.
TIK
B
HA
HA
HOO
SO, THIS IS THE PLACE, HUH? SEEMS A LITTLE WARM.
DAD!
YOU CAME! I CAN'T BELIEVE IT!
WELL, WELL, WELL--
SALAZAR, LISTEN, I JUST WANTED TO--
NO NEED. WE HAVE ALL THE TIME IN THE WORLD. I'M GLAD YOU'RE HERE.
LET ME SHOW YOU AROUND...
THEY PLAY A GAME CALLED *WAND BALL*, AND *BUILD SAND CASTLES*, AND THERE'S *SO MUCH* TO TELL YOU!

RESA'S RUBY RED RETREAT

Recipe by John "Hambone" McGuire

2oz	Coconut Aberrant
2oz	Dark Aberrant
1oz	Freshly Squeezed Lime Juice
1/2oz	Orange Juice
1/2oz	Ruby Red Grapefruit Juice
1/2oz	Passionfruit Syrup
1/2oz	Sugar Syrup

Add all ingredients into a shaker filled with ice and shake.

Strain into a **Tornado Tumbler** filled with ice, top off with **Pamplemousse Club Soda** and let this **tropical twister** take you away!

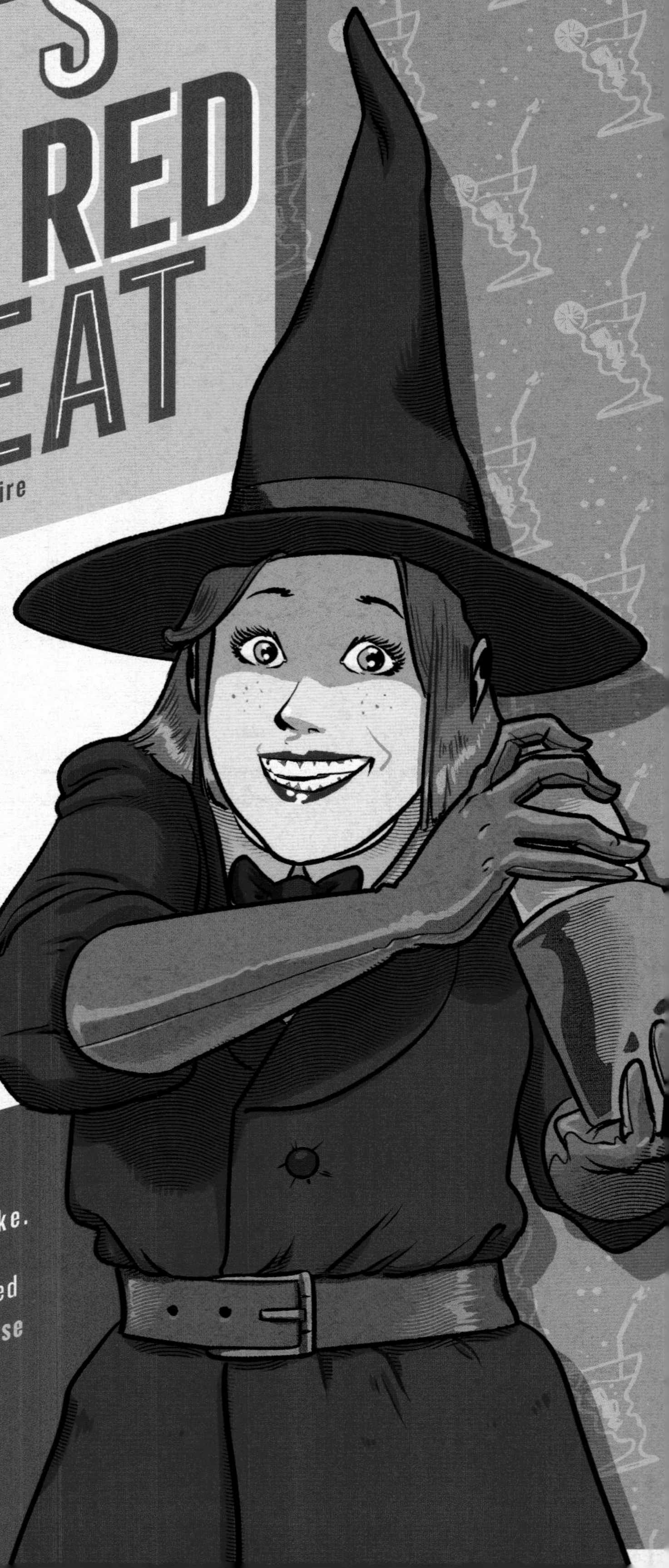

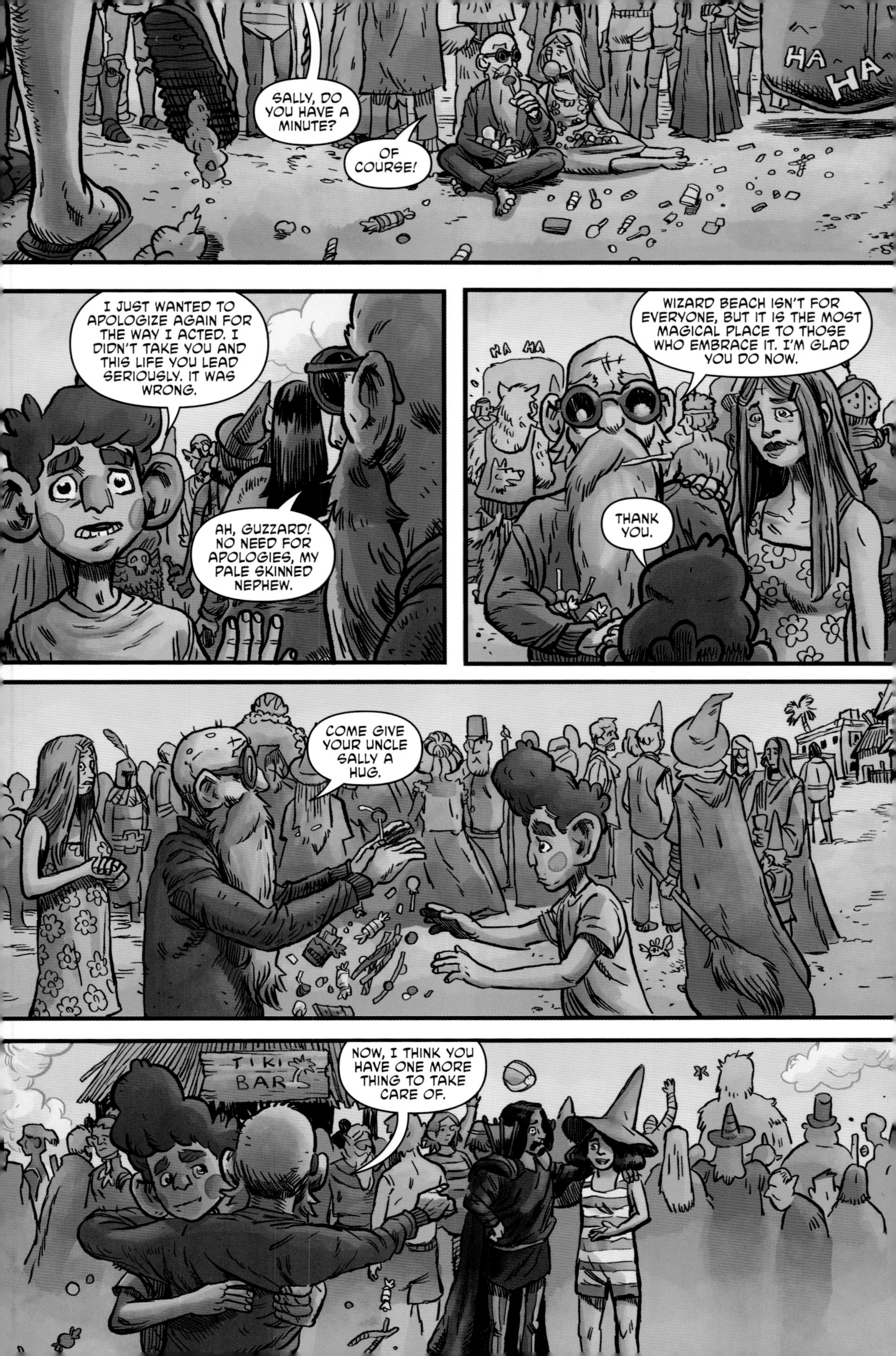
SALLY, DO YOU HAVE A MINUTE?
OF COURSE!
HA HA
I JUST WANTED TO APOLOGIZE AGAIN FOR THE WAY I ACTED. I DIDN'T TAKE YOU AND THIS LIFE YOU LEAD SERIOUSLY. IT WAS WRONG.
AH, GUZZARD! NO NEED FOR APOLOGIES, MY PALE SKINNED NEPHEW.
HA HA
WIZARD BEACH ISN'T FOR EVERYONE, BUT IT IS THE MOST MAGICAL PLACE TO THOSE WHO EMBRACE IT. I'M GLAD YOU DO NOW.
THANK YOU.
COME GIVE YOUR UNCLE SALLY A HUG.
TIKI BAR
NOW, I THINK YOU HAVE ONE MORE THING TO TAKE CARE OF.

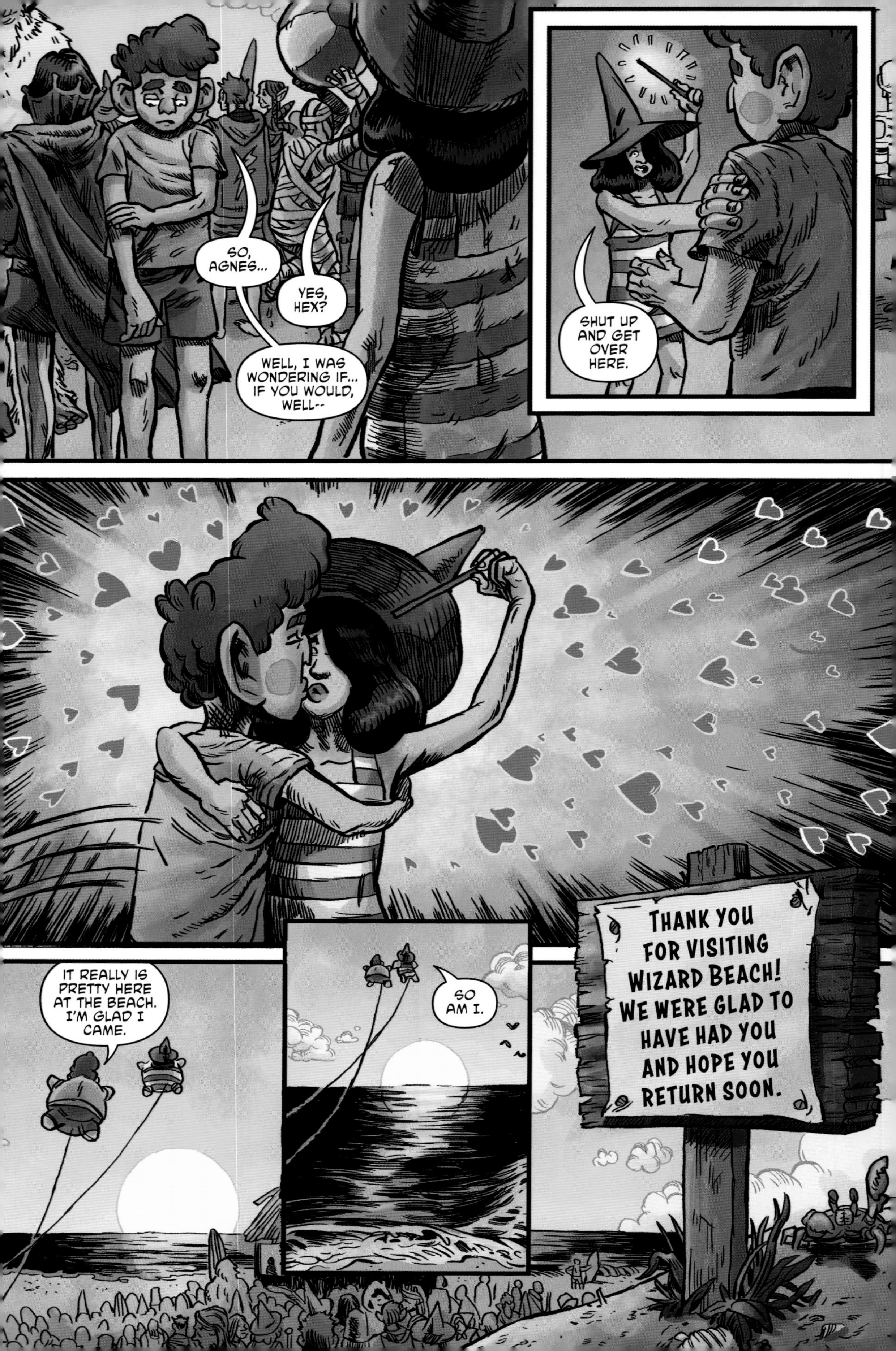
SO, AGNES...
YES, HEX?
WELL, I WAS WONDERING IF... IF YOU WOULD, WELL--
SHUT UP AND GET OVER HERE.
IT REALLY IS PRETTY HERE AT THE BEACH. I'M GLAD I CAME.
SO AM I.
THANK YOU FOR VISITING WIZARD BEACH! WE WERE GLAD TO HAVE HAD YOU AND HOPE YOU RETURN SOON.

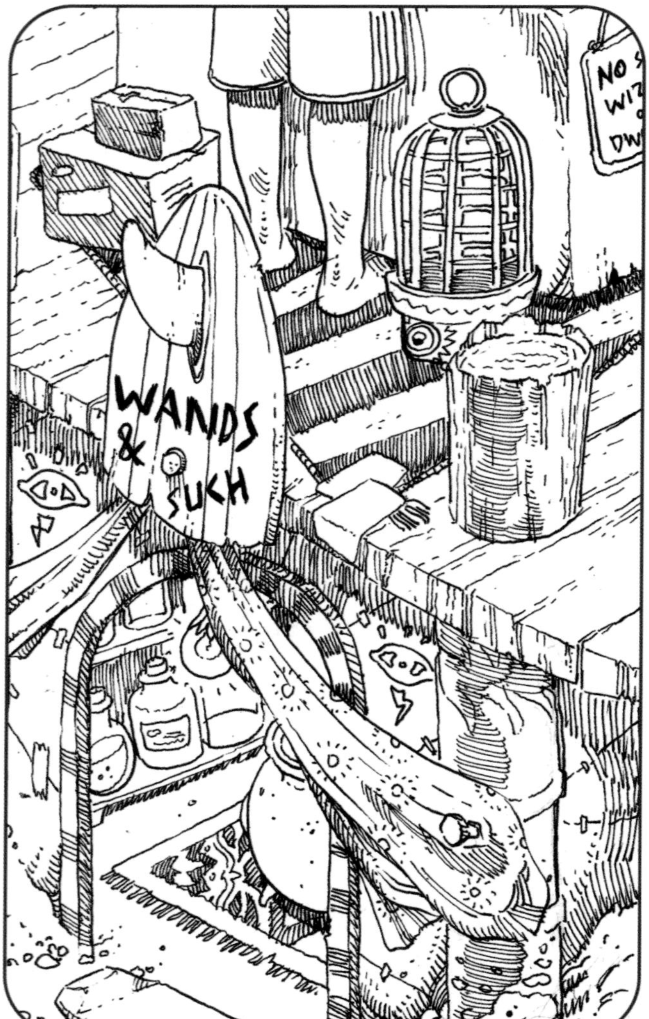
WANDS & SUCH

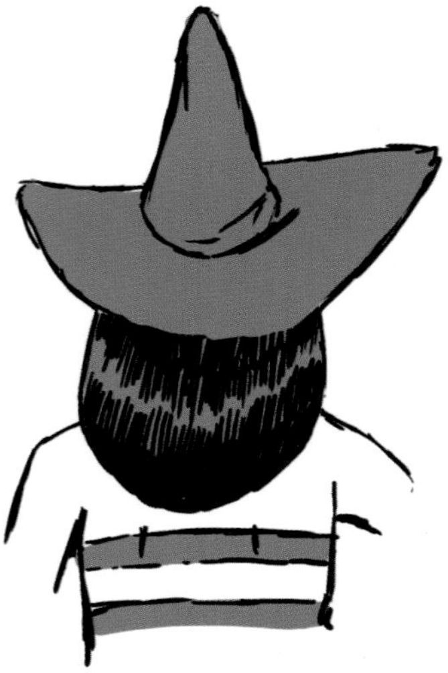

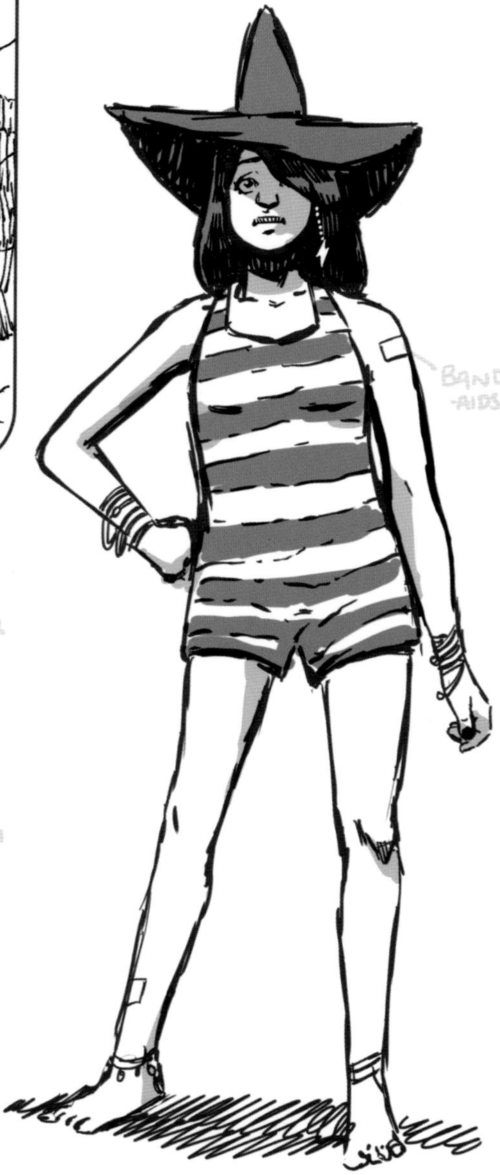
BAND-AIDS

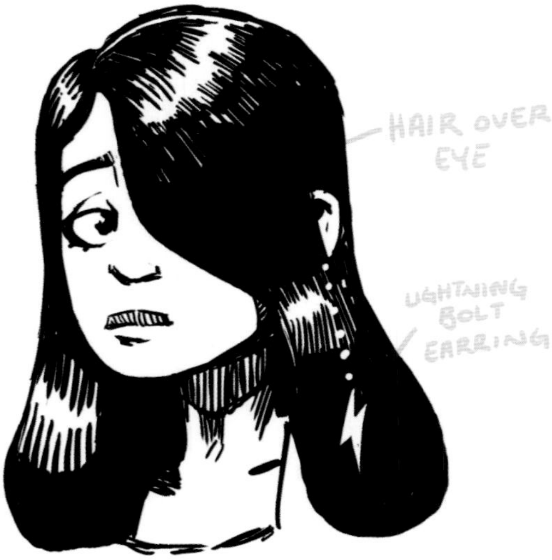
HAIR OVER EYE
LIGHTNING BOLT EARRING

CHARACTER AND SET DESIGN BY
CONOR NOLAN

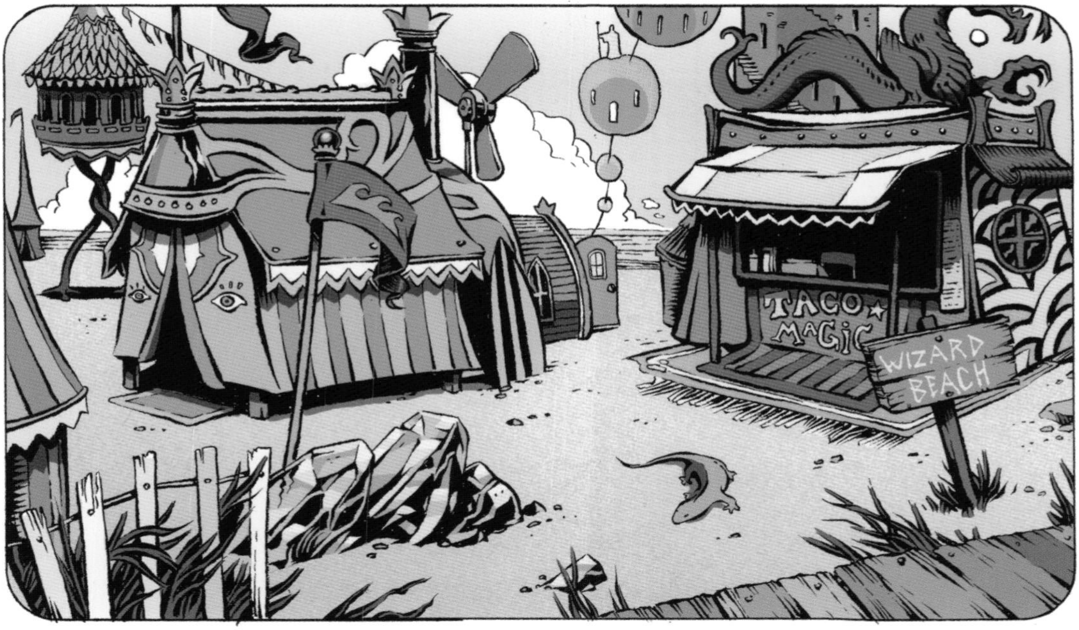
TACO ★ MAGIC
WIZARD BEACH

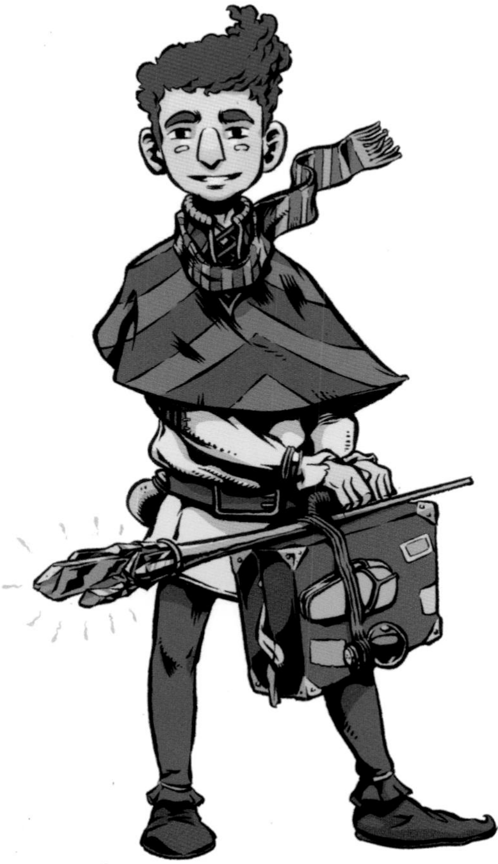

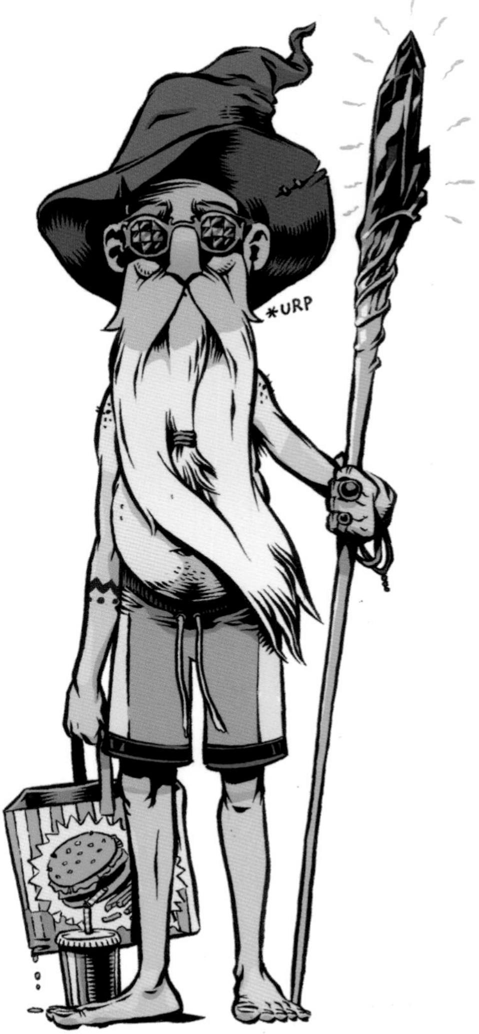
*URP

ABOUT
THE AUTHORS

CONOR NOLAN

Conor Nolan is an illustrator based out of Rhode Island. He splits his time between comic work and his illustration practice. More of his work can be seen in *Jim Henson's The Storyteller: Giants* and *Bedtime Games*. You can find more of his work at **ConorNolan.com**

SHAUN SIMON

Shaun Simon is a writer from the Northeast. His other works include *The True Lives of the Fabulous Killjoys*, *Neverboy*, *Art Ops*, and *Collapser*.